T0114421

More Praise
for '78

"Reynolds does a remarkable job enlightening readers about Boston's neighborhoods in 1978 and the social, racial and economic conflicts that were tearing the city, or parts of it, apart. . . . The playoff game between the Boston Red Sox and their hated rival—the New York Yankees—provides a dramatic thread linking all the events in the years that led up to the classic clash of the titans." —*Deseret News* (Salt Lake City, UT)

"[Reynolds's] book is a worthy chronicle of a decade lots of people who live in Boston would just as soon forget, except, perhaps, for the home run Carlton Fisk hit during the 1975 World Series, and for the early and middle innings of the game with which the Red Sox season ended in 1978." —Only a Game

"[A] good book . . . ['78] entertains and educates. . . . Reynolds masterfully uses a sequential account of the one-game playoff between the Red Sox and Yankees that would decide the American League East to pace his story's advancement, while otherwise freeing himself for extemporaneous exploration of race, busing, and baseball in Boston . . . [He] skillfully explores the yin-and-yang relationship of busing and the Sox on the city of Boston, tracing each back to its sixties' roots while grounding everything with new firsthand accounts from folks who lived it. . . . Reynolds describes a Fenway Frank such that the spicy mustard will burn your sinuses as you read it." —Boston Sports Media Watch

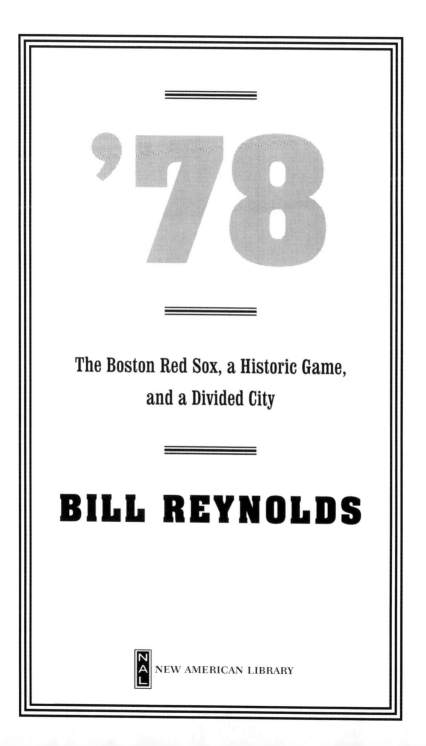

'78

The Boston Red Sox, a Historic Game,
and a Divided City

BILL REYNOLDS

NEW AMERICAN LIBRARY

NEW AMERICAN LIBRARY
Published by New American Library,
a division of Penguin Group (USA) Inc.,
375 Hudson Street, New York, New York 10014, USA
Penguin Group (Canada), 90 Eglinton Avenue East, Suite 700, Toronto,
Ontario M4P 2Y3, Canada (a division of Pearson Penguin Canada Inc.)
Penguin Books Ltd., 80 Strand, London WC2R 0RL, England
Penguin Ireland, 25 St. Stephen's Green, Dublin 2,
Ireland (a division of Penguin Books Ltd.)
Penguin Group (Australia), 250 Camberwell Road, Camberwell,
Victoria 3124, Australia (a division of Pearson Australia Group Pty. Ltd.)
Penguin Books India Pvt. Ltd., 11 Community Centre,
Panchsheel Park, New Delhi - 110 017, India
Penguin Group (NZ), 67 Apollo Drive, Rosedale, North Shore 0632,
New Zealand (a division of Pearson New Zealand Ltd.)
Penguin Books (South Africa) (Pty.) Ltd., 24 Sturdee Avenue,
Rosebank, Johannesburg 2196, South Africa

Penguin Books Ltd., Registered Offices:
80 Strand, London WC2R 0RL, England

Published by New American Library, a division of Penguin Group (USA) Inc. Previously published
in a New American Library hardcover edition.

First New American Library Trade Paperback Printing, April 2010

 REGISTERED TRADEMARK—MARCA REGISTRADA

New American Library Trade Paperback ISBN: 978-0-451-22922-9
The Library of Congress has cataloged the hardcover edition of this title as follows:

Reynolds, Bill, 1945–
'78: the Boston Red Sox, a historic game, and a divided city/Bill Reynolds
p. cm.
ISBN 978-0-451-22602-0
1. Boston Red Sox (Baseball Team)—History. 2. Baseball—Social aspects—
Massachusetts—Boston. 3. Boston (Mass.)—Social conditions—20th century.
4. Boston (Mass.)—Race relations. 5. New York Yankees (Baseball team)—History.
6. Sports rivalries—United States—History. I. Title. II. Title: Nineteen seventy-eight.
GV875.B62R47 2009
796.357'640974461—dc22   2008052765

Set in Fairfield LH
Designed by Elke Sigal

146119709

To my sister, Polly Reynolds,
whose spirit in the midst of daily adversity,
is a constant inspiration.

And to Lizzy, for her ongoing support
and encouragement.

ACKNOWLEDGMENTS

A special thank-you to:

David Vigliano, my agent and professional adviser for twenty years now, who saw that this could be a book when it was just an idea floating around in my head.

Dan Ambrosio, who shepherded the idea through the world of New York publishing.

Mark Chait, who edited this book, shared the same vision of it that I had, and made it better at the crucial time when it needed it most. No writer can ask for more.

Art Martone, the sports editor at the *Providence Journal*, whose insight into the Red Sox in the seventies was instrumental in the beginning of the process.

The Red Sox, specifically Dick Bresciani and Pam Ganley, who went out of their way to be helpful.

Liz Abbott, whose help in research and in acquiring the pictures was invaluable.

Isabelle Brogna, my techie wizard, who saved me from falling into a technological swamp, and Katie Myers, who helped with the pictures.

'78

On September 25, 1978, the *Boston Globe*'s Ray Fitzgerald wrote a column on the sports page titled "Lunacy and the Red Sox Fan."

Its premise was that an unidentified man had been found walking aimlessly on a Back Bay street, "talking to lampposts and trying to interest a wire-haired terrier in a game of cribbage." So he was brought into a clinic and placed on a cot, a tag around his neck.

The doctor read the inscription on his tag.

"I am a Boston Red Sox fan and no longer responsible for my actions. If found, bury me at home plate, next to the team's pennant chances."

The doctor shook his head.

"Another one of those. It's close to an epidemic."

Yes it was.

And the Red Sox's collapse wasn't supposed to have happened, of course.

They were just three years removed from losing in the seventh game of the '75 World Series. They were a talented, tested team in its prime, with the iconic Carl Yastrzemski and Carlton Fisk, the regal catcher who seemed as solid as the New Hampshire of his youth. They had the strong-armed Dwight Evans in right field, the sure-handed Rick Burleson at shortstop, and the graceful Freddie Lynn in center, who had swept across that '75 season like a supernova in his rookie year. They had George Scott, the old Boomer himself, one of the last holdovers from the "Impossible Dream" team of 1967, one of the first black stars with the Red Sox, now trying to hang on, no longer able to pull the ball, his best days all in the past. They had Jim Rice, in the middle of what would turn out to be an MVP season, the most feared slugger in the game.

They also had quality starting pitching, no insignificant thing for the Red Sox, whose history always seemed to be a lineup that looked at the friendly left-field wall as a siren song but whose pitching forever seemed to betray them, my kingdom for an ace. Now they had four of them: the crafty Luis Tiant, with his trademark cigars in the locker room and a pitching motion that seemed like the baseball version of some guy running a three-card monte game on a street corner, now you see it, now you don't, complete with turning his back to the batter in the middle of his windup; the flamethrowing Dennis Eckersley, who always looked as if he were on his way to Studio 54 in New York with his long hair, mustache, and chiseled features, and had his own language to match, a combination of California slacker and surfer dude; Mike Torrez, who had been with the Yankees the year before but was now with the Red Sox, this gun for hire; and the irrepressible Bill Lee, "the Spaceman" himself, baseball's counterculture hero whom Eckersley called "Sherwin Williams" because he was a master at painting the corners of the plate.

The same Bill Lee who had said three years earlier that the only person in Boston with any guts was Judge W. Arthur Garrity, the man who had ordered the forced busing that had torn the city apart.

In the middle of July they had an amazing fourteen-game lead on the Yankees and were eight ahead of the Milwaukee Brewers, and seemed to be on cruise control to win the division, especially since the Yankees were in a free fall, a dysfunction in pinstripes, a melodrama masquerading as a baseball team. It was as if this was the Red Sox team all of New England had been waiting for ever since 1918, the last year the Red Sox had won a World Series. They were the best team in baseball. The record said so.

Then the swoon had started.

There had been a combination of reasons, certainly, everything from injuries to the theory that manager Don Zimmer played his regulars too much, and thus burned them out, to the vagaries of the game itself. All this had combined with the Yankees starting to play appreciably better after manager Billy Martin suddenly resigned in another installment of the miniseries that had become the Yankees, and was replaced by Bob Lemon, a move that quieted the chaos and began to bring the curtain down on all the drama.

In early September the Yankees came into Boston for a four-game series in Fenway Park, and by this time they were only down four, so close now the Red Sox could hear their breathing. When they left Boston the two teams were tied, and the Yankees had outscored them 42–9 over the four games, four games in

Yet in a funny way the pressure was now off.

Hadn't they already blown it? Hadn't they let a near-invincible fourteen-game lead wither away? Hadn't they been endlessly killed in the papers and on talk radio? Hadn't they been called chokes and gutless and all the other epithets fans could heap on them? Hadn't they seemingly played out all of New England's worst fears, the feeling that, in the end, as sure as death and taxes, the Red Sox would find a way to lose?

Then somehow, some way, they managed to find another life after their public disgrace.

Whatever the reason, somehow in their collective shame they had found a way to start winning games again, their season reborn, and had come into the last weekend of the season having won five straight. The problem was the Yankees also had kept winning, and on the last day of the season it was a gray, overcast day in Fenway, the clouds close and heavy, what one writer called "a perfect day for a funeral."

All the Yankees had to do was win one more game against the lowly Cleveland Indians in the stadium and the Red Sox season would be over, no matter what they did in their last game of the season against the Toronto Blue Jays. The obits already had been prepared. Summer was over, and so were the Red Sox.

Then at a little after two in the afternoon, Luis Tiant, who had left his native Cuba to chase his baseball dreams, was about to pitch to Toronto's Roy Howell. A roar began building in the bleachers. It spread to the right-field grandstand, then through the rest of the crowd, building in intensity. Transistor radios had told the fans that the Indians' Andre Thornton had hit a two-run homer in New York.

Tiant, whom the celebrated New York columnist Red Smith

once described as looking like "Pancho Villa after a tough night of looting and burning," seemed almost puzzled, like he was getting an ovation for simply toeing the rubber.

It certainly wasn't the first time Tiant had been given an ovation in Fenway. Yastrzemski was more beloved, the legacy of '67 with his iconic status, and Fisk might have been more respected, for his steely resolve, the native son living out every New England kid's sandlot fantasies. But maybe no one was more downright popular than Luis Tiant.

He had come to Boston in June of 1971, after having once started an All-Star Game with the Cleveland Indians. But he had failed in Minnesota, courtesy of a sore shoulder, and it hadn't worked out in spring training with the Atlanta Braves either, before he signed with the Sox's Triple A team in Louisville. In his first start in Boston he gave up five runs in the first inning.

But by the following year it was as if pixie dust fell from the sky and settled on Tiant's shoulders. By the end of the year he was their best pitcher, and one September night, as he walked to the bullpen to get ready for the second game of a twi-night doubleheader, the Fenway crowd gave him such an ovation that his teammates joined in, "Loo-Eee . . . Loo-Eee" floating in the air like some religious chant. When he came to the plate to hit in the bottom of the eighth the chant began again, one that lasted throughout his at-bat, through the break, and during the top of the ninth inning.

"I've never heard anything like that in my life," Yastrzemski said.

That began Tiant's cult status in Boston.

In 1975 Fidel Castro, after some pressure from the South Dakota senator George McGovern, had allowed Tiant's elderly parents to leave Cuba to come see their only child. Tiant hadn't seen his father in fourteen years. He met them at Logan Airport with his wife and three children, along with a swarm of media. Tiant embraced his parents, tears streaming down his face. Five days later his father, who once had been a great pitcher in Cuba and had pitched for a while in the Negro Leagues in the United States, threw out the first pitch in Fenway Park.

Now Tiant was going to pitch a game the Red Sox absolutely had to win.

Twelve minutes later, Yastrzemski coming to the plate, the Fenway message board flashed that the Yankees had tied the game in New York at two apiece, which was followed by a crescendo of boos everywhere.

At 2:27, as Sox center fielder Fred Lynn stepped into the batter's box, there was a standing ovation. Another Indian had hit a home run in New York. Lynn was so confused he tipped his cap.

Six minutes later a Toronto player walked to the plate to another standing ovation, as the Indians had gone ahead 4–2.

That's the way it was for the rest of the afternoon, the fans cheering at the wrong times, as if watching some giant movie where the sound track was out of synch.

"When I saw the Indians go ahead, my knees started shaking," Jerry Remy, the Red Sox second baseman, who had grown up in a small Massachusetts town about an hour south of Boston, said later.

The Sox would get two runs in the fifth inning on a Remy double to break a tie, then shortstop Rick Burleson, nicknamed "the Rooster" because his hair had once seemed to stand on end after a workout, lifted a two-run homer into the screen in left, and the Sox were in command.

Then at 4:12 the message board flashed that the Indians had beaten the Yankees 9–2, and Fenway erupted in a massive lovefest. And at the end of the game the message board read, "Thank you, Rick Waits," in homage to the Cleveland pitcher who had beaten the Yankees.

"There's no more hoping that someone else will do it," Yastrzemski said. "It all comes down to us now. We've got to do it ourselves."

He was sitting in the Sox locker room, a room in back of the first-base dugout. Most of the players were there, answering the same questions over and over, as wave after wave of reporters approached them. They were smiling, for the pressure had been lifted. They had won twelve out of their last fourteen games, each one a pressure game. More important, they had averted one of the worst flops in Red Sox history. Burleson was saying how he was sick of all the psychological reasons that had been given for the collapse, that they had blown their big lead and that was that, but that they had played well for the past two weeks and no one could say they had choked.

The day before, Ray Fitzgerald had written another column in the *Boston Globe*. He was fifty-one, had been at the *Globe* since 1965 after working a dozen years for the *Springfield Union*, and had been writing columns for three years. The premise for this column had been that the Red Sox had been playing two games the past couple of weeks, the one on the field and the one on the scoreboard that revealed how the Yankees were doing.

He had asked Yastrzemski if he believed in fate.

"Fate," Yaz said. "All I believe is that the Indians have to score more runs than the Yankees tomorrow."

"Aha," Fitzgerald said. "Then you believe in Santa Claus?"

"There is one, isn't there?" Yastrzemski said.

On this last day of the regular season it seemed like there was.

The pitching matchups for the next day already had been announced as the Red Sox were in their clubhouse. Ron Guidry, who had finished the season 24–3 and led the American League in almost every pitching category, one of the great all-time seasons, would pitch for the Yankees. Mike Torrez, who had been signed as a free agent last fall, would pitch for the Red Sox, even if he had faltered down the stretch. No matter that he was arguably the Sox's third best pitcher. Eckersley, who was twenty-three, had pitched a great game on Saturday for his twentieth win. And it had been Tiant when they had needed it most, another big game from a big-game pitcher.

It would turn out to be Tiant's last game for the Red Sox, although no one knew it. Yastrzemski had said that "in a game you have to win, he's the man I'd flip the ball to." He supposedly was thirty-eight, although there always were doubts about his true age, and he was adored by his teammates as well as the fans, both for his infectious, freewheeling personality and his ability to have his best games when it seemed to matter the most, complete with the wonderful nickname "El Tiante." He had the unique ability to make his teammates laugh, no small thing in a clubhouse where you could almost see the pressure right there in the lockers, along with the next day's uniform.

He called Yastrzemski "Polacko" and Torrez "Taco," and he seemed to have a nickname for everyone, but constantly poked fun at himself, too. He took showers while smoking his ever-present cigars, and was infamous in the Sox clubhouse for coming out of the shower and standing in front of a mirror and calling himself, in his Spanish accent, in a loud voice so that everyone could hear, "a good-lookeen sonofabeech."

Now he had just pitched a two-hitter, had won the game the Sox had to win.

"Can he pitch tomorrow?" Yastrzemski asked in a jubilant Red Sox clubhouse.

No, he couldn't.

So it would be Torrez.

And there was a slice of irony about that, no question about it. He had signed with the Red Sox in the off-season after winning two games in the World Series for the Yankees. It had been a symbolic signing, one that said the Red Sox were serious about coming after the Yankees, that they weren't just going to sit back and watch the Yankees have their pick of the free-agent litter. He was a classic power pitcher who threw a live fastball, curve, and used his slider as his out pitch, but as the Red Sox had turned sour so had he, not having won in his last eight starts.

Yet this is what he made big money for, and as he sat in the Sox clubhouse he was confident he would pitch well tomorrow.

"How many days in Kansas City?" he asked third baseman Butch Hobson, for the American League Championship Series would begin Tuesday in Kansas City, with either the Red Sox or the Yankees playing the Royals.

"Two," Hobson answered.

"When are we supposed to leave?" Torrez asked.

"Tomorrow, after the game," said Hobson.

"Bring your suitcase," said Torrez.

The Yankees had arrived in Boston on Sunday night, just a few hours after their loss to the Indians, and settled into the Sheraton in the Prudential Center, which had been the tallest building in the city until the John Hancock Tower had opened two years earlier.

They had made the short flight from New York City into Logan Airport, where people had said, "We'll kill you tomorrow" and "We'll kick your ass," and others had good-naturedly booed as they walked by and gave them the thumbs-down sign.

They had had drinks on the plane, the mood was loose, and that meant that nothing was sacred. This is how the Yankees handled pressure, by ripping each other and telling each other not to choke, and generally acting like a bunch of kids on the way to a high school game. This was the culture of the Yankees, and by the time they checked in to the hotel it was a loose team, a confident one.

Eventually, several of them found themselves in Daisy Buchanan's, a bar on nearby Newbury Street named after Jay Gatsby's golden girl in the famed novel *The Great Gatsby*. It was a popular watering hole, the kind of place that in the seventies had come to be called a singles bar, and it was on a fashionable street full of shops and restaurants that was about halfway between the Boston Common and Fenway Park.

To sit on Newbury Street on that early October evening in 1978, on the eve of a huge playoff game between the Red Sox and the Yankees, there was no way you'd have ever thought that this was a bruised and battered city, still in the midst of its most turbulent time in its modern history, the schools ruled by a federal judge.

Just down the street, past Kenmore Square, was Boston University. Across the Charles River was the Massachusetts Institute of Technology, the number-one engineering school in the country, and the ivied elegance of Harvard, the oldest college in the country. Farther down Commonwealth Avenue, in neighboring Newton, was Boston College. On the other side of Fenway, so close they were almost in the shadow of the light towers, were three women's colleges, Simmons, Wheelock, and Emmanuel. A few blocks away, behind the large, stately Museum of Art, which was on the other side of Fenway Park, was Northeastern. Then there were the several junior colleges throughout the city, Tufts in nearby Medford, and the Boston branch of the University of Massachusetts in adjoining Dorchester.

All these students were all back in school, giving Boston its annual shot of youth, arriving in the city every fall like an invading army. Most of them came from somewhere else, and to them, busing in Boston was happening somewhere else, in the parts of the city they didn't go anyway.

As it was to the Red Sox players.

Yastrzemski and the Boston Bruins star Bobby Orr had done some public-service spots on television in the days before busing in September '74, saying, "It's not going to be easy, but that never stopped Boston." For the most part, though, it was something that was rarely discussed, as if it were happening on some far-off planet. Most of the players lived in the suburbs, came into Boston to play games. Many had no emotional connection to the city, didn't know its history, except in the most rudimentary of terms. In the reality of professional sports, they were all hired guns, here from somewhere else.

But busing hovered over the city like Banquo's ghost, even for people whose daily lives weren't directly touched by it. On this eve before the playoff game it had been the topic of four years of newspaper headlines and TV news spots. In a sense it was like living in a city under siege, even if for many their daily lives went on as they always had. The fallout from busing was always there, in the city's psyche, in the civic conversation, in the way Boston was viewed by others. Decades later, a few of the Red Sox players admitted that the busing controversy had taken its psychic toll, even if they had been unwilling to publicly deal with it at the time.

How could it not have influenced them?

And for the people who lived in Boston, especially those in the neighborhoods, it was unavoidable. It determined where their kids went to school. It determined what was talked about. It determined whom they voted for. It determined what they thought about their government, their country, their leaders, their city, their lives. In short, it determined everything.

The mood among the Yankee players inside Daisy Buchanan's that early October night, on the eve of the game, was the feeling that this was as it should be, the two best teams in one last game to decide things once and for all, like two old gunfighters in the middle of some dusty street in some bleak Old West town about to slap leather, all the while knowing that only one was going to walk away. There was no sense that they had blown everything in the loss to the Indians, no anguish. Not only had they come back from being down fourteen games, they also had survived all the drama of Billy Martin and George Steinbrenner in the middle of the year, and considered themselves fortunate to still have their season alive. They also were less than a month removed from their four-game sweep of the Red Sox in Fenway, so there was no sense of being intimidated playing there; the game was to be played in Fenway because the Red Sox had won a coin flip. And they had Guidry, the best pitcher in the game, who had one-hit the Red Sox in Yankee

Stadium in mid-September, and whom they had the utmost confidence in.

They were certainly familiar with the Red Sox, and there was a certain respect, too, even amidst the fact that the two teams didn't like each other very much. Both free agency and the vagaries of the game had already taught them that players' loyalties were not so much to the franchise and the city they played in but to their teammates, for players came and went. Torrez, who was to pitch for the Red Sox, had been a Yankee the year before. Lyle had once played for the Red Sox. In the new baseball world, who knew what the future was going to bring for any of them?

Still, the two franchises had a bitter rivalry that stretched back to the beginnings of the game itself. Certainly the fans had a certain hatred for each other, especially in Boston, where the merest sight of the Yankees inflamed passions and resurrected old wounds, almost as if the Yankees always had been the big brother, the one that won all the championships, while the Red Sox were the envious little brother, always wanting what the big brother had but never getting it. Maybe it was this simple: Since the Sox had let Ruth get away to New York in 1920 the Yankees had won twenty-two world titles and become the greatest organization in all of sports, and the Red Sox had won none.

There also was little question that Fisk and Yankee catcher Thurman Munson had a visceral dislike for each other, the legacy of their fight at home plate in Yankee Stadium five years earlier and the pervading sense that Munson was jealous of Fisk, saw him as one of the darlings of the national media, saw him getting attention he thought should be going to him. Either that, or it was more elemental: Fisk, tall and movie-star handsome, Munson, short and stumpy, with a mustache and bushy hair that crawled out from under his cap.

There also had been the ugly brawl in Yankee Stadium two years earlier, the one in which Fisk and Yankee outfielder Lou Piniella had gone after each other after a brutal collision at the plate, and Lee had been punched by Yankee center fielder Mickey Rivers, then thrown to the ground by Graig Nettles, injuring his shoulder. And it was no secret that the Yankees had no use for Lee. They hadn't liked his remark in '73 that they had fought like "hookers swinging purses," nor did they like being called George Steinbrenner's "brownshirts," as he had called them in the aftermath of the '76 fight. They considered him a loudmouth, and more than a few of them had liked it when Nettles had thrown him to the ground two years ago, essentially affecting the rest of his season. There also was the sense that they were disappointed with Torrez, not because he had left to go with the Red Sox, for that was only business and all players understood business, but because he had made some remarks about the Yankees that some of the players didn't like, their feeling that he had a short memory.

Yet there was an acknowledgment that these were two great teams that would be playing the next day, two teams that had survived tumultuous seasons, two teams that had come to understand that baseball could be like a lover you never really can know, a game that always surprises you just when you thought you had it figured out.

"I remember that we all thought it was ironic justice that these two good teams should end up tied after a hundred and sixty-two games," the Yankee outfielder Lou Piniella would later say. "Like it was just meant to be."

What Piniella could not have known that night was that this game was taking place at exactly the right time, and in the right place.

For it had been four very difficult years in Boston, four years no one ever could have envisioned, four of the most ugly and tumultuous years in the city's long history. It had been four years of bleak newspaper headlines and TV stories and the perception that Boston was a racist city, all the residue of the worst school busing crisis in American history. Boston needed a great baseball playoff game, needed something that could serve as some form of civic catharsis—needed the Red Sox, the one thing that always had had the potential to bring everyone together, if only for a while.

In many ways this playoff game was more needed than the '75 World Series had been, even though that had taken place in the same autumn that the second phase of the city's busing plan had started, the second autumn of violence and demonstrations. That had almost been too raw, the disconnect between what had been happening in Fenway Park and what had been happening in the city existing as if they were in parallel universes.

Now it seemed less so.

Maybe it was the simple fact that this was now three years later, with the growing realization that none of it had really changed anything. The violence. The demonstrations. All the angry rhetoric. None of it. Maybe it was the realization that by this October evening in '78 busing in Boston, and the ugly ramifications that came with that, were beginning to seem like a movie you'd seen too many times.

Whatever the reasons, a certain resignation had seemed to set in. There was the sense that the fallout from busing no longer had the power to shock the way it once had. It was as though busing had become like sets in some stage play, always there, but in the background, no longer center stage. It was still there, certainly, still an embarrassment, still adding to the perception of Boston as a racist city. Yet it had somehow became easier to accept, as though busing was just part of the landscape and that was just the way it was.

Maybe it was this elemental: people needed a win. Needed to feel good about themselves again. Needed to feel good about their city. Needed to get beyond the past four years.

So Boston needed this playoff game, needed a civic boost. Needed something symbolic, something that could say the worst was over, even if no one was really sure. And if it's simplistic to say that afterward Boston instantly began to heal, as if the wounds of the past could easily be wiped away by a dramatic baseball game played out on a national stage, most of the violence did seem over on this October evening. A new school year had started and, so far anyway, there had been none of the major disruptions of the past four years. As if everyone was depleted, the battle played out. As if Boston was finally ready to move toward a better future, as slow as that movement often would seem to be.

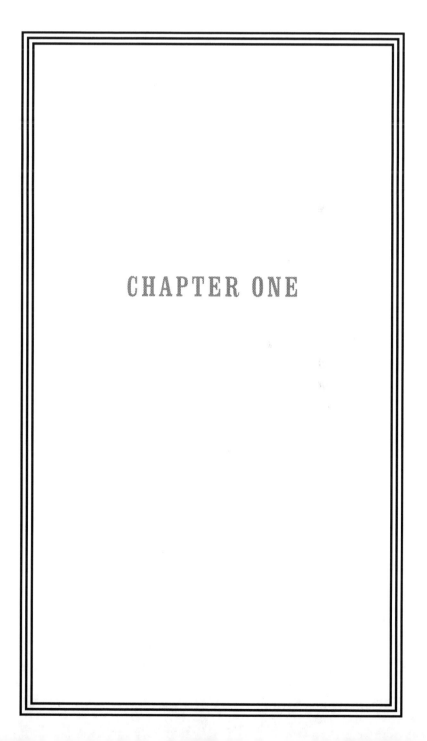

CHAPTER ONE

By 10:00 a.m. there already were throngs of young people swarming outside, even though the game was not scheduled to start until 2:30.

Drinking was taking place everywhere in the street. The metal doors on Jersey Street that ran alongside the front of the park were being repeatedly banged upon, even though it already had been announced that the game was sold out. There were innumerable near fights, and everywhere you looked you could see both blue-shirted police along with police on horseback.

Obscenities were everywhere, both shouted and on the T-shirts of young men and women, causing one *Boston Globe* writer to say it was "a public display that a sociologist might plumb for significance."

This was all taking place outside the brick façade of Fenway Park, which had been there since 1912, back when William Howard Taft was president and World War I was still in the future. John "Honey Fitz" Fitzgerald, who later would be the grandfather of John F. Kennedy, threw out the first pitch in the 1918 World Series, his daughter Rose two seats away from him. All taking place in this storied old ballpark that essentially had stayed the same, while everything else around it in Boston had changed.

For the Boston of legend was the Boston Tea Party and Paul Revere's ride. It was the Old North Church and the Freedom Trail, the "cradle of liberty." It was the ivy-covered walls of Harvard, and the austere, geometric buildings of MIT across the Charles River in Cambridge. It was the national image of a graceful, cosmopolitan city, the symbolic home of the Kennedys, America's unofficial first family. It was the sense that Boston was the heart of academia, this city where the nation's first high school had opened, this city so steeped in tradition that the past was always there, almost palpable, what locals called "the Hub," short for hub of the universe. To walk its streets was, in many ways, like walking through American history, this old city that once had been called "the Athens of America."

But on this beautiful morning Boston had become a city full of little individual duchies, the Irish in South Boston and Charlestown, the Italians in East Boston, the blacks in Roxbury and parts of Dorchester, an essentially segregated city that was at the tail end of its worst crisis since the fight for independence from England two hundred years earlier. A city where the beginning of court-ordered school busing just four years earlier had punctured the city's façade and put it on the nightly news in all its violence and all its hate and all its shame, called "the Little Rock of the North."

The images of police in riot gear shepherding black schoolchildren into all-white schools in all-white neighborhoods had rocked the city in ways no one could have predicted. It was as though all the hate and anger and violence had blown up all the myths of what Boston had thought it was, the realization that beneath all the history and all the tradition this was a city that had never dealt with race and class and all the other hidden issues that didn't make the travel brochures.

For this wasn't some Southern city, some place where America's racial shame was played out for all the world to see.

This was Boston?

What had happened?

You certainly didn't ask the Red Sox players for the answers. Marie Brenner, a New York writer who would be hired by the *Boston Herald* to cover the team the following year, quickly learned that you don't ask the players about busing in Boston, dope, Woody Allen, or the lobster at Locke-Obers, the downtown restaurant that was one of the symbols of the city's establishment. Instead, you stuck to safe topics like rock groups and how much Friendly's, a Massachusetts ice cream company, was paying them in endorsements.

"They wear their psychic scars like so many pilgrims doing time at Lourdes," she would write.

Even though many of the players now wore the accoutrements of youth culture, the long sideburns and bushy hair that snuck down the backs of their necks, the open shirts and gold chains, as if they would be off to the disco as soon as the game was over, the soul of the game was still rooted in small-town America and its small-town values. The majority of the players still believed in those most American of beliefs of hard work and sacrifice, of listening to the manager, of playing the game the right way, even if these values were constantly being questioned in the America of the seventies.

But not all of them.

The country was changing, though, no question about that. The end of the Vietnam War. Watergate. The energy crisis. They all contributed to what President Jimmy Carter would call "our national malaise." But it was more than just the obvious things, the events that led the nightly news. The changes were more profound than that, would turn out to be more lasting, as if the seventies were a Maginot Line that got crossed, and afterward there was no turning back. Attitudes about sex, about race, about ethnicity, and how we came to feel about both government and institutions, all were shaped by the seventies, as though the tumult of the sixties became mainstreamed. Change was everywhere, as in the wind as a fly ball in Fenway. From the faces that stared out from high school yearbooks as if on their way to a Sgt. Pepper reunion to the pulsating disco beat of *Saturday Night Fever*, it was as though everything was being transformed. People. Institutions. American life as we once had known it.

But baseball's appeal is that it was one of the few constants in a sea of change, the game that had grown up with the country in ways so many other sports had not.

The Red Sox had been playing in Boston since 1901, as much a part of the city as Beacon Hill and the swan boats in the Public Garden, had been around so long that if you didn't know better you might have thought that Paul Revere had once played second base. Baseball was the game that had grown up with the country in ways other sports didn't, a rural game that had been born in the small towns of an earlier America, called the National Pastime for a reason. It's been immortalized in literature, and once had been one of the first places where the idea of the melting pot had been actualized, at least for white America. It was the first sport to be broadcast on radio, the first to be televised, a timeless game that comes wrapped in history in ways so many of the other sports don't.

And here it was, another great baseball moment in a city that already had seen so many of them, complete with Tip O'Neill, the Speaker of the House, the man famous for saying all politics were local, Mayor Kevin White, and Senator Ted Kennedy, who was making noises that he was going to make a run at Carter in two years and try to get the Democratic nomination, all sitting in choice seats.

Just four years earlier, a few days before the first phase of busing had begun, Kennedy had appeared at an antibusing rally at Government Center in downtown Boston. There were roughly eight thousand people there. He had not been scheduled to speak, and when he approached the podium people began jeering and booing, as Kennedy and Judge W. Arthur Garrity, the man who had put busing in place, were known to be close.

"You're a disgrace to the Irish."

"Yeah, let your daughter get bused, so she can get raped."

"Why don't you put your one-legged son on a bus?"

The ugly shouts came at him, rapid-fire, as he started to speak, a crescendo of noise.

Kennedy's face tightened, but each time he attempted to speak the catcalls only intensified.

As he left the podium and started across the plaza toward the federal building that was named for his slain brother, a thrown tomato hit the ground and splattered his pin-striped suit. Another tomato and some eggs rained down on him as Kennedy hurried on, pursued by people screaming at him. One small woman, with a tiny American flag pin in her hair, struck him on the shoulder. He stumbled, then righted himself, and hurried on as an elbow hit him in the ribs.

"People have strong emotions and strong feelings, and they've certainly expressed them," he said, once inside the building. "They have a right to their position."

But pouring cream into a cup of coffee, his hand trembled. These were the people who had sent John F. Kennedy to Congress thirty years before, and who had helped send Ted Kennedy to the Senate in 1962, even when it was widely understood that Ted had been the least qualified of the three brothers, the people who always had been there for the Kennedys.

That day it had been six years after Chappaquiddick, the night when Mary Jo Kopechne, who once had worked in his brother Bobby's Washington office, had died on Martha's Vineyard in a car Ted Kennedy had been driving, a tragedy complicated by the fact that Kennedy had swum to safety while Kopechne drowned in the car. Kennedy had pled guilty to leaving the scene of an accident, and received a suspended sentence of two months in jail, and the tragedy had complicated Kennedy's presidential hopes. But he was still Ted Kennedy, still the last of the Kennedy brothers, still with the aura of American royalty.

"Now in the heart of Ted's own city," J. Anthony Lukas would later write in *Common Ground*, "in the plaza beneath his own office, in the shade of the federal building dedicated to his brother, these people not only had deserted him, they had publicly humiliated him."

Could there have been a more symbolic moment that busing was ripping apart a city's soul?

Baseball had been a balm to that, at least on the surface. Sports always have been the great escape, especially the Red Sox in Boston. The antibusing forces hated the *Boston Globe*, the most dominant paper in the city, for the *Globe* had supported busing. To them, the *Globe* had sold them out, had forsaken the neighborhoods in its desire to become a national paper. In the early days of busing, shots had been fired into the *Globe* building on Morrissey Boulevard. To them, the *Globe* had become everything they despised, liberal, elitist, run by rich, hypocritical men who lived in the suburbs and didn't have to deal with busing, yet told them how they should think, a paper that had turned its back on its roots.

It had gotten so ugly that eleven shots had been fired into the *Globe* in two nights, until the police department had to put snipers on the roof. There were bumper stickers reading "Boycott the Globe," there were pickets outside the paper's downtown business office, there was a demonstration with mothers stepping in front of *Globe* delivery trucks, delaying trucks for three hours, until the police were called. There was the slashing of the tires on a delivery truck in South Boston, and there was the night another delivery truck was hijacked at gunpoint and then pushed into the water at Fort Point Channel.

And yet, many of them still bought the paper.

Why?

For the sports.

To see how the Red Sox did. As if sports and the Red Sox were somehow exempt from the hatred and tension that ran through Boston, the one island of refuge in an ever-churning sea, even if race always had been the elephant in the living room for the Red Sox, the legacy of the Sox being the last team in baseball to integrate.

They were Red Sox fans, through the good years and the bad, part of the generations of fans who always had given their hearts to this team, the undying loyalties that decades later would become known as Red Sox Nation. These were the people whose fathers had taken them to Fenway Park when they were kids, and now they took their own kids there, as if the players changed, and the decades changed, and everything changed, yet their affection for the Old Towne Team never did. They were the ones who always had the radio on in the background, the sound track of summer in Boston, the ones whose allegiances to the Red Sox were passed down through the generations like a family heirloom.

As if there was politics, and there was baseball, and never the twain shall meet.

Until they did, of course.

How could some fans cheer for Tiant and Rice yet not want black kids bused into their neighborhoods?

In a sense it was the great conundrum of sports, how fans could cheer their black athletes yet not necessarily want them living next door. Was it this simple? That they came to see the black players on the Red Sox as people, not like the blacks they didn't know, the ones they dealt with in stereotypes? Is that why a white kid in South Boston could throw rocks at black students bused in from Roxbury while idolizing Rice?

Or was it more layered, the fact that all athletes are viewed from a certain distance, are often regarded as special, apart, almost mythic? The fact that the black players weren't trying to take people's jobs, or send their kids to neighborhood schools, or do any of the things that were viewed as threatening? The fact that the Red Sox in Fenway Park were somehow exempt from the realities of real life?

Whatever the reason, there's no question that the black play-ers in Fenway were both cheered and supported, even during this traumatic time when blacks and whites in Boston seemed forever to be staring at each other from a distance that seemed as wide as the Continental Divide. Then again, race always had been a complicated issue in Boston sports. Back in the sixties when the Celtics had been the best team in all of basketball, they always had played before smaller crowds in the Boston Garden than the Boston Bruins played to, even though the Bruins had nowhere near the success the Celtics had then.

Had it simply been because Boston always had been a great hockey town?

Had it been because the Celtics had had a predominantly black starting team then?

Or had it been a mixture of both?

At one level, it seemed very simple in Fenway Park in '78: talent trumped race.

Rice was having a great season and was cheered every step of the way. Tiant was not only good but a great showman besides, all but dripping with charisma, as the Fenway crowd roared its appreciation. Yet Scott, once a fan favorite, was now appreciably less so, as his batting average dropped, his talent in decline.

The message?

Red Sox fans surely wanted to see their team win.

But did that shape attitudes about busing and the integra-tion of the city's schools and neighborhoods?

It didn't seem to.

Maybe if Rice and Tiant had been more outspoken on the subject. Maybe if the Red Sox had used their considerable clout to comment on the issue, outside of Yastrzemski doing his public-service spots before it all began. Maybe, maybe, maybe. It didn't happen. Or as a woman who grew up in South Boston then said, "They liked Freddie Lynn more, but they cheered for Jim Rice, too."

Maybe in Boston, in 1978, that was as good as it was going to get.

Now, though, the Red Sox were going to play the hated Yankees in Fenway Park in the first American League playoff game in thirty years, and it all seemed somehow inevitable. For this wasn't the Sox playing the Orioles, or the Brewers, or anyone else for that matter. This wasn't even the World Series, as big as that had been just three years earlier. This was the Yankees, complete with all the history that came with that. This was the Yankees, whose success the Red Sox always had chased, and never had caught. As if for the Red Sox to truly exorcise all their demons, they had to beat the Yankees.

It was October 2, 1978, and about the only thing in Boston that remained unchanged was baseball in Fenway Park. As if the decades came and went, everything changed, yet Fenway was still timeless.

It had opened the same week that the *Titanic* had sunk, and was situated between Lansdowne and Jersey streets. It had been called Fenway Park because it was in the "Fens," a residential area of the city dominated by a large park that had been designed by the famed landscape architect Frederick Law Olmstead as part of his emerald necklace that cut through Boston. The Red Sox were owned at the time by John I. Taylor, whose father, General Charles Taylor, owned the *Boston Globe*, and since his father also owned the Fenway Realty Company and was looking to expand the area around the new ballpark, Taylor no doubt figured the publicity wouldn't hurt.

It had once been the home of Babe Ruth, and later of Ted Williams, two of the towering names in the game's history, had long been one of the great cathedrals in the game. Tom Yawkey, the longtime Red Sox owner who had died in 1976, had said in June of 1967 that Fenway was outdated and that he wanted a new stadium out of the city, maybe somewhere off Route 128, the highway where all the new companies were going, someplace that was bigger and had more parking, like all those new stadiums that were sprouting up all over the country. But the Sox had come out of nowhere to win the pennant that year, and fans had flocked to Fenway, as if it were a shrine to the game, so Fenway was still here. It had survived two world wars, the Depression, and the Vietnam War. It had seen presidents from William Howard Taft to Jimmy Carter, had hosted World Series, although the Sox hadn't won one since 1918. The Boston Patriots had played there for four years in the sixties, and thirty years ago Fenway Park had hosted the first American League playoff game between the Red Sox and the Cleveland Indians, one that the Sox had lost.

Now it was going to host another one, a script written by the baseball gods, both teams having gone through tumultuous seasons to get to this day in Boston.

It was a beautiful fall afternoon, one of the last gasps of summer, the temperature almost 70 degrees, a light breeze blowing in from over the Green Monster in left. Even years afterward, everyone would remember the weather, the perfect afternoon. The Great Blizzard of the previous February, one of the worst in

New England history, seemed like ancient history as Mike Torrez warmed up in the bullpen in right field, as the sellout crowd continued to file into Fenway. He had eaten light, for he didn't like to pitch on a full stomach, and he felt good warming up. He didn't throw hard until the last couple of minutes. He looked over at Ron Guidry warming up in the adjoining bullpen and waved to him, wishing him good luck, as the year before they had been teammates. Guidry reciprocated. Then Torrez walked out of the bullpen and across the green grass of right field on a beautiful afternoon in Boston to begin the game he would end up being most remembered for.

The year before he had won two World Series games against the Dodgers for the Yankees, and he already had come so very far from the Topeka, Kansas, of his childhood.

Over the winter he had signed with the Red Sox for $2.7 million for five years, and he had seemed like the perfect free agent. He was tall and glib and confident. He wore shirts that seemed open to his waist and usually had gold chains around his neck. He used hairspray and his cologne often stayed behind him after he had left the room. His wife had been a model in Montreal.

And he wanted the ball.

Torrez had been thinking of Mickey Rivers and Munson when he'd been warming up in the bullpen, how they were the keys, hitting first and second in the Yankee order, and how he had to keep them off base.

Then he proceeded to walk Rivers on four straight pitches, none of them close to being a strike.

Rivers, the Yankee center fielder, was five feet ten and had grown up in a Miami ghetto. He also was one of those great baseball characters, to the point that when he heard teammate Reggie Jackson say his IQ was 160, he said, "Out of what, a thousand?" He also had once told the mercurial Jackson, whose full name was Reginald Martinez Jackson, "No wonder you're mixed up. You've got a white man's first name, a Spanish man's middle name, and a black man's last name." He often called people "Gozzlehead" and "Warplehead," words he had learned in his Miami youth, and once said that his goals for a new season were to hit .300, score one hundred runs, and stay "injury prone." Then there was the time he had pulled his Cadillac into the Yankee parking lot only to be confronted by his irate wife, there in her Mercedes. She proceeded to smash her Mercedes into his Cadillac, continuing to do this several times. Then, as the story went, she went home and burned all his clothes, and walked around in an Adidas sweatshirt for a week or so.

Rivers was in his third season with the Yankees, and to Red Sox fans he was a villain, thanks to his fight with Bill Lee two years earlier. Since then whenever he was in center field in Fenway he was pelted with just about anything fans in the bleachers could think to throw at him, everything from bottle caps to small batteries, and people would derisively call him "Monkey Rivers." The last thing the Red Sox wanted was Rivers on base, for he was one of those players who seemed to make things happen with his speed—he was called "Mick the Quick"—even if he was famous for walking so slowly to the plate that he looked like some old man on his way to a rocking chair.

It was not the way to start the game.

And now Torrez had to face the dangerous Munson, hitting second because Willie Randolph, normally the Yankee second baseman, was out with a hamstring problem. After he threw a ball on his first pitch, his fifth straight, the Red Sox reliever Bob Stanley got up to start throwing in the bullpen. There would be no margin of error. Not on this day.

But Torrez eventually struck out Munson, even if Rivers had gone to second on a pitch in the dirt that had gotten by Fisk, then got Piniella to ground out to backup third baseman Jack Brohamer, who was playing because Butch Hobson, the regular third baseman, had bone chips in his elbow and could no longer throw the ball across the infield to first base.

Enter Reggie Jackson.

He was arguably the biggest superstar in baseball, the one that transcended the sports page. In a sense, it was like a sneak preview of the future, a time when to be truly a celebrity in America it had to be about more than what you did on the field. You had to be able to get yourself on the gossip pages, too, to be seen as outspoken, controversial, culturally edgy, something that made you a household name, known to people who didn't know the Yankee infield from the infield fly rule. You had to live in celebrity's crosshairs, and no one in baseball in 1978 did that better than Reginald Martinez Jackson.

Part of it was New York, certainly, as he had become the Yankees' first black superstar. Part of it had been his three home runs in the sixth game of the World Series the year before. But that was just part of it. In a changing America, one that was now, on the surface anyway, more receptive to black athletes, Jackson was outspoken, intelligent, made a lot of money, and drove a silver Rolls, a gift from Steinbrenner for signing with the Yankees two years earlier. Maybe more important, he always knew where the camera was.

Jackson, a left-handed hitter, swung and missed the first

pitch, Torrez's first great fastball of the game. The third pitch was another fastball, on the outside part of the plate, and Jackson went with it and sent a fly ball toward left field and the short green left-field wall, only 310 feet away. Once upon a time it had been covered with advertising, large ads for things like Lifebuoy soap and GEM blades, but those had been removed in the forties when Ted Williams had complained. So now it was a dark shade of green thirty-seven feet high, with a screen on top to prevent every home run from going out on to Lansdowne Street that ran behind it.

Anything hit deep to left in Fenway leaves the bat with promise, and this was no exception, especially off the bat of someone as powerful and muscular as Jackson. But the little breeze that was there was blowing from left to right and it held the ball up a bit. Yastrzemski, who might have played the wall as well as anyone who ever lived, ran toward the left-field corner and caught it for the last out of the inning.

Torrez had gotten through the first inning, leaving Rivers at second base.

George Steinbrenner was sitting in the first row beside the Yankee dugout. He had said hello to Boston mayor Kevin White, whom he had known in college at Williams, a small, elite, liberal arts school in western Massachusetts, and had noticed both Ted Kennedy and Tip O'Neill. Steinbrenner used to come into Boston once in a while from Williams, both to explore the city and to run in some college track meets in the Boston Garden, but had never been to Fenway until he bought the Yankees five years earlier, and discovered the Sox fans were throwing nuts and bolts at the Yankee players in the outfield.

Welcome to the rivalry.

He was in his sixth year as the Yankee boss, a new breed of owner, new money, CEO as superstar, a sneak preview of the future.

He had been part of a group that had bought the Yankees from CBS. He had been forty-two at the time, a former assistant football coach at Northwestern. He had made his fortune by taking over his father's shipbuilding company in Cleveland and by expanding it, and from the beginning he had gravitated to sports. He had owned the Cleveland Pipers in the American Basketball Association, and later had a part interest in the Chicago Bulls. He had his own racing stable. He helped finance a couple of Broadway plays. To Steinbrenner, baseball was show business, no different than a Broadway show.

He had said at his first press conference that he was probably going to be an absentee owner, given all his businesses and other interests, but it was quickly apparent those were just words. He loved both the limelight and the cachet that came with owning the Yankees, and quickly became the kind of owner no one could have envisioned, as loud and brash as New York itself, a man who understood the power that came with being splashed across the back pages of the New York tabloids.

The day before, he had been despondent after the Yankees had lost to the Indians, but he had seen Guidry in the Yankee Stadium parking lot afterward. Guidry had been with his wife and young son and he had said, "Relax, I'm going to do it for you."

Guidry was the best pitcher in the game, as improbable as that would have seemed just a few years earlier. That was when he was being sent down to Triple A Syracuse and, with his wife in the car, began driving south from New York City instead of north to Syracuse.

"Where are we going?" his wife asked.

"Back home," he said.

"And what are you going to do when you get there?" his wife asked.

Home was Louisiana, where he had grown up in Cajun country, a backwoods kid who liked to hunt and fish and was called "Gator" by his teammates. He had spent five years bouncing around the minors before getting called up to the Yankees midway through the '75 season, but hadn't found himself until midway through the '77 season when he went 10–2 after the All-Star break. He was only five feet eleven and 160 pounds, but he had a great fastball that tended to all but explode as it reached the plate, and once he found a great slider to go with it, a pitch that had been taught to him by teammate Sparky Lyle, he was almost unhittable. He didn't say a whole lot, and some days he looked like he couldn't have weighed much more than 150 pounds, the negative he'd had to overcome back when there were baseball people who thought he was simply too small to be a power pitcher, but he had an ERA of 1.72, the lowest of any left-handed pitcher in almost half a century, and the Yankees with the ball in Guidry's hand didn't lose very often.

He also loved pitching to Munson, who from the beginning had told Guidry that regardless of the pitch he called, Guidry didn't need to worry about the target as much as simply throwing the best pitch he could. In that sense, Munson made it easy for him. That, too, was one of Munson's gifts as a catcher, something his pitchers appreciated. Munson made things simple.

But Guidry was pitching on three days' rest, instead of his usual four, only the second time all year he had done that.

Now, in the bottom of the first, having struck out shortstop

Rick Burleson and gotten second baseman Jerry Remy to fly weakly to left, he faced Jim Rice. And if Guidry was the best pitcher in the game, Rice was the most feared hitter, someone who hit for both average and power, and was the odds-on choice to be the MVP of the American League in his fourth full season.

Rice had come up to the Red Sox in September of '74, the month the first phase of busing had started, a kid from Anderson, South Carolina, about twenty miles from Clemson University. It was a sleepy town with its one-way streets and a main street full of small stores and small white frame houses that sat under leafy trees. It all seemed like a page out of another time.

This was where James Edward Rice grew up, the fourth of nine children. His father was a factory supervisor, and it was a disciplined home, where the children said, "Yes, sir," and "No, ma'am," and didn't talk back.

It was still the segregated South, where whites and blacks lived in different worlds.

"That was the way it was then," said William Roberts, who first met Rice when Rice was twelve and coached him in football and baseball at all-black Westside High School. "He was a nice kid. He never was a problem. I wouldn't classify him as moody. He was treated just like all the rest of the kids."

From the beginning Rice's athletic ability set him apart. He was a starter for Westside High School while only in the eighth grade. As a sophomore he supposedly hit a ball five hundred feet, something that became part of the town's oral tradition. He also was Ed Rice then. Or Jim Ed Rice. Never Jim Rice.

It was about then that he met a man named Olin Saylors, who coached the town's American Legion team. One night Rice and a couple of his friends came over for a tryout, the first time blacks had shown up. Rice immediately began knocking the ball out of the park, the ball jumping off his bat. But the next day Rice didn't come to practice. So Saylors went looking for him, found him hanging outside a variety store near his house drinking Pepsi and eating potato chips. Saylors asked him why he wasn't at practice. Rice replied that he wasn't going to waste his time playing baseball, he was going to get a job so he could buy some clothes.

"I don't know anything about clothes," Saylors told him, "but I know something about baseball. You stick with baseball, and someday you'll be wearing silk underwear."

It was just before Rice's senior year that, in retrospect, was the turning point for him. It was sixteen years after *Brown v. Board of Education*, the landmark legislation that had brought civil rights to the South; almost a decade after the civil rights marches; two years after Martin Luther King Jr. had been assassinated in Memphis. But integration was coming to Anderson. Although he lived close to his school, Rice was bused to the all-white Hanna High School on the other side of town, even though his sister wasn't. School officials denied gerrymandering, but there was strong sentiment in Anderson that Hanna wanted Rice to play both football and baseball for them.

"They used him," said Beatrice Thompson, a guidance counselor at Westside High School. "He knew they only wanted him there to play ball for them."

Yet the opportunity to go to Hanna undoubtedly helped Rice's career. Even as late as the late sixties black high schools in the Deep South often played in obscurity, all but ignored by scouts. But after hitting .500 at Hanna High School he became the Red Sox's first pick in the 1971 draft, turning down football offers from North Carolina, Nebraska, and nearby Clemson to sign with the Sox for $46,000.

Three years later he was in Fenway Park.

And for a young black kid from South Carolina it must have seemed like a different planet.

And complicating everything was that both he and Fred Lynn were at Pawtucket together, both billed as can't-miss prospects, yet it was Lynn who was called up to Boston first, even if Rice had the more impressive numbers. Tony Pennachia, his agent at the time, would later say that it definitely affected Rice when Lynn went to the big leagues ahead of him.

The next year both Rice and Lynn were officially rookies, and they both burst into the American League as if propelled off a launching pad. They were called the "Gold Dust Twins," coming of age at the same time, linked together. Only Lynn was everything Rice was not. He was graceful in the field, smooth, articulate, the college kid from USC. He also was white.

"I had been to college and had represented my country three times," Lynn said. "I had played in Japan and Colombia and been all over the place, had been exposed to a lot of different things. Jimmy was a kid from a small town in the South who went right to professional baseball. By the time we both got to Boston I was much more prepared for what we were getting into than he was."

So maybe it was inevitable that Lynn instantly became the media darling. Then shortly after the playoffs, Rice broke his wrist. He spent the '75 World Series sitting in the dugout in relative obscurity, while Lynn spent it under the media microscope. And then Lynn was named the American League MVP.

"I was hurt by all the attention he got at the time," Rice would say in 1985. "Anyone who looked at the stats had to think I deserved the MVP as much as he did."

Whatever the reason, even in this magnificent season, the wall Rice erected around himself was still there, almost impregnable. He seldom gave interviews. When he did they were perfunctory at best, given to baseball, and baseball only. There have been virtually no peeks at Rice the man, what he thinks, what he feels, who he is. There seemed to be a controlled anger about Rice, the sense that he wanted to be left alone. He didn't want to be a spokesman. He didn't want to be a leader. He didn't want to speak for black players. What he really wanted to do was let his numbers speak for themselves, as if they were enough.

"Jimmy was coming into a volatile environment, given what was going on in the city, and his best defense was not to say much," Lynn said. "I think it's very understandable."

What did Rice think of the irony that he had first come to Boston in the same month that busing had started, this man who had been bused to an all-white high school in his senior year?

What did he think of the pressures of being a black player in such a racially charged atmosphere?

No one knew, not really.

Yet there were hints.

"I think race has been a factor in the way I've been used," he had said that year, "because the front office let it be a factor. Lynn can hit .240 in the minors and I can hit .340, and he gets a starting job before I do."

A decade later, the writer John Hough spent a year following the '86 Sox and he said of Rice: "He won't look at me, won't say hello, carries an indifference to me and my business that is so colossal, so absolute, that the sheer weight of it seems aggressive."

In that same time frame Rice had said about the media, "They don't write down what you say. They stand in the back and don't hear everything, or else they get it from somebody else and put it in the paper anyway. And they don't respect that sometimes I want to be alone. If they don't respect me, why should I respect them? Or they want me to talk about my teammates, or what's wrong with the team. Well, I'm not going to do that. And if I have to tell a lie to please them, then I'm not going to do that. I wasn't raised that way. And what did they ever do for me anyway?"

Even by '78, though, he was quickly becoming one of the least-known superstars in the history of Boston sports, the Red Sox's existential man, proud, imperial, mysterious, enigmatic. Back home in South Carolina the people who had known him when he was a kid felt that his behavior was little more than a defense mechanism, a survival tool for dealing in a world he hadn't been prepared for.

"I can understand if he went into a shell," said William Roberts, Rice's old coach, a decade later. "From what I hear Boston's as segregated a place as it used to be down here. Maybe he dealt with it the best way he could."

Yet Zimmer loved him, and why not? He always came to play. He played hurt. He played hard. He worked to get better in the outfield. His teammates respected him. In a sense, he was a throwback, a player from another era, someone who came to the park early, worked on his game, and never gave the manager any problems. Later, Don Baylor would question why he wasn't more of a leader, but in '78 no one really expected him to be. Not on a team that had Yaz and Fisk, older players. Rice was still a young player, just seven years out of high school, and in a sense it had all come so very quickly.

Any true insight into Rice would come much later. One of the best portraits would be in Howard Bryant's excellent 2002 book, *Shut Out*, an examination of the Red Sox and race. Rice was forty-nine then, long retired, but still essentially enigmatic, still closed, as if long ago he had erected a moat around his true feelings, and he wasn't too keen about taking it away now.

"I had a job to do," he said in *Shut Out*. "I wanted to do my job and go home. That's it. I didn't want to be the highlight. Reggie Jackson enjoyed it. I didn't. I wasn't going to go out there and draw attention to myself all the time because I didn't enjoy it."

He was six feet two and built like the high school football star he once had been. Everyone always talked about his incredible strength, how he could be fooled on a pitch and still drive it out, the kind of strength that stood out, even in the big leagues. No one knew it at the time, but this would be the season of Rice's life, that for all the numbers he would put up in the future, this had been the year when he was the undisputed most feared hitter in the league, the kind of season he never would replicate again.

His dealings with the media grew worse throughout his career, and he became more of a mystery, adding to the sense that it could have been different. His anger was more on the surface in those later years, as if he had positioned himself into a place where he didn't get both the attention and adulation he undoubtedly could have had if he had been more accommodating, and was feeling a certain bitterness that he didn't get it.

Rice was a coach in the Red Sox's minor-league system when Bryant spoke with him. The interview took place at Legends Field, the Yankees' spring training home in Tampa, and if Rice certainly wasn't trying to reinvent himself, he wasn't trying to run from the past either, eventually saying some things he no doubt had kept bottled up for years.

"Here I am coming into a situation," he said. "They had Freddy Lynn. He was supposed to be the Golden Child. Mr. Everything. And here comes this nigger from South Carolina who was every bit as good, and was one of the top five players in the American League, and it was a different story. It didn't work out the way everyone thought it would. They didn't know what to do. I wasn't white. I wasn't Irish and I wasn't from Boston. But I knew the rules. I wasn't going to say or do anything that was going to put what I had in jeopardy."

Now, on this October afternoon in 1978, Rice stood in against Guidry in the classic baseball showdown: the great pitcher against the great hitter. The two men who were the favorites to be the American League's MVP.

Guidry struck him out, getting him with a slider.

The first inning ended with no score.

CHAPTER TWO

The story of Boston's beginnings are familiar to every schoolchild. Religious dissenters sailed across the ocean to a land sparsely populated by Native Americans. And from the beginning those Puritans cared about government.

"For we must consider that we shall be as a city upon a hill. The eyes of all people are upon us," said John Winthrop, the first governor of the Massachusetts Bay Colony.

Those early Yankees built a society that led the revolution against the British, and their city became a citadel for learning and culture. The first public school was built in 1635. A year later Harvard was founded, the first college in this new land. Boston Common became the country's first public park. By the early nineteenth century Boston blossomed as a center of learning and political and social activism. The antislavery movement, women's rights, civic disobedience, and the philosophical movement known as Transcendentalism: all have Boston roots. As does much of this country's literary tradition, a list that includes Emerson, Thoreau, Hawthorne, Longfellow, Louisa May Alcott, Julia Howe, John Greenleaf Whittier.

The first wave of immigrants came from Ireland, fleeing the Irish potato famine of the 1840s. It was the first movement in what the Boston native and historian Theodore White would later call the "ethnic ballet" that would make the city home for Europe's downtrodden and remake the city's politics and culture. For more than a century the ethnic fissure in the city would be between Irish Catholic and Yankee Protestant, and the Yankees did not take kindly to the waves of Irish flooding into the city, dramatically changing it. It didn't take a visionary to see the future, one in which simply by sheer numbers the Irish, with their Catholicism and their immigrant culture, were going to be the majority group in Boston.

By the late nineteenth century this happened. The Irish took control of city government and used public jobs as engines of upward mobility. Politics were played out on a local level. It was a serious game, "an ethnic contact sport," the longtime *Boston Globe* reporter Martin Nolan once said.

Once upon a time African-Americans had gotten along very well with the Brahmins, Boston's traditional ruling class, the ones who ran the banks and the government and lived in the stately brownstones on Beacon Hill, a fly ball away from the Boston Common. Slavery had been ruled unconstitutional as far back as 1783, and by the middle of the nineteenth century blacks in Boston had achieved a degree of freedom unprecedented in the United States, complete with desegregated schools. Boston also had been the center of the abolition movement, the home of the fiery speeches of William Lloyd Garrison, and many blacks were educated, cultured, and closely aligned with whites.

But by the sixties Boston's dirty little secret was that beneath all the history and all the tradition Boston was a parochial city, full of underperforming schools and run-down neighborhoods. From 1940 to 1960 the city's black population had tripled, many arriving from the South uneducated and unskilled, ending up in housing projects. Not only did this cause tensions and divisions in the black community, these new arrivals also competed for marginal jobs with the white working poor. By the early seventies the blacks were in ghettos, primarily in the South End, Roxbury, and parts of Dorchester and Mattapan, that the different white ethnic groups left behind in the old neighborhoods after their more affluent cousins had bailed out to the suburbs.

This was the Boston of three-decker tenements and shots and beer at the corner bar, the Boston that's come to be immortalized in movies like *Mystic River* and *The Departed*, the Boston that's never had anything to do with Harvard and the city's literary heritage, the one that never was in the Freedom Trail brochures.

Boston in the sixties was a city of neighborhoods, neighborhoods that would come to feel they were under attack a decade later.

"You were defined by three things then," remembered Mike Gorman, who grew up in the Dorchester section of Boston and went on to be the television voice of the Boston Celtics for the past twenty-five years. "Your neighborhood. Your parish. And your ethnicity. You wore your ethnicity like a badge back then."

Dorchester was primarily Irish-Catholic then, 100 percent white, a section of the city Gorman calls South Boston overflow.

It was only five miles from downtown, but to get to Filene's, the downtown department store on Washington Street that was a Boston institution, Gorman had to walk to Ashmont Station, take the "green line" into downtown. To get to Boston Latin School, which was over by Fenway Park, he had to take three trains, a trip that took about an hour. Boston Latin was the city's prestige high school, which was overwhelmingly white and where 90 percent of the graduates went on to college. Virtually across the street was Boston English High School, which was predominantly black and where roughly a third of the graduates went on to college.

"Your parents tried to convince you that you were middle class," Gorman says, "but the more you traveled around the city you never really believed it. To most of my peers, the goal was to buy a house down the street from your parents and replicate the experience. The other goal was to get a job at the post office, or else on the police and fire departments. Either that, or be a teacher."

Carlo Brogna is another who grew up in the Boston of the sixties and seventies. His neighborhood was the North End, a tiny enclave about a jump shot away from the Boston Garden on Causeway Street, where both the Celtics and the Bruins played, a neighborhood that was overwhelmingly Italian.

"When I was a kid most of the business in the North End was conducted in Italian," he says, "and the wiseguys were everywhere, and everyone knew who they were."

Brogna lived in a small apartment that was hard by the Old North Church, once one of the cornerstones of Paul Revere's ride signaling the townsfolk that the redcoats were coming. It was not far from Prince Street, where the Boston mob boss

Gerry Angiulo had his office. Brogna's father was a butcher, his mother a seamstress in Chinatown, which was downtown. Nearby, across the Mystic River Bridge, was the Irish world of Charlestown. The North End was a self-enclosed little world where the old men played bocce, the old women always wore black, and non-Italians were referred to as "Americans."

"It was the neighborhood," he says. "Why would you leave?"

Today, the North End is a place where the Old World is shopped to tourists, gentrified in many ways, but back then it was poor, ethnic, where many people showered every day at the community bathhouse. In many ways it was a world unto itself, and while Brogna, too, went downtown to Filene's, the North End was his world. When he was ten his family moved to Medford, one of the blue-collar suburbs that were the first stops for immigrants on their way to the American Dream.

"It was only seven or eight miles away, but it was a million miles in culture," he says.

Still, the family was always going back to the North End. It was where his mother went to shop. It was where his cousins lived. It was where everyone went to celebrate the numerous feasts. It was where the roots were, and in Boston then roots were everything.

Bill Russell was arguably the first public figure to say that Boston had a racial problem, even if no one was really listening at the time.

He was the first black superstar in Boston, arriving in December of 1956, fresh from winning two national titles at the

University of San Francisco and winning at the Olympics in Melbourne. But he was more than just a great basketball player, one who would soon turn the Celtics into the best basketball team in the world. He also was a young, proud black man, and in many ways Boston wasn't ready for him. By the time he arrived he already had a strong sense of racial pride, already had decided he was not going to be the stereotype of the Negro, the good-natured laughing boy just wanting to please. He already had decided that he would speak when spoken to, offer little, and do everything he could to help his team win, but on his terms, no one else's.

He already had learned about both the ephemeral quality of sports fame and his place in fifties America. The year before he had been invited to the White House to be on President Eisenhower's commission on physical fitness, part of a group that included Celtics great Bob Cousy, baseball luminaries Willie Mays and Hank Greenberg, and boxers Gene Tunney and Archie Moore. Afterward, he had traveled to Louisiana to visit relatives, only to quickly discover that it didn't matter that he'd led his college team to two national championships, or been invited to the White House. In the Deep South he "was just another black boy, just so much dirt, with no rights, no element of human courtesy or decency shown to me and mine."

These were the lessons he brought with him to Boston. Not only was he the first black superstar in the NBA, he was a young man positioning himself for a changing America. He knew what he thought. He knew what he believed. And nothing was going to get in the way of that.

It was soon apparent he had little use for Boston. Not the Celtics organization, whom he never had a problem with. Not his teammates, whom he always got along with. Not Red Auerbach, the autocratic coach he respected. For Boston. He was not someone who aspired to be a "credit to his race," like the prizefighter Joe Louis, not someone who was going to acquiesce to the status quo. It also was soon apparent that Bill Russell was a sports star the likes of which Boston had never seen before. He called Boston a racist city, said it had been difficult to buy a house in suburban Reading, and that he and his family had been the targets of discrimination.

But what was he talking about?

Hadn't the Celtics been the first team to put five black players on the floor at the same time? Hadn't they been the first NBA franchise to hire a black coach, Russell himself in 1966?

Hadn't the Boston Bruins had the first black hockey player in the NHL back in 1958, Willie O'Ree?

Hadn't the Boston Patriots always had black players ever since they began in 1960?

What, pray tell, was Russell's problem?

That seemed to be the consensus then, the sense that this outsider had come into Boston and was making public accusations that no one had ever said before. Complicating things, though, was the fact that the Red Sox didn't have a black player until 1959, the last team in the major leagues to integrate.

The irony is they could have had both Jackie Robinson and Willie Mays. Or at least they had a chance to have them, Robinson and two other black players having come into Fenway Park in April 1945 for a tryout, two years before Robinson broke baseball's color line in 1947. The tryout came after constant pressure from a Boston city councilman named Isadore Mushnick, who threatened to take away the Red Sox's special license to play games on Sundays if the three black players weren't given a tryout, and even then it came reluctantly. The three players had to sit around Boston for a few days, and even then the tryout had been nothing more than a cursory look, little more than a baseball version of a dog-and-pony show. Near the end of it someone yelled, "Get the niggers off the field."

Robinson forever disliked the Red Sox for the sham of a try-out, and years later called Yawkey the most bigoted man in base-ball. The Red Sox also once sent a scout to watch the great Willie Mays, then a kid in Birmingham, Alabama, but the game got rained out, and rather than stay around and wait for Mays to play, the scout left and later filed a report saying Mays couldn't play.

This was the history, and when asked about it in those days Yawkey always said that he wanted to sign a good black player but his scouts never found him any. That was the party line, anyway, along with the theory that since the Red Sox had two of their top farm teams in the South, it probably wouldn't have been fair to have subjected a young black player to that in the fifties. Yet Al Hirschberg, a respected Boston sportswriter at the time, and the man who had done Celtics' star Bob Cousy's first book in 1957, wrote that manager Pinky Higgins had told him in the late fifties, "They'll be no niggers on this team as long as I have anything to say about it."

In 1958 Elijah "Pumpsie" Green was brought to spring training in Scottsdale, Arizona. He was not allowed to stay in hotels the Red Sox used, and instead stayed in Phoenix, seven-teen miles away. He also was soon sent down to a Sox farm team in Minneapolis, even though he had hit well, a demotion that caused the Boston chapter of the NAACP to complain. He was brought up to the Red Sox in June, where he was first befriended

by Sox great Ted Williams, who always would warm up with him
before games, and also by Bill Russell, who often would drive
the young Green around town in his Cadillac, all the while talking about how racist Boston was, how lonely and miserable he
often was, how difficult he found Boston, going on monologues
like he was sitting on some therapist's couch.

Sometimes Russell would go to nightclubs in Roxbury like
the Hi-Hat and Slades, leftovers from the time before World
War II when the intersection of Massachusetts Avenue and Columbus Avenue in the South End had been Boston's version of
Harlem. There had been jazz clubs that attracted some of the
biggest musical names of the time, from Count Basie to Duke
Ellington. There had been ballrooms and restaurants, bars and
jukeboxes, pool halls and neon lights. It had been the center of
black nightlife, talked about in Malcolm X's autobiography, as
he had lived for a while in Boston.

But it was mostly just memories now, save for the few restaurants and clubs that were farther down Washington Street,
and for Russell it was further evidence that when it came to race
in Boston the whites were in denial, and the blacks were passive, as if both groups were clinging to the adage that this is just
the way it is, the way it always had been.

By 1967 the Red Sox began the season with three black
starters, and they all knew they were under a microscope. They
knew that they had little room for error, and were held to different standards. They knew what Pumpsie Green had learned:
you got along on the Red Sox by going along. Not that they
said a lot about it. Bill Russell might be able to get away with
saying something about being a black athlete in Boston. They
couldn't.

At least in the beginning.

The two most talented black players then had been George Scott and Reggie Smith. Although they were both young players, they also brought vastly different experiences to Boston. Scott was from Mississippi, from Faulkner country, with its old ghosts and tortured history, its racial hell. He had grown up with both segregation and poverty, living in a tar-paper shack. It was the early sixties, still a couple of years before civil rights workers would come to Mississippi and change it forever, but to Scott it was just the way things were. When he signed with the Red Sox for $10,000 on the night he graduated from high school, he had no idea where Boston was, or anything about it.

"I went to play ball," he would later say. "I didn't know anything else."

Inside the lines of a baseball diamond the world made sense. Outside the lines, it made little sense. He had grown up with both prejudice and discrimination so he was used to that. But the Mississippi of his youth, for all its horrible flaws, had been structured. Everyone knew the rules. His second year in the minor leagues, in Winston-Salem, North Carolina, in the summer of 1964, he was the only black on the team. Sometimes people brought black cats to the games.

"This is your sister," they would yell at Scott, holding up the cat. "This is your mother."

He got to Boston in 1966, and in his view he lived in two separate compartments: he worked in Fenway Park, and he socialized in Roxbury, two places he soon came to know had nothing in common.

Smith was different from Scott.

He was from Compton, California, and he was what was

called a "five-tool" player, someone with many physical gifts for the game. But much like Russell a decade earlier, Smith didn't like Boston either. He, too, was young and proud, and from his rookie year in 1967 he never felt comfortable in Boston. In the beginning he had praised Yastrzemski for helping him in his adjustment to the Red Sox, but it was the city he didn't like, its social stratification, the idea that there were places he wasn't supposed to go. Eventually, he began to carry his anger with him, as if it was always there, right beneath the surface, like some virus that had gotten into his system that he couldn't get out. Peter Gammons, the *Globe* baseball writer who had carved out a national reputation during the fishbowl that had been the '75 World Series, would later say that in his thirty years of being around Boston baseball Smith was the unhappiest player he'd ever seen.

"Smith had a lot of problems playing in Boston," Bill Lee wrote in his '84 book, *The Wrong Stuff*. "Reggie received some hate mail that began 'Dear Nigger,' and then it got nasty. The letters could only hurt his psyche. That wasn't enough for some crazies. They took to throwing hard objects in the outfield at him, forcing him to wear a batting helmet when he was out there."

It was in June of '67 that a riot erupted in the South End and in Roxbury, a four-square-mile area that contained roughly sixty-five thousand blacks and Puerto Ricans, roughly 10 percent of the city's population. It had started when a group of welfare mothers, complaining of long waits to see social workers and then being insulted and harassed when they did get to see them, demanded to see the city's welfare director. The women locked themselves in the office on Grove Street and prevented welfare workers from leaving the building. Police then charged through the windows.

That night the police fired shots into the air, and the next night a police officer was wounded by a sniper in another night of rioting and looting. Mayor John F. Collins called it the worst riot in the city's history, and several black leaders blamed the police for the escalation of violence. The next night, the first night of hot summer weather, police in full riot gear patrolled Roxbury and parts of the South End. Blue Hill Avenue, one of the main streets through Roxbury, was closed to traffic. There was more looting, more violence, more gunfire, more stones thrown at passing cars, more fire alarms, more sirens wailing into the night. There were nineteen hundred police called to the area.

"I prayed for something like this riot," a twenty-three-year-old black woman told the *Boston Globe*. "I generally hoped for it because you see this way we have to get along. We have to have unity now."

But did they have attention?

Not really.

The country was preoccupied with the Vietnam War, the one that came into people's living rooms every night with its grisly images, the first televised war. It was curious about the hippies, these strange kids with their long hair and love beads, their drugs and their sexual freedom, their acid rock and protests, as if the entire country seemed to be on the verge of a national nervous breakdown. There was the sense that everything was unraveling, everything old and familiar was under attack.

Besides, African-Americans had no clout in Boston. There were none on the city council. There were none on the school committee. And their neighborhoods were mostly out of sight, to the point that it was possible to come into Boston, see a show in the theater district, go to the Garden to see the Bruins, go out to eat, go to a club in the Back Bay, go to Fenway, hang around the colleges, do just about anything there was to do, and see very few black people. Certainly Fenway was like that, where you saw more black faces on the field than you did in the stands, and that wasn't a whole lot either. George Scott had been right: Fenway Park and Roxbury truly were worlds apart.

The city was run by the Irish, just the way it had been since the turn of the century. And to the Boston Irish, politics was serious. It was the way they controlled everything, the lesson they had once so painfully learned from the Brahmins, back when they had run Boston with an iron fist, and the signs, both visible and buried in the psyche, were "No Irish Need Apply." The Irish had learned this lesson well. They controlled the city's government. They controlled the city jobs. They controlled the schools. And they weren't going to willingly give that up, for to give that up was to give up power. It's been said that the Irish treated others the way the old Yankees had once treated them. That's probably too simplistic. The Irish ran Boston the way they did because they could. It was their club, and they made the rules.

There was more trouble the following year, following the assassination of Martin Luther King in April of 1968. Riots broke out in over 160 cities across the country, and once again Roxbury blew up. Angry bands of youths stoned cars and buses on Blue Hill Avenue. Rocks were thrown at police cars. There were numerous fire alarms, liquor stores were looted. A furniture store was set on fire. There were fires and vandalism and packs of out-of-control kids, a neighborhood unraveling.

"A massive mob of youths were milling around the Heath

Street housing project in Roxbury wielding clubs and swinging chains," reported the next day's *Boston Record-American*.

Roving bands of black youths posted flyers in shops reading "This store is closed until further notice in honor of Dr. Martin Luther King, the fallen martyr of the black revolution." A crowd estimated at four hundred, complete with bullhorns, invaded Jeremiah E. Burke High School in Roxbury, where they burned the American flag, ripped up a picture of John F. Kennedy, vandalized classrooms, and pulled two teachers from their cars in the parking lot and roughed them up. The looting and stoning of cars continued.

That September, another school melee in Roxbury resulted in a clash between kids and police in a violent brawl that lasted a half hour. It had started because the black students wanted to wear African-style clothing to school, and it continued the next day with police being pelted with rocks from rooftops and rocks being thrown at passing cars.

Boston's black ghetto had become like kindling just waiting for a match.

The signs had been there for a while, certainly, just like they had for the rest of Boston's poorer neighborhoods, if anyone had really stopped to look.

But who really cared about the neighborhoods anymore?

Not the scores of commuters who came in every day and worked in the new skyscraper office buildings that were beginning to dot the landscape, the influx of commuters for whom the Boston neighborhoods were just something to drive through on the way home, signs along the highways. Not the power brokers, the city's establishment. They were the ones building the "New Boston," one that had everything to do with downtown urban renewal, and attracting new business, trying to take Boston into the future.

"Boston went down the tubes after World War II," said Scott MacKay, a former *Providence Journal* reporter who is writing a book about New England politics. "It de-industrialized. The shoe industry went bust. The textile industry went bust. They all moved out in search of cheaper labor. You had three generations of people living in public housing. And these were white people. There was very little opportunity. So everything became either a federal or a city job, and to get those you had to know somebody. Politics was the way you moved up. Everything became political. People came to Boston to go to school, but the people in Boston never left. Once you got past Harvard and the veneer of the old Brahmins, Boston in the seventies was a working-class, ethnic, tribal town."

By the seventies ancestry was destiny in Boston. The plumbers union was Italian. So was the carpenters union and the laborers. The Teamsters were Irish. So were the teachers and the cops.

The melting pot?

Truth be told, it didn't melt a lot back then.

But things were changing downtown. Urban renewal had almost obliterated the old West End neighborhood, knocking down the old Scollay Square, with its burlesque houses, tattoo parlors, and sailors bars. The Boston Redevelopment Agency had begun in 1957, and by 1970 it had changed the landscape. The Government Center, a downtown behemoth with all the warmth of a Soviet office building, opened in the late sixties, a dramatic modernist building designed by I. M. Pei that spoke of the future. The Prudential Center in Copley Square, maybe the first symbolic act, had opened in 1964, the second tallest building in the country at the time. The John Hancock Tower was even bigger than that, coming along twelve years later. This coincided with the ascension of hospitals like Massachusetts General, Beth Israel Deaconess Medical Center, and Brigham and Women's, hospitals that had national stature. Schools such as Harvard, MIT, Boston University, Boston College, and Northeastern attracted scores of students from other places in the country, making Boston arguably the best college town in the country.

This was the "New Boston," a city waking up from decades of slumber, a city with national aspirations, not just regional ones anymore. Maybe this was the Kennedys' real legacy to their old hometown, this sense that the horizons got expanded. Certainly they had for the new mayor, Kevin White, elected in 1967, the son of a Massachusetts pol but also someone with big dreams, a man who had gone to private schools and college at Williams, a man who had a bigger vision for himself than simply being the mayor of Boston. The new businesses on Route 128, the ring road that all but circled Boston, was making Boston a player in the new high-tech world.

And all the while the neighborhoods felt more and more under attack, as if left behind in this march toward the future.

But the white neighborhoods had found their voice, however unlikely she initially appeared to be.

Her name was Louise Day Hicks. She was the daughter of a popular South Boston judge, and though at first glance she was dowdy and seemed to come from a bygone era with her flowered hats and white gloves, she was the first Boston politician to tap into the discontent that was smoldering in Boston's white neighborhoods. She also seemed to have stepped out of the pages of *The Last Hurrah*, the Edwin O'Connor novel supposedly based on the infamous James Michael Curley, the longtime Boston mayor who once had been elected while being in jail. She was a woman full of contradictions, as complicated as the neighborhood she had come of age in, someone who started out as a reformer and became forever known as anything but.

Women didn't go to law school in the fifties. Not in South Boston. But she worshipped her father, a man known for helping the people of South Boston, and when he died she promised herself that she would continue his legacy. That was the legend, anyway, and as she began her ascent through Boston politics that's what she became, a blend of fact and fiction, until at the end she became only a symbol, someone who seemed to exist in the public arena as a sound bite, the incongruous sight of the matronly housewife with the tough talk, all the while clinging to her manners and her diction lessons.

She was thirty-nine when she received her law degree, getting up at four in the morning so she could study before class, for she already had a family. She first got elected in 1961 and two years later she was chairperson of the Boston School Committee, winning an amazing 74 percent of the vote in a citywide election. And from the beginning she was never Louise Hicks, her husband's surname. She was Louise Day Hicks, just in case anyone had forgotten that Day Boulevard ran through South Boston, named for her father.

She had first run on the slogan "The only mother on the ballot," and essentially had run as a reformer, someone who had promised to keep politics out of education. Talk about a Herculean challenge. Since the early part of the century the school committee had been dominated by the Irish, and the perk of being on it was that each member controlled a certain number of jobs, everything from teachers to custodians.

In 1963 there were thirteen inner-city schools that were 90 percent black. Eleven percent of them were at least fifteen years old, and in that spring the Boston chapter of the NAACP demanded a public acknowledgment of de facto segregation in the city's public schools. That same day the Alabama governor George Wallace stood on the steps of the University of Alabama and symbolically blocked a court order that said the university had to admit two black students who had been admitted. That night, on national television, an emotional President Kennedy told the nation that he'd introduced legislation to deal with the desegregation of the nation's schools, calling it a moral issue.

At the same time three hundred people stood in the rain outside a meeting of the Boston School Committee singing "We Shall Overcome."

But the school committee refused to accept the premise that there was de facto segregation in the Boston public schools. It understood that many of the schools were underperforming and too old. Not that this was a new revelation. In 1964 Jonathan Kozol, who had grown up in the suburb of Newton, gone to Harvard and been a Rhodes Scholar, went to work as a fourth-grade teacher in Roxbury, first in a freedom school, then in a public school. His book, published in 1967, called *Death at an Early Age: The Destruction of the Hearts and Minds of Negro Children in the Boston Public Schools*, won the National Book Award, a public shot across the bow.

So the school committee had no quarrel with the argument

that the schools should be better. How could they? But the committee believed in neighborhood schools, and if those schools
had children in them of a certain race, that was about sociology,
not education. Or so their reasoning went.

And Louise Day Hicks quickly became the most popular
politician in Boston.

She declared that children were simply the pawns of racial
politics. She could speak. She was forceful. And when she talked
it was as if the white neighborhoods were talking through her,
as if she had found a way to channel both their fears and hopes.
She might have been what was called "lace curtain" Irish, might
have been perceived as matronly with her styled hair and bright
suits, but she was tough and unyielding, too, and people who
underestimated her did so at their peril.

"Boston schools are a scapegoat for those who have failed to
solve the housing, economic, and social problems of the black
citizen," she said. "If the suburbs are so interested in solving the
problems of the Negro, why don't they build subsidized housing
for them?"

She soon became nationally known as the staunch opponent
of busing to attain racial balance in the schools. Her notoriety
grew. She had two police officers assigned to her around the
clock, and became the most visible symbol of the burgeoning
antibusing movement. She ran for mayor in 1967, complete
with a slogan that said, "You Know Where I Stand," a campaign
that caused the *Boston Globe* to make its first political endorse-
ment in seventy-two years, backing Kevin White. She also said,
"I will continue to defend the neighborhood school as long as I
have breath left in my body."

And while she went on to lose to White by only twelve thousand votes, she proved that she had become a major player in Boston politics.

People did know where she stood.

"She looked nice enough, like someone's grandmother, a tubby older woman with a flowery, old-fashioned dress like Nana wore and a small church hat perched on top of her round Irish face," Michael Patrick MacDonald would later write in his powerful memoir about growing up in South Boston called *All Souls.* "People said she was from Southie, but she had a face that didn't look like she had been through much. Her father was a judge and she lived in a big beachfront house on City Point, but she was okay with us. 'She's the only one sticking up for us,' someone said, so I liked her too."

For the people in the neighborhoods, the ones who felt left behind, the ones who were seeing both their city and their country change all around them, the ones who felt betrayed by so many of their leaders, she became their voice. She knew them. She walked the same streets, shopped in the same stores, had the same fears. She was them, even with her law degree and her pearls and her waterfront house on City Point. She argued with civil rights leaders. She spoke out against the downtown politicians. To her supporters, she was the only one who stood for them, while the politicians and the *Boston Globe* and all the television commentators had abandoned them. And the controversy that surrounded her only added to her appeal, made her a star, put her on the cover of *Newsweek* in 1967, and profiled in *Life*, even if many in the national media denounced her, saw her as some Northern version of Bull Connor, the Alabama sheriff who had become the poster child for Southern bigotry. Even if, through it all, she maintained she was not a racist.

"The important thing is I'm not bigoted," she said. "To me, that word means all that dreadful Southern segregationist, Jim Crow business that's always shocked and repulsed me."

Her mantra was "neighborhood schools for neighborhood children," a phrase that resonated throughout the white neighborhoods, but more than anything she came to represent the traditional values of neighborhood and church, country and flag, all the things that seemed to be becoming more and more demeaned. For two years she served a term in Congress, then came back to run again against White, again losing. But she was famous now, and when Judge Garrity ordered that the first phase of busing to achieve racial balance in the schools would begin in September 1974 she had found her moment.

CHAPTER THREE

Free agency was changing the game, and both the Red Sox and the Yankees were testimony to it.

Baseball always had been run like a plantation, the players the indentured servants, lorded over by paternalistic owners who ran their teams like benevolent despots.

The Red Sox had been the classic example, run by Yawkey, a South Carolina plantation owner and gentleman farmer who long had been accused of running a baseball version of a country club. His uncle, who had adopted him when he was a baby, had owned the Detroit Tigers, and one of Yawkey's earliest memories was playing catch with the baseball immortal Ty Cobb on his uncle's lawn. He had played club baseball at Yale, and when he turned thirty he inherited a large trust fund, and later the family lumber and metals business in Canada.

By the time he bought the Red Sox in 1933, the franchise was below the crosstown Boston Braves in popularity and never had seemed able to recover from selling Babe Ruth to the Yankees in 1920 and seeing Ruth become not only the centerpiece of the great Yankee teams of the twenties but the most famous athlete in the country. Between 1933 and World War II Yawkey had spent millions trying to bring a winner to Boston, pouring money into Fenway Park, but he never could catch the Yankees, finishing second to them four times.

When he first bought the club he loved to work out with his players, loved being around them. They were his stars, and he seemed to idolize them as much as the fans did. He loved baseball, had his own locker in the clubhouse, and when the club was on the road often had picnics on the outfield grass with his wife. He would often invite some of his players to South Carolina in the winter to hunt with him. He paid them handsomely, never cut anyone's salary, and was known as the most benevolent owner in the game, to the point that the Red Sox often were referred to as "Yawkey's Millionaires," even in those decades when they weren't.

The only real knock on him then was that he tended to surround himself with cronies, either drinking buddies or men he felt comfortable with, even if they turned out to be incompetent. The Red Sox had started the fifties as one of the best teams in baseball, only to get progressively worse as the decade played out, a victim of poor scouting and poor organization. And as he got older his relationship with the players changed. Always shy and reclusive, Yawkey only felt comfortable around a handful of people, all the while continuing to dote on his stars, one of the reasons why the Red Sox always were criticized as a selfish team, a team full of stars who always seemed to be circulating in their own individual solar systems, the famous "25 cabs for 25 players" quote, which lasted for decades. One of Yawkey's pets had been Ted Williams, the only player who called him by his first name, so maybe it was only fitting that Yastrzemski, Williams's successor, became another. In a sense they became the sons he never had.

He would arrive from South Carolina in June, to his suite in the Ritz-Carlton Hotel, one of Boston's swankiest, that overlooked Boston Common. He then would arrive somewhat surreptitiously at Fenway Park, where he sat by himself in his private box and watched his team. By the sixties he was rarely seen in public, more and more of a recluse. He was rarely quoted in newspaper stories. For years the only pictures of him in the newspapers showed a man of middle age, looking fairly robust. But by 1967 Yawkey was frail, old, emaciated, someone who could walk through Fenway during the middle of a game and go unnoticed. There were rumors he was dying of cancer.

The '67 season rejuvenated his passion in his Red Sox. Most of the sixties had been a dreary time around Fenway. Williams was gone, the team was mediocre, the crowds were down. Yawkey looked around Fenway and saw it as old and obsolete, belonging to some lost era. He threatened to move the Sox out of Boston if the city didn't build him a new stadium within five years.

Then the Sox came out of nowhere to win the pennant, and a whole new generation flocked to Fenway, as if it were a sacred shrine, and Yawkey became reborn as the gentleman sportsman, a Boston institution, even if history would not always be kind to him.

In many ways Steinbrenner was the antithesis of all that.

He was not a gentleman sportsman.

He wanted to win, period.

When he had taken control of the team in 1973 it was not

a good time for New York, not with a dwindling population and a collapsing base. It tried to call itself "Fun City," but the fun seemed all gone, replaced by too much crime and too much trash that never seemed to get picked up on time. New York had become a symbol of liberalism run amok, a city burdened by its municipal unions and too many social services, and too much debt. In many ways it seemed a microcosm of the country's fears, a fractious place that simply didn't seem to work anymore. The worst time, at least symbolically, had come two years later, when the city essentially was bankrupt, and went to Washington looking for a bailout. President Gerald Ford said no, summed up in a front-page headline in the *New York Daily News* that said in big black type FORD TO CITY: DROP DEAD.

In a country that often seemed to be falling apart at the seams, coming out of a long, unpopular war and mired in the Watergate scandal, a country where drugs were in every high school and interest rates kept rising like the thermometer on a summer morning, New York seemed like the center of the chaos that seemed to be becoming more and more a part of American life. As if something had gotten lost and no one knew where it had gone.

The Yankees seemed to mirror this, the once-proud franchise whose glory days seemed behind them. The past seven or eight years had not been kind to the Yankees. In 1966, in the twilight of the great Mickey Mantle's career, they even fell into last place, and on a day late in the season only 413 people rattled around in cavernous Yankee Stadium, a crowd so embarrassingly small that the television cameras were ordered not to show shots of the empty stands. The neighborhood around the stadium was rapidly deteriorating.

By the mid-seventies entire neighborhoods of New York seemed to be disappearing, full of abandoned buildings and forlorn streets, worn down by years of neglect. In a sense, the South Bronx became a symbol for all of them, a once bustling neighborhood that had turned into urban despair. People from the suburbs no longer liked driving into games at Yankee Stadium, the "House That Ruth Built," which had opened in 1923. Nor did they even want to take the subway into the South Bronx, as if it all seemed interrelated, the Yankees only a remnant of what they once had been, and urban blight all around it. Somehow it all seemed symbolic, the good times gone.

But if other teams feared free agency, afraid it would ruin the game, Steinbrenner embraced it. When Jim "Catfish" Hunter, the great A's pitcher, went on the open market in 1975 due to a loophole in his contract, the Yankees paid him $3.75 million for four years, an amazing contract at the time, one that went out across the baseball world like a neon sign in the middle of the desert, one that spoke of the future. This wasn't the kind of contract other teams gave out, one signed in virtual secrecy, the figures not made public, the way things usually had been done in baseball's past. This was public, all over the news, a contract as a marketing ploy, one that screamed out to fans, one visible symbol that Steinbrenner and his Yankees would spare no expense to win, that the rules they were a-changing.

Midway through a disappointing season Steinbrenner dumped Bill Virdon and hired Billy Martin to be his new manager. That, too, was another symbol. Not only did Martin bring the Yankee past and the memories of the glory days into the manager's office with him, he brought the kind of passion that Steinbrenner demanded, even if the most stoned-out scriptwriter never could have envisioned how their relationship would ultimately play out.

Martin, the fiery ex-Yankee second baseman who always seemed to be in a sprint to his next personal crisis, was one part managerial genius, one part as if he had just checked out of *One Flew Over the Cuckoo's Nest*, the Ken Kesey novel that had been turned into a hit movie starring Jack Nicholson in 1975. He already had managed in Minnesota, Detroit, and Texas, where his reputation was of a hard-driving, passionate manager who made teams better, even if he sometimes left scorched earth behind. Beneath his passion and his temper, which he all but wore on the back of his uniform, right there with the number 1, his insecurities always were a minefield everyone had to tread softly on.

If the prevailing wisdom in baseball is that the season is too long to get emotional over a particular game, Martin didn't manage that way. Each game was life and death, an island in itself. Losing tore at him, resurrected old hurts. He didn't have the emotional temperament to be able to put losses into perspective, so he rode his teams hard. In a perfect world all he wanted to do was to be left alone to manage his team, but working for Steinbrenner was far from a perfect world.

Steinbrenner had loved nothing better than signing Jackson in November of 1976, after which Jackson said, "He courted me like I was a broad." The lavish press conference at the Americana Hotel. The walking down Fifth Avenue. The big dramatic statement, all played out in big bold print in the New York tabloids. This was vintage Steinbrenner. This was what being the owner of the Yankees was all about. It was all a long way from Cleveland.

It was inevitable that he and Martin would clash. They both needed to be the center of attention, both needed control, as if to not have it was a sign of weakness. Martin dismissed Steinbrenner as a fan, felt he didn't know anything about baseball. But, as Steinbrenner loved to point out, "I sign the checks."

In spring training Lou Piniella had said that he couldn't go through another year like '77, even though the Yankees had won their first World Series in fifteen years. But to Piniella, it had been too emotionally draining, the constant turmoil, the endless drama, the never-ending media attention, the ongoing Billy and Reggie show, as if always playing in a middle of a fishbowl.

Then Jackson had showed up forty-eight hours after everyone else to spring training, and it all had started again. His excuse was that he'd been in New York with a candy company in preparation for the upcoming Reggie Bar, for as he once had said while playing in Oakland, if he played in New York they would name a candy bar after him, just the kind of statement that angered his teammates. Or as Red Smith, the famed columnist of the era, once wrote, "There isn't enough mustard in the world to cover the hot dog that's Reggie Jackson."

The summer before, his first year with the Yankees, Jackson had blasted Munson in a *Sport* magazine article, saying that Munson may be the Yankee captain but that he was the "straw that stirs the drink." That set the tone, and many of the Yankees never forgot it, even if Jackson said that the writer had sandbagged him. They came to see Jackson as forever drawn to the limelight like a moth to a flame, came to resent both his self-centeredness and that his presence contributed greatly to the circus atmosphere that surrounded the Yankees. Even Rivers, who once had idolized Jackson, and wanted to be just like him, didn't like the way he acted when he joined the Yankees.

"Thurman and a lot of guys played it off like it was a black and white thing, which it wasn't, it was an ego thing," Rivers would say years later.

But Jackson had hit three home runs in the Yankees' win over the Dodgers to win the World Series in the fall of '77, the night that forever cemented his baseball legacy, and it no doubt helped his status in the Yankee clubhouse. Yet it only seemed to complicate his troubled relationship with Munson, who was both jealous of Jackson and bitter that he no longer was the highest-paid Yankee, a distinction he said had been promised to him by Steinbrenner. Munson had spent the off-season saying he wanted to be traded to the Indians, to be nearer to his Canton, Ohio, home, and came to spring training refusing to talk to reporters, walking by them and saying, "I've got nothing to say to you fuckin' guys." The Yankee beat writers, in turn, nicknamed him "Grumpy."

Munson had been the product of a dysfunctional family, to the point that when a Yankee scout had come to his house to sign him, his father growled, "He ain't too good on pop flies, you know." In his autobiography he gave his father little more than a passing reference, essentially saying that things in the house went much smoother when his father wasn't there. But Munson carried those scars with him, as if there was a big chip on his shoulder and he was just daring you to try and take it off, and if it was part of what fueled him and made him a great player, he paid a price for it, too.

So in the first half of the '78 season Martin and Jackson were still locked in their self-destructive dance, Martin hating

Jackson, and Jackson essentially oblivious to both Martin and his teammates, the star of his own movie.

When he did finally arrive in camp, Jackson started telling the beat writers that his great World Series performance had been for everybody, the rich and poor, black and white, and that the most important thing was that he and his closest friends, and the Yankees, had done it as a team. And all reliever Sparky Lyle could think of was, "Who are these closest guys he's talking about? They're certainly not his teammates."

And if this weren't enough, Lyle, who had won the Cy Young Award the year before, wanted to be traded.

"This isn't about pride," he had said. "It's about money. Trade me anywhere for a wet jockstrap."

In short, it was another installment of a long-running soap opera. It was only spring training, the Yankees were the reigning world champions, and already tension and discord were right there on the roster, as though last year's glory already had become yesterday's news. As if every year was a clean slate, and nothing mattered but the present tense.

"Billy better start buckling down, or we won't repeat," Steinbrenner said after one spring training loss.

The year before, in a Saturday afternoon game in a hot and steamy Fenway, the tenuous relationship between Martin and Jackson had unraveled, on national television, no less.

Jackson had let a fly ball fall in front of him in right field, a play Martin thought he hadn't hustled on.

Martin went out to the pitcher's mound, where Munson was already there with Torrez, then pitching for the Yankees. Munson, in particular, was incensed at Jackson, thought he had loafed on the play.

"Take that sonofabitch spook out," raged Munson. "That sonofabitch doesn't want to play today. Something must be bothering him. Maybe he's got a hangnail or something."

Martin didn't have to hear that twice.

He told Paul Blair to replace Jackson, even though replacing a position player in the middle of an inning almost never happens in baseball. Jackson was oblivious to all this, as he had turned to talk to someone in the Yankee bullpen, his back to the field, one arm casually draped over the bullpen railing.

When he finally realized what was happening he pointed to himself with a "You mean me?" look on his face.

"What the hell is going on?" he asked Blair.

"You've got to ask Billy that," Blair said.

As Jackson trotted in, all this being played out on national television, he seemed more puzzled than angry, coming down the dugout steps with his hands spread, palms up.

Martin met him at the bottom of the steps, face contorted in rage.

"What the fuck do you think you're doing out there?" he asked.

"What do you mean?" Jackson asked. "What are you talking about? Why did you take me out? You must be crazy to embarrass me in front of fifty million people."

"You know what the fuck I'm talking about," Martin countered. "You want to show me up by loafing on me. Fine. Then I'm going to show your ass up. Anyone who doesn't hustle doesn't play for me."

Jackson put his glasses down, and approached Martin, as Joe Garagiola said on television, "They're going to confront each other right there in the dugout."

"I don't give a fuck," Martin snarled. "I ought to kick your fucking ass."

"Who the fuck do you think you're talking to, old man?" Jackson said. "Don't you dare show me up again, motherfucker."

Martin tried to get to Jackson, as Garagiola said, "There they go." But it was broken up.

"You don't like me—you've never liked me," Jackson shot back, as he went down the ramp that led to the visiting clubhouse.

Jackson later said he was planning to fight Martin in the clubhouse, away from the fans and the TV cameras, but was convinced by backup catcher Fran Healy, his best friend on the team, to shower and leave the ballpark. He did, eventually walking back to the Sheraton in Copley Square, about a mile away.

After the game Martin sat in the cramped manager's office in the visiting locker room. Again, he clung to his theme that if a player shows up the team, he was going to show up the player, as if to back down, or admit he might have made a mistake, would have been weakness. He looked haggard and gaunt, the blood drained from his face.

"Did you consider a more conventional means of discipline?" he was asked.

"How do you fine a superstar, take away his Rolls-Royce?" Martin shot back.

"Do you think the incident was bad for baseball since the game was on national television?"

"I don't care if it went out over the whole world," Martin said.

That night, in his room in the Sheraton, Reggie got a phone call from Jesse Jackson, then thirty-five, a decade after he had

been standing on the balcony in Memphis when Martin Luther
King had been shot. The two had begun a friendship early in the
year, and now Jesse Jackson was telling Reggie Jackson to calm
down.

Later in the evening, he was joined in his hotel room by the
Yankee beat writers Phil Pepe of the *New York Daily News* and
Paul Montgomery of the *New York Times*, who was filling in for
Murray Chass. Jackson was sitting on the floor. His shirt was
off, three gold chains dangling from his neck, a big red Bible
open on his lap. Also in the room was Torrez. A woman, staying
with Jackson, was in the shower.

"It makes me cry the way they treat me on this team," he
said, the emotion running through his voice. "I'm a good ball-
player and a good Christian and I have an IQ of 160, but I'm
a nigger and I won't be subservient. The Yankee pinstripes are
Ruth and Gehrig and DiMaggio and Mantle. They've never had
a nigger like me before."

But now it was a year later, and even though the Yankees
were coming off a World Series win, it was as if nothing had
really changed. Winning had only been a brief reprieve, spring
training had been chaotic, and the start of the season had done
little to change that. Throw in some injuries, and once again the
Yankees were walking along some emotional fault line.

By the middle of July they were an amazing fourteen games
behind the Red Sox, a season that had never gotten going and
now seemed about to unravel like some old baseball left outside
in the rain. The hidden theme had been the self-destruction of
Martin, as if he had some managerial death wish. He had almost
gotten into a fight with Munson on a plane trip when Munson
had periodically removed his earphones and his Neil Diamond

music reverberated throughout the cabin. Martin had chastised him for not being a better leader, and Munson had shot back, "The only reason you're saying this stuff is that there's nine guys between us."

Never backing down was the one article of Martin's faith, the trait he had carried with him from his hardscrabble childhood in Berkeley, California, to the biggest baseball stadiums in the country, and he wasn't going to back down now. He went after Munson, people broke it up, and once again the Yankees had become the Bronx Zoo.

It became the subtext of the season, the little flare-ups, appearing as quickly as spontaneous combustion, a team moving from crisis to crisis as it moved through the season.

So much of it was Martin's volatile personality, his insecurities, his temper, a witch's brew all fueled by his nightly drinking. He couldn't deal with Steinbrenner, who he believed constantly second-guessed him, constantly meddled, unable to stay in the background and simply let him manage the team. He couldn't deal with Jackson, whom he had almost a visceral hatred for, part racial, part based on the belief that Jackson felt he was too big for the team, immersed in too many individual agendas that had little to do with how the team played. He couldn't deal with the brooding Munson, who though respected by his teammates had his own demons that were as much a part of him as his shin guards and chest protector.

But mostly he no longer seemed able to manage in New York, where he always felt he was on the precipice of getting fired, that whatever he did Steinbrenner sat in daily judgment, like some stern father there was no pleasing.

And it all blew up in Kansas City.

Martin had been drinking at a bar inside O'Hare Airport in Chicago when he ran into two beat writers, Henry Hecht of the *New York Post* and Murray Chass, and the talk invariably turned to Jackson and Steinbrenner. It was just a few days after he had suspended Jackson for five games for bunting when he wasn't supposed to, a move that once again was all over the papers in New York, another crisis in a season where the Yankees seemed to move from one to another. Martin essentially said that Jackson and Steinbrenner were made for each other.

"One's a born liar, and one's convicted," Martin said.

That did it.

It was one of those lines that would take on a life of its own, and go out across the baseball world like lightning in the middle of the night. An emotional Martin quit the next day in Kansas City, complete with dark glasses and tears and the feeling among many of the reporters present that they were watching a man having a nervous breakdown. He had been replaced by Bob Lemon, who had been fired a few weeks before by the White Sox, and from the beginning Lemon essentially said he was going to keep out of the way and simply let the Yankees play.

"You guys won last year, which means you must have been doing something right," he told his team. "So what do you say you go out and play like you did last year? And I'll try to stay out of the way."

In short, he was going to be the anti-Martin.

The Yankees' Willie Randolph, the black kid from Queens who would go on to become a Yankee coach and a Mets manager, wasn't sure Lemon even knew the names of all of the players, simply calling them all "Meat."

Regardless, the Yankees responded to Lemon's laid-back

style, and quickly began playing better. They also got healthy, and Jackson got hot. In fact, one of the few times Lemon showed his displeasure was the last day of the regular season, when the Yankees had lost at home to the Indians. He had closed the clubhouse to the media and had gone after Rivers for not hustling on a play in the outfield. It was out of character for Lemon, and because it was, it had the intended effect, not like Martin's temper tantrums and tirades that had become so frequent they were easy to tune out.

But Lyle thought that Martin's legacy was that the Yankees had become a tough, scrappy team, a team that always battled, a trait that was overlooked because of the circus atmosphere that always surrounded it. It also was a team with many strong personalities—Munson, Jackson, Lyle, Goose Gossage, Piniella, Graig Nettles—a team that learned to depend on itself through all the turmoil. One way had been by the constant needling of each other, a climate where nothing was sacred. Rivers would later say that if you struck out, or made a bad play in the field, your teammates would get on you, that every day someone seemed to get their turn. He believed that that was the reason they had become winners, simply because they were always fighting each other, that there was no room for losing. That, and the fact that they were able to quickly move beyond losses.

Munson, in particular, was great at this: when the game was over it was over. It was one of the reasons why he was so respected in the clubhouse. Not only was he the ultimate gamer, he was one of the guys who made everyone else loose, a leadership style defined both by the passion he played the game with and the irreverent way he looked at everything else.

They also had been aided by the fact that the New York City

newspapers went on strike in early August. No longer was the Bronx Zoo on the back pages of the New York tabloids every day, the daily diary of dysfunction. No longer were there innumerable reporters in the locker room every day, looking under rocks, asking difficult questions, stirring everything up. Not only were the Yankees getting healthy and playing better, the volume had been turned down, and in this new reality they had flourished.

Now they were in the second inning of a playoff game with the Red Sox, and who could have believed that at the All-Star break?

CHAPTER FOUR

If the Yankees had survived their own peculiar drama, so had the Red Sox, surviving not only their four-game humiliation in early September and their fall from grace, but also the fissures that were running through their own clubhouse, most notably the generational clash between Zimmer and Bill Lee, and the ramifications that came from that.

Zimmer was the ultimate baseball lifer, one of those men who had come of age squinting across innumerable parched infields, a former teammate of Jackie Robinson with the old Brooklyn Dodgers. He had been married at home plate when he was a minor leaguer, and once had been hit in the head by a pitch and had a metal plate in his head as a reminder. He lived inside the game, had come of age in an organization that did things the right way, the textbook way of Branch Rickey baseball, old school before anyone used the term.

But it wasn't easy being the Red Sox manager, never really had been.

The only one the fans had really liked had been Dick Williams in '67, who had come in and immediately changed the culture. He was a manager out of some old dog-eared baseball novel, a remnant from the time when a manager ran the clubhouse like a marine drill sergeant ran a bunch of Parris Island recruits. There was a dress code, there were rules, and it was a court with no appeals. Then he went out and took a team that had been given no chance at the start of the season and won the pennant with them, the season forever remembered in Boston as "the Impossible Dream."

He was gone after the '69 season, as his relationship with several of the veteran players, including Yastrzemski, began to deteriorate, and Yawkey sided with Yastrzemski. But after that, everyone who succeeded him was compared to Williams and found wanting, at least by the fans, who had loved Williams's "my way or the highway" approach. Zimmer had replaced Darrell Johnson shortly before the end of the '76 season, even though Johnson had guided the Sox to the World Series the year before. But everyone knew managers were hired to be fired, right? No one went on their own terms. Not in Boston anyway.

Everyone knew that Bill Lee called him "a gerbil." Everyone knew Zimmer had feuded the year before with a group of players who called themselves "the Buffalo Heads," the Red Sox versions of the counterculture, who considered Zimmer some antediluvian relic from some lost era, a dinosaur in a Red Sox uniform.

He was roly-poly and bald, and he always seemed to be chewing something, his cheeks all puffed out, and after games he would sit at his desk and all but grunt some answers to questions, all the while dunking cheese squares into mustard and

popping them into his mouth. Zimmer looked like a cartoon figure, and when things started to unravel, he was like a batting
practice fastball just waiting for someone to take a whack at it.

It wasn't the Boston newspaper guys, not really. Most of them
liked Zimmer, especially the older ones. Sure, he said "fuck"
about every third word, but he was a baseball guy and baseball
writers tend to like baseball guys. In a sense, the sportswriters
mirrored the Sox players. The older ones liked Zimmer because
he acted like a manager was supposed to act. The younger ones
looked at him and saw some guy who still thought he was living
in the fifties. In that sense Zimmer became a lightning rod for
the generational clash that was taking place, not only in his own
clubhouse but throughout baseball. No one was immune to the
realities of the seventies, not even old-school baseball guys.

"Zimmer was one of those old-fashioned guys who ran the
ship the way it always had been run," said Leigh Montville, a
Boston Globe columnist at the time. "But now there were bells
and whistles all over the ship, and it was like he didn't want
to deal with the bells and whistles. He just wanted to run the
ship."

If the team was changing, so was the way it was being covered, and one of those changes was the rise of sports talk radio
in Boston. There was *Calling All Sports* on WBZ with Bob Lobel
and Upton Bell, who had taken over from Guy Mainella, one
of the trailblazers for sports talk in Boston. There was *Clif-'n'-
Claf* on WITS, Cliff Keane being a former sportswriter for the
Boston Globe, Larry Claflin a columnist for the *Herald*. There
was *Sports Huddle* on Sunday nights, hosted by Eddie Andelman, an irreverent look at the local sports scene that would, in
many ways, become the template of the sports talk that would

follow, where the key was entertainment and sports knowledge, not inside baseball. They all took calls, and for the first time the average sports fan had a voice, if only for a minute or so.

Once, the newspaper columnists had been the only real voice, their insight and opinions going out every morning to innumerable readers, their circulations giving their opinions a certain clout, a certain gravitas. That was changing. Not only did the talk show hosts each have their own voice, but so did the callers, one after another until it sometimes felt like a chorus. And as the Sox season had plummeted there was an almost daily barrage against Zimmer and the crumbling of the Red Sox. Making it worse was that Zimmer listened. He would put the show on when he left the park at night and hear "Vinnie from Dorchester" and "Joe from Revere" question his every move and call him an idiot, and a moron, endless venom over and over, one that only intensified as the Sox saw their lead dwindle. During games in Fenway he would hear the people near the dugout calling him names, and then on his ride home he would hear it all over on the talk shows, as though he couldn't stop himself from listening.

"It ate at him," said Fred Lynn. "That was his downfall."

Lynn had quickly learned as a rookie in '75 that the way to survive in the hothouse that was the Red Sox clubhouse, with its unrelenting media, was to keep low and not say a whole lot. Even with playing on the best college team in the country at USC, he hadn't been prepared for life under the microscope that was playing for the Red Sox. He soon learned that there were two ways of being a Red Sox star: you either embraced it, what Tony Conigliaro had once done, when he had been the unofficial Pope of Kenmore Square, and what Lee was doing now, all but running for microphones as though they were respirators and he was out of breath; or you didn't go out very much.

He had found that out early. It had been an off day and he had been at a tourist site north of Boston, just doing something different and trying to get to know the area, and all of sudden someone asked him for an autograph and he turned around and there was a train of people behind him.

"I used to sneak away by myself and go fishing," he said. "Just find some little place in the middle of nowhere and get away from it all."

The last thing he was going to do when he left the park was listen to talk shows. But he understood the pressure of playing in Boston, knew that some guys couldn't really handle it, and he saw what it was doing to Zimmer, how the constant criticism and the constant second-guessing chipped away at him, diminished him.

Zimmer believed that Bill Lee had started most the venom, that Lee would go to the media and tell them his nicknames for him, and because the media loved Lee, who was always good for a quote, it just grew from there, a drum continually pounded.

"I think that rubbed off on some of the fans and they started booing and it became sort of a ritual," Zimmer would later say. "I learned to live with it."

But it had become very personal with Lee, so ugly that Zimmer would later say that of all the people he'd met in baseball during his long career Lee was the only person he would not invite into his home.

Lee was in his tenth season in Boston, a California kid who had all but mainlined the counterculture. He was irreverent, he was funny, he was insubordinate, and above all he was outrageous, as if someone had put Abbie Hoffman into the middle of a major-league clubhouse and given him a uniform and sent reporters to interview him afterward. Lee was many things, sometimes all at once, but he always was a lightning rod. In a game where players relied on clichés as if they were life rafts, you never knew what was going to pop out of Lee's mouth.

Is it any wonder that reporters flocked to him?

Any wonder that Boston's large youth culture loved him, and many older fans thought he was some kind of baseball hippie, someone they couldn't come close to understanding?

In a sense, the generational clash inside the Sox clubhouse mirrored the one in the country, and the Red Sox were one of the few things that brought the generations together in New England. The world of Red Sox fandom was the one place where fathers and sons could agree that the Sox didn't have enough pitching, or Zimmer was an idiot, or any of the themes that ran through the season. The one place where fathers and sons could talk about the infield fly rule and not politics, the one place that seemed like a sanctuary from the divisiveness that seemed to run through the country like some out-of-control virus.

The counterculture might have begun in the late sixties, but youth culture flourished in the seventies, when it often seemed as though there were two Americas, where parents and children seemed to be communicants in different churches. The old order was being attacked by the new, traditional values were under assault by a youth culture that had very different attitudes on everything, a youth culture that wanted nothing more than the transformation of the society their parents had built. This was the psychodrama running through the country, and it was all there in the Sox clubhouse, too, with the constant skirmishes between Lee and Zimmer, like some dysfunctional family right out of a Eugene O'Neill play.

You could see it in the bleachers at Fenway, baseball as a party, complete with beer and marijuana, and the unquestioned belief that Zimmer could have been a foot soldier in the Nixon White House. This was a snapshot of the generational clash going on in Boston, this city that had become one of the battlegrounds of the new America, one that was more about lifestyle than about the traditional trappings of success, a city where it was possible to live the countercultural life. Or at least the illusion of it.

Eventually, that same generational clash would even affect the busing controversy. For youth culture, in its ideal anyway, was meant to be inclusive. It had been born in the politics of the sixties, and even if much of that had become diluted by 1978, there were still some sacraments that essentially were unquestioned: antiwar, antiracism, anti-oppression. So even in the blue-collar neighborhoods of Boston, in the midst of busing, there were kids who began to question the attitudes and actions of the adults they saw around them, even if this got little attention, a little story lost in the middle of the larger one.

Karen Maguire, who grew up in South Boston and went on to become a newspaper editor, remembers going off to college in the mid-seventies and not wanting to tell people she was from South Boston, that she had found both the racism and the violence repugnant.

Carol Shedd, who also had grown up in South Boston and had been bused to a black school, remembers becoming friends with several of the black kids.

So there undoubtedly were changes in attitudes as busing

began to drag on, especially among the young people perceptive enough to realize that their childhoods were being sacrificed in a dispute where they were merely the pawns on some civic chessboard. Undoubtedly, there were kids in the city's blue-collar neighborhoods who were both a product of the growing youth culture and influenced by it, too. You couldn't be a kid in the seventies and be completely immune to it, even if your daily life was spent in the middle of busing. Even if you were caught in the contradictions of liking black music and black athletes, but still not wanting black kids bused into your neighborhood every morning.

How much significance did this actually have in much of the violence diminishing by the fall of '78?

Who can say?

But there was no question that by the fall of '78 things seemed more muted, regardless of the specific reasons.

Lee was called "the Spaceman," courtesy of the time he was doing a pregame interview on the radio and spoke more about the country's space program than baseball. Or maybe it was because the time he first saw Fenway Park and looked at the wall staring in on him, he asked, "Do they leave it there during games?" Take your pick. It was all part of the package by '78, to the point that no one knew what was real and what wasn't anymore, as if it were all a show, Bill Lee as baseball's Merry Prankster. He said that he had learned more baseball in one year at the University of Southern California than he had in ten years in the Red Sox organization. He said his wife would go to singles bars in Boston with male models when he was off on road trips. He said he used to sprinkle marijuana on his pancakes in the morning. He said just about anything and everything that popped into his head, as if there was no filter, and everything he said, the more outrageous the better, simply added to his emerging celebrity. And every time he said something outrageous it was as though the steam was going to come out of Zimmer's ears.

He also loved to go out on the town, and one of his places was the Eliot Lounge on Massachusetts Avenue in the Back Bay, one of those cult bars that attracted an eclectic mix of reporters, intellectuals, and various antiestablishment types, a place where bartender Tommy Leonard became one of those great Boston characters, a working-class Renaissance man who seemed to know everyone and became the greeter for the Boston Marathon. It was a place about which Charles Pierce once wrote, "once there was a place where nobody batted an eye the night the horse walked in. The horse stopped to visit with everyone sitting at the bar, and then it took eight people to get him out again, and nobody in the place thought it at all remarkable."

It had been the reference point for one of Lee's more enduring lines, which had happened three years earlier in the World Series, when Lee had said, about Don Gullett, the great Cincinnati pitcher, whom he had been matched up with, "Don Gullett is going to the Hall of Fame and I'm going to the Eliot Lounge."

His buddy Bernie Carbo, one of the stars of game six of the '75 World Series, had been jettisoned at the All-Star break, back when the Sox were riding high, essentially given away to Cleveland for a bag of balls, as the old saying went. Lee had been so incensed at hearing the news that he had left the team for twenty-four hours, angrily saying the Red Sox had just sold the pennant, an act of petulance that so enraged Zimmer that, when Sullivan told him he had to take Lee back, Zimmer said, "I want to have a circle of guys in the dressing room and let me go at him."

So Lee was the only Buffalo Head left, the small cadre of counterculture players on the team, so named because pitcher Ferguson Jenkins thought the buffalo was the dumbest of all animals, and that the buffalo reminded him of Zimmer.

In a *Sports Illustrated* story in early August, called "In an Orbit All His Own," the writer Curry Kirkpatrick, who once upon a time had been on the student paper at the University of North Carolina with the *Globe*'s Peter Gammons, tried to examine the phenomenon that Bill Lee had become in Boston. The article caught the outrageousness of Lee, everything from his fascination with the British rocker Warren Zevon to his obvious attraction to the counterculture to his flaunting of any of the rules of decorum that Zimmer and the Red Sox tried to enforce. Like wearing an old warm-up jacket on plane trips when he was supposed to be wearing a sports coat, for what was more a "sports coat" than a warm-up jacket? Or his fondness for wearing sandals and loud Hawaiian shirts, and generally treating Zimmer's rules as if they were just empty words, words with no meaning. It said that Lee often argued frequently and vehemently with Fisk during games, and how once Reggie Smith had beat him up. More important, it painted Lee as arguably the most unusual player in the game, intelligent, irreverent, subversive, someone who would have been equally at home in a student demonstration on some college campus somewhere as he was with the ball in his hand on the pitcher's mound in Fenway Park.

It also caught the sense that Lee was almost a walking contradiction, a great competitor whose off-the-field comments had complicated his career.

"He is an enthusiastic supporter of the Save the Whales movement, but around his neck he wears a Yin-Yang symbol that looks suspiciously as if it is fashioned from a whale's tooth," wrote Kirkpatrick. "He lobbied against sugar, but he's the only one in his family who takes his coffee sweet."

He had his supporters in the Boston media, though, especially the younger ones, many of whom tended to view the world the same way Lee did, only turned down a few notches. One was George Kimball, an irreverent, iconoclastic bear of a man who wrote for the alternative weekly the *Boston Phoenix*. He said that "nobody who can count doesn't like Bill Lee." And the television commentator Clark Booth, another of Lee's friends in the Boston media, said, "It all started out as a joke, a put-on. Bill entertained us, and amused us and it was, you know, 'all seriousness aside' and that routine. Somewhere along the line, though, Bill started to think he had to keep it up. He was like a little kid who wanted to please his elders. Maybe he still wants the role and all the attention. But maybe he's tired of it, too."

No matter.

To Cliff Keane on the *Clif-'n'-Claf* radio show, Lee was the devil himself, and the fact that both Zimmer and Red Sox management let him continue to exist was a sure sign of the organization's growing incompetence. Keane was what would later be called old school, a crusty guy who had been a sportswriter for the *Globe* for years and tended to call everyone "bush." There were some who thought Keane was racist, as illustrated by an incident described in the book *Shut Out*, when Larry Whiteside, who had been hired by the *Globe* in 1973 as their first black sportswriter, heard Keane making references to "niggers," and went over to Keane and calmly said, "If I ever hear that word out of your mouth again, I'm going to knock the shit out of you." Yet Keane supposedly was the one who had covered the ill-fated tryout of Jackie Robinson and two other black players in Fenway Park in 1945, when someone from one of the windows upstairs had yelled, "Get those niggers off the field." Keane had reported it, keeping the story alive.

If nothing else, though, by 1978 Keane was a product of another time, one in which the press box was all white and blacks were often viewed in nasty stereotypes, and whites could throw around pejoratives they simply couldn't say in an integrated setting. The following year, in a Marie Brenner article in *Esquire*, she recounted the story of seeing Keane approach Scott one day and say, "Hey, Boomer, you old bush nigger, you." But when she told that to Zimmer, he had gruffly said that she must have heard it wrong.

There was no question, though, that Keane had no use for Lee.

"Did Lee get a cortisone shot in the shoulder or in the head?" he had asked general manager Haywood Sullivan at a June press conference after Lee's twenty-four-hour disappearance. "If this team has any class you'll tell him to shove it."

Keane kept up a constant barrage against Lee on the air, calling him an "imbecile," "goon-head," and "drug addict," among other things.

No matter.

If nothing else, Lee was the most obvious symbol of the new youth culture in a staid old game that always had fought off change like a good hitter fights off a pitch on his hands. That had changed. Baseball always had been a conservative game, operated like mills used to work in a different America. They were a fiefdom run from the top down, and the players were expected to play and be subservient. That's the way it always had been, as fundamental as the infield fly rule, essentially unquestioned.

A decade before, baseball players were still products of the fifties, with their crew cuts and their general lack of awareness to the changing cultural tides. The '67 season had taken place during one of the most turbulent summers in American history, with riots in several cities, the Summer of Love in San Francisco, and the feeling that the country was coming apart like an old baseball. Yet inside the game it could have been 1957.

But now baseball was dealing with many of the issues that the rest of society was dealing with: longer hair, mustaches, bushy sideburns, recreational drug use, rock music, and more significant, both a questioning of authority and a disrespect for it. It had been one of the underlying tensions on the Yankees under Martin, and it was in the Red Sox clubhouse, too, with Lee at the epicenter. And Lee survived for only one reason, and it really had little to do with his popularity with Boston's burgeoning youth scene. He was a left-handed pitcher who from '73 to '75 had won seventeen games each year.

But the generational clash inside the Red Sox clubhouse was as much a part of the landscape as the batting order that was posted on the wall every day. It wasn't just coincidence that the Red Sox had purged themselves of the Buffalo Heads, a group that once had included Bernie Carbo, Ferguson Jenkins, and Jim Willoughby, in addition to Lee.

Zimmer had hated them.

General manager Haywood Sullivan, the former backup catcher for the Sox in the fifties, had hated them, too.

In a sense they were an affront to everything old-time baseball people believed in, heretics in a sacred church. More important, on a team that was collectively fragile to begin with, they were a distraction at best, potentially divisive at worst.

Zimmer had all but buried Lee in the second half of the year, taking him out of the rotation. He believed Lee had never been the same pitcher after Nettles had thrown him to the ground in the Yankee Stadium brawl two years earlier. Lee believed it was a form of managerial revenge, Zimmer's way of getting back at him. Whatever the reason, the Lee-Zimmer feud had transcended a player-manager dispute. It had become intensely personal, to the point that years afterward it was still a relationship full of bitter animosity.

Zimmer had gotten to the ballpark at eight thirty, something he always did for day games. Two years earlier, when he'd been a coach, Yawkey would often come down to the clubhouse in the morning and sit next to his locker with a cup of coffee and the two would talk baseball. Zimmer remembered that Yawkey's favorite line about something that had gone wrong was "it wasn't meant to be," as if that explained everything.

And for a while there in the second half of the season, as the injuries kept coming, and everything that could go wrong did go wrong, and the boos and the criticism kept mounting, from one talk show caller after another, it must have seemed as if he could hear Yawkey's fatalistic old line in his sleep. As his team slumped and the criticism mounted it must have seemed like it just wasn't meant to be, as if that was as good a reason as any.

Once, one of his adult daughters had come to a game, and on the way home she had started to cry in the car. What's the matter, he had asked, and she had answered that she couldn't deal with the people booing him.

"Get used to it," he had said.

Now, here at the start of the second inning, he was only a game away from redemption.

The first Yankee hitter was Nettles, a left-handed hitter who once had played for Billy Martin with the Minnesota Twins. A tough, hard-nosed player, he was in his sixth season with the Yankees, a steady third baseman with home-run power, good enough to lead the league in home runs two years ago. He had long ago learned to live in the bizarre climate that was the Yankees in New York. He didn't suffer fools gladly, tended to shy away from the media, and just went out and played, even if the drama that always seemed to surround the Yankees sometimes seemed to drag him down, as if he had come to learn that Steinbrenner wanted a certain amount of controversy, for it kept the team on center stage.

He had hit twenty-seven home runs and batted in ninety-three runs, was a dangerous power threat. He also was upset at Torrez for making some derogatory comments about the Yankees during the season, and wanted nothing better than to beat him. Before he stepped into the batter's box, though, there was a stoppage of play, as some fans in center field had put up some signs that the umpires thought might affect a hitter's vision.

"It was a party out there," said Scott MacKay, then a first-year reporter at the *Burlington Free Press*, Vermont's largest newspaper. He and a friend had bought two tickets from a scalper in the swarm of people on Jersey Street outside Fenway as the national anthem started. They cost ten dollars each and looked like something you would get at a county fair. The tickets were in the last row of the center-field bleacher. "Beachballs were being slapped around. There was a lot of drinking, the smell of weed everywhere. At one point a fight broke out, two guys arguing about Reggie Jackson. Periodically, there were chants of 'Monkey' Rivers."

Nettles settled in and popped to the shortstop Burleson on the second pitch, then Chris Chambliss hit a vicious line drive that George Scott speared at first, and Torrez followed by striking out Yankee left fielder Roy White for an easy inning.

"Winning a pennant isn't as easy as it looks," Yastrzemski had said in June.

He was thirty-nine, and it had been eleven years since the great '67 season when he had won the Triple Crown and carried the Red Sox to the World Series, one of the all-time great individual seasons in modern baseball history. That was the season that secured his status as a New England icon, someone who was as beyond reproach as Caesar's wife, even if he hadn't had a season that had come close to his '67 heroics.

But no one believed him that day in June when he said it wasn't easy to win a pennant, not after the Sox had gone 23–7 in May, and in the middle of June already were up six games on the Yankees.

Before that '67 season, the one that made him a New England icon, he had been burdened with the baggage of replacing the great Ted Williams in left field, baggage that had worn him down as much as the losing did, to the point that sometimes it seemed as if it was going to get in the way of his great potential. The Red Sox in the early sixties were going nowhere in a hurry, and there was pressure on the young Yastrzemski.

Hadn't Ted Williams himself supposedly told him to "never let anyone change your swing" the first time he had seen Yastrzemski hit, like a message from Mt. Olympus?

Hadn't the baggage of trying to replace the great Teddy Ballgame been not only heavy but amazingly unrealistic?

Hadn't he sensed that several of the older players in those first years resented him, jealous of his big signing bonus and all the attention he was receiving, saw him as Yawkey's new pet?

Yastrzemski didn't have either the temperament or the personality to handle that. Then again, no one could have. Williams had been such a towering presence in Boston. From his movie-star looks to his infamous battles with the sportswriters, whom he derisively called the Knights of the Keyboard; to his charisma to the fact that he had left baseball for nearly five years to go off and fly airplanes in both World War II and Korea; to the fact that when teams played a shift against him, all but inviting the left-handed Williams to hit the ball to the left side of the field, he stubbornly refused to do so; to the fact that everyone knew he refused to wear a necktie; to the fact that for years he lived alone in the Hotel Somerset, the iconoclastic Williams was larger than life. All that, and he had been the last player to hit .400 for a season. If that weren't enough, he had hit a home run in his last at-bat in a late-season game on a dreary afternoon in Fenway Park in 1960, a feat turned into literature by John Updike in a magazine piece called "Hub Fans Bid Kid Adieu."

Not only had Williams been one of the all-time greatest hitters in the history of the game, his study of the art of hitting almost legendary, he also had been Yawkey's surrogate son. He had been treated like the city's celebrity in Boston, and in many ways that's what he had been, as everything from his marriages to his refusal to tip his cap to the fans to the sense of mystery that always seemed to surround him became fair game to a voracious press core that knew that Williams sold papers, that there was an insatiable appetite for any news about him. Over a nineteen-year career he had, in many ways, been the Red Sox, the one that people came to see, his name transcending the sports page, such a Boston institution that the city would one day name a tunnel after him.

Some young kid was going to replace him?

What should have been a great story, the Polish kid from the wrong side of the tracks in the Hamptons, the kid who had grown up playing on the town team with his father and his uncles, the kid who had all but grown up as an apprentice in a baseball workshop, shaped by his father, who once had seen his own baseball dreams sacrificed to the Depression, had instead got layered. What should have been a great story, the kid who had come of age chasing a childhood dream and now had it right in the palm of his hands, instead became simply more pressure, the incredible presence of Williams hovering over him.

The first year Yastrzemski went to spring training he was given a locker next to Williams, then in the last year of his career. You didn't need to be an English major to see the symbolism, the baton being passed. Williams was always talking to the young Yastrzemski, as if hitting a baseball was as complicated as nuclear fission. Yastrzemski never knew what he was talking

about. To Williams, hitting was science, something to be ana-
lyzed like some lab specimen under a microscope. To Yastrzemski, it was instinctive, something he had done all his life.

Those first years with the Red Sox had been difficult, to
the point that he had bickered with manager Billy Herman in
1966, Herman thinking he didn't hustle enough. He had the
ceremonial title of captain, a position he didn't necessarily want,
or wasn't particularly suited for. He didn't really get along with
Tony Conigliaro, the local kid who embraced being a star like a
starlet takes to a photographer. He wasn't particularly close to
many of his teammates, dating back to his first spring training
when his wife, Carol, away from home for the first time, was
lonely and couldn't make any friends, and his only friend on the
team had been Chuck Schilling, whom he had played against as
a kid on Long Island. With the exception of veteran Frank Mal-
zone, no one on the team had gone out of their way to befriend
him, and it would take him years to get over that.

At the end of the year there were rumors the Sox were thinking of moving him, and he didn't want to leave. He had just
bought a house in Lynnfield, a suburb north of the city. He had
come to like Boston and he didn't want to uproot everything and
go somewhere else and start all over again.

Then came '67 and his life changed.

It's a part of Red Sox lore how Yastrzemski rededicated himself that previous winter, how he found a Hungarian trainer
who set out to rebuild his body and get him in the best shape
of his life. If now off-season conditioning is a part of being a
major-league player, it wasn't then. Most players had jobs in
the winter, needed the money in those days before big salaries.
Besides, working out year-round was not part of the game's cul-

ture. There were no strength coaches. No one ever talked about nutrition or flexibility. No one ever talked about transforming your body, making it better. Lifting weights was seen as making someone muscle-bound, frowned upon for athletes. And wasn't spring training for getting in shape, stretch in the sunshine, jog a few laps in the outfield? Wasn't that what getting in shape meant?

It was no secret that in those early years Yastrzemski had been moody, even petulant at times, developing a reputation as someone who didn't run out routine ground balls. Years later he would say that that first spring training had changed him, made him more wary. And even though he won the batting title his third year in the league, he was far from a fan favorite. He wasn't Williams. And the team was going nowhere, the ballpark half empty, a few bright spots against the dark canvas of mediocrity.

The '67 season changed all that. No only did it resurrect passion for the Red Sox, it immortalized Yastrzemski. Not only did he win the Triple Crown, he seemed to carry the Sox on his back, heroics after heroics, as if he had come direct from central casting in the role of baseball hero. In the final twelve games he hit over .500, and on the last weekend of the season, the Sox needing to beat the Twins twice to avoid a three-way tie with them and Detroit, he had gone seven for eight and hit a three-run homer in the first game. Never again would he have a year like that, but ultimately it didn't matter. Nor would it matter that he was never really a leader, that he was too self-absorbed for that, too moody, too uncomfortable in that role. He had given New England one of its all-time great baseball summers and that was enough.

Even at thirty-nine, and even with all his aches and pains

he was still a great fastball hitter, even if it was known that you could get him out with the slower stuff.

He had been nervous before the game, even though he had been in so many big games before. But he knew the magnitude of this one, knew that at thirty-nine he was in the shadows of his career, and who knew how many chances would come after this? They had come so close in '67, and again in '75, yet he had never won a World Series, and now he was on the best team he'd ever been on and they were in a playoff game with the Yankees.

Guidry had been trying to get a fastball in on Yastrzemski, but it stayed out over the plate and Yastrzemski turned on it, pulling it down the right-field line. Fair? Foul? For a second or two no one seemed to know where the ball would land, but it was fair, and at the end of the second inning the Red Sox led 1–0.

Yaz had come through once again.

CHAPTER FIVE

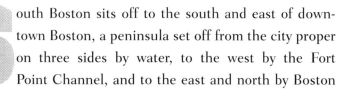outh Boston sits off to the south and east of downtown Boston, a peninsula set off from the city proper on three sides by water, to the west by the Fort Point Channel, and to the east and north by Boston Harbor.

Somehow it seems symbolic.

For South Boston always has thought of itself as different from the rest of the city, removed geographically as well as spiritually. In 1776, on a hill behind what would become South Boston High School, George Washington had ordered a fort built. It was from that site that Washington and several thousand men forced the evacuation of Boston Harbor by the British, and the site is marked by the 115-foot-high Dorchester Heights Monument.

Back in the 1840s it had been considered almost a recreation spot, complete with houses on the water, but by the early 1900s it had become a tight-knit neighborhood of three-deckers, a working-class neighborhood of mostly Irish who considered South Boston theirs, to the point that going downtown was called "going to Boston." They were from South Boston, and proud of it, and if the years after World War II saw the migration to the suburbs, what remained was a tight, insular neighborhood, people who wore the old values of family and turf as easily as the old Irish songs about love and loss in ole Kilarney blared out from the bars on the boulevard on St. Patrick's Day, and people, their voices all but choking with emotion, sang "Southie Is My Hometown."

"In the distance soared the pale towers of Yankee Babylon," wrote the Boston political icon Billy Bulger in his memoir, *While the Music Lasts*, "their alien frigidity made beautiful by what we perceived as the warm colors of the hanging garden, South Boston, where we lived. Family wash danced . . . like brazen flags of an ethnic country."

Even in South Boston, though, there were class divisions. The more fortunate lived in City Point, where there were water views and the remnants from when South Boston had been a prestigious address. The less fortunate lived in the more industrial Lower End, where there were four large housing projects, most of them full of mothers with too many kids and no fathers, the white urban poor, although few sociologists wrote about them back then. The one thing they all shared was "Southie" pride, which they wore like a merit badge. From the kids who had "Irish Power" on their arms in makeshift tattoos made with green ink and sewing needles to the project walls that had shamrocks and "IRA" spray-painted on them, South Boston was as much an idea as it was a place. And it came with an attitude that said we take care of our own, and we take no shit from anyone.

An attitude that said this is who we are, and no one is going to tell us to be any different.

This is what Louise Day Hicks appealed to, this sense that this was their neighborhood and now everyone wanted to change it, the courts, the politicians, the suburban liberals, the outside world, everyone. This was what was so threatening in the early seventies with the specter of busing, the sense that change was on the horizon, change they didn't want and promised to change the life in the South Boston that they knew.

It's little wonder that the people of South Boston felt under siege. All around them were the symbols of a changing America, one that had evolved out of the upheavals of the sixties. The antiwar movement, the women's movement, civil rights, the counterculture—all of them, in their own way, had been body blows to blue-collar, working-class neighborhoods like South Boston.

In the late sixties they had seen blacks win a suit forcing both the city's police and fire departments to become more in-clusive, no longer just the domain of the Irish. They had seen blacks begin to move into some of the other unions that also had been controlled by the Irish and the who-do-you-know world of Boston politics. In short, they had seen the others start to take pieces of a pie that was dwindling anyway, what with recession and the Vietnam War.

And now they were going to bus black kids into South Boston and bus some of their kids to Roxbury?

Busing was something they could do something about.

Or so they thought.

The issue had been going on for over a decade now, ever since the Boston School Committee had said in 1963 that they would not agree with the statement that the schools were segregated, the ill feeling thrown back and forth as if it were a football, the tensions ratcheted up. It had surely been there in 1972 when a case shepherded by the Boston chapter of the NAACP, a case that became known as *Morgan v. Hennigan*, was assigned to W. Arthur Garrity, a federal judge who had grown up in Worcester, gone to the nearby College of the Holy Cross, and then Harvard Law School, and was in the Kennedys' inner circle.

Garrity was the essence of the American Dream. His great-grandfather had come to Boston from Ireland in the 1840s, and his father, Wendell, had gone to both Holy Cross and then Harvard Law School, graduating in 1909, one of the few Irish to do so then. He also had been a member of the NAACP, back in the fifties, when few whites were members.

So maybe it's not surprising that his son, Wendell Arthur Garrity Jr., followed him to both Holy Cross and Harvard Law, or that he went to work on Jack Kennedy's campaign for the Senate in 1956. Kennedy was the new breed of Irish politician, highly educated, ambitious, far removed from the Irish neighborhoods of Boston.

"They were second- and third-generation Irish-Americans," wrote J. Anthony Lukas in *Common Ground*, "who after the war had moved out of Boston's ethnic enclaves, finding homes in the suburbs and making their way in law, medicine, or business. In the elaborate hierarchy of the Boston Irish, they were the 'two toilet' Irish, an emerging professional class no longer comfortable with the claustrophobic world of their fathers."

In 1960 Garrity ran the Milwaukee headquarters in the Wisconsin primary for Kennedy, and in return became a U.S. attorney a year later when Kennedy became president and his brother Bobby became the attorney general. Five years later he became a federal judge, recommended by Ted Kennedy, and two years later he was assigned the Boston school busing case. He was considered a careful, methodical judge, a slight man with an almost shy aura about him.

In June of 1974, after two years of review, Garrity announced his decision.

He ruled that the Boston School Committee "knowingly carved out a systematic program of segregation," and had "intentionally brought about and maintained a dual system."

And here was the kicker.

"The entire school system of Boston is unconstitutionally segregated," he said.

It was announced that the first phase of busing would begin that September, with eighteen thousand kids to be bused, and that the two main school districts involved would be Roxbury and South Boston, some white kids from South Boston going to Roxbury every morning, some blacks kids going into South Boston.

So throughout that summer the antibusing rallies had started in South Boston, and as September and the start of the school year beckoned, newspaper stories began the countdown, fueling the climate, adding to the tension. Throughout South Boston there was the growing sense that the start of the school year was going to be unlike any start of school in the city's history. The signs were everywhere: "Resist" . . . "Never" . . . "Hell No Southie Won't Go."

"Where are we not going?" Michael Patrick MacDonald wrote in *All Souls*, for he was just a kid then, eight years old. "One of the mothers said, 'They're trying to send you to Roxbury with the niggers. To get a beatin',' she added. Someone else told her not to say that word to kids, that they were blacks, not niggers. 'Well, it's no time to fight over that one,' someone else said. 'It's now time to stick together.' When I asked who was trying to send us, someone told me about Judge Garrity; that a bunch of rich people from the suburbs wanted to tell us where we had to send our kids to school; that they wanted us to mix with blacks, but their own kids wouldn't have to mix with no one, because there were no blacks in the suburbs."

South Boston High School sat at the top of a hill. Once upon a time it had been a showcase. But those days were long gone. It was a brick fortress surrounded by a circular driveway, a school that wore its age like some tired old dowager. But it still existed as a symbol of "Southie Pride," the one place where so many of its residents once had been young together.

This was their line in the sand.

The lid came off Boston on September 12, 1974.

It was the first day of busing, and as soon as the yellow buses carrying black children headed for South Boston High School were seen coming over the hill, all the planning and all the hopes that this could work peacefully shattered into pieces.

"Niggers, Go Home."

"Go Back to Africa."

"Here We Go, Southie, Here We Go," as if this were a football game.

People lined the streets around South Boston High School. They chanted. Some threw rocks. Everywhere you looked you could see police, over a hundred of them, many in riot gear.

Sirens wailed. There were police on motorcycles. There were helicopters overhead. Some people had started crying when they first saw the buses. A brick was thrown through a bus window. Then more, as the police began moving through the crowds with their billy clubs, as the air filled with "Here We Go Southie, Here We Go."

Six hours later, as the buses pulled away from South Boston High School, they were pelted by eggs, beer bottles, and rocks, shattering windows on some of the buses and injuring nine students.

These were the images that went across the country that night on the TV news, images that became stamped in the national memory. This wasn't Little Rock, or Birmingham, or Nashville, wasn't some Southern city where the battle for civil rights already had become part of American history. This was Boston, and the *Boston Globe* said, "Boston is supposed to be an enlightened city, the Athens of America. Now our collective concern is stunned by brutal attacks on children in school buses, and in innocent citizens going about their business on our streets."

This became the new reality.

Three weeks later there was a riot inside South Boston High School that had started with a food fight in the cafeteria, in which the school's headmaster was knocked down, and one teacher described the scene as "mass hysteria." Two days later seven thousand people marched down Broadway in South Boston in an antibusing rally, and two days after that a thousand people protested outside police headquarters claiming there had been police brutality in a raid over the weekend at a South Boston bar.

On October 7, a black man from Haiti went into South Boston to pick up his wife, who worked at a Laundromat. While he was stopped at a red light, a gang smashed the windows in his car, and he was running to get to a nearby house when hit in the head by a lead pipe. That was reciprocated by a group of black youths stoning cars and attacking whites in Roxbury.

That night Mayor Kevin White went on Boston television and said that the city could no longer control the situation. He was highly thought of, a big-city mayor who was polished enough for the Boston establishment to hold him in high regard, and liberal enough for both the blacks and the young to see him as progressive, a man who entertained aspirations of being president. He had a certain charisma, and was someone who looked like a mayor should look in the early seventies, someone who understood the different factions of the city and had both the skill and clout to be able to navigate his way through them. But no mayor was going to come through the minefield that was busing in Boston unscathed. By the end of the decade, even if he was still the mayor and would remain so until 1983, whites called him "Mayor Black," blacks and liberals thought he had sold out to the white establishment, and he would see his national aspirations turn to dust.

And White had to have sensed that in the early weeks, as he saw his city on the nightly news, saw the violence and the hate, saw his city becoming a symbol of racism in ways that would have once been unimaginable, that it was his fate to be the mayor of Boston at the worst possible time. He asked for federal troops, a request denied by President Ford. The next day there were television images of gangs of black youths roaming through Roxbury, smashing windows and dragging a white man who had been driving by and beating him up.

On Columbus Day, over a thousand antibusing demonstrators protested outside the Sheraton in Copley Square, where a Democratic Party fund-raiser was being held. That night, at Anthony's Pier 4 restaurant on the waterfront, where Senator Kennedy, Congressman Robert Drinan, Speaker of the House John McCormack, and gubernatorial hopeful Michael Dukakis were having dinner, a group of protestors essentially held Kennedy inside for two hours before letting him leave. The next day Massachusetts governor Francis Sargent ordered 450 members of the state's National Guard into armories around Boston.

"Welcome to Boston. The city is occupied. A boycott exists. The people are oppressed."

That was what the large sign read, one that hung over the head of Louise Day Hicks at another one of the seemingly endless rallies.

This was Boston in the fall of 1974.

And it didn't get better.

For these were just the highlights, snapshots of the chaos. All the while attendance was down at South Boston High School, and the black and white kids circled each other like wary alley cats, hostility everywhere, violence occasionally lashing out like spontaneous lightning. Ione Malloy, an English teacher, published a diary called *Southie Won't Go*, an amazing daily account of a situation out of control, with high absenteeism, hostility, almost daily skirmishes, and a climate better suited to Northern Ireland than an American high school.

The diary was like dispatches from behind the lines, and what comes through over and over again was that South Boston High School was not a school anymore as much as it was a lab experiment, some giant sociological study with both the kids and the teachers studied as if they were rats inside some maze designed as a school.

On Thanksgiving morning, one of the traditional high school football games was South Boston versus East Boston. The year before, the game had decided the city championship, no small thing in South Boston, where sports were both important and a point of civic pride, a star player's heroics living forever in South Boston, giving him a sliver of immortality. Only that year the game came with an asterisk. Because the whites and blacks refused to play together, South Boston did not have a team. Instead, they had a club team, an all-white one. That was the team that played a club team from East Boston before five thousand people, a game that would be described as an antibusing rally. At one point, an old yellow school bus was driven onto the field. Out came caricatures of White, Garrity, and the police commissioner.

Then the school bus was burned.

One day in December a group of white kids began banging on the door to South Boston High School, which was locked. The students were inside. The kids outside began throwing rocks and bottles at the police, a police car was overturned, and the black kids within the school were told to stay away from the windows. This from Ione Malloy in *Southie Won't Go*:

"Louise Day Hicks addressed the mob. 'Let the blacks go back to Roxbury. Let them out of the school.' The mob refused. They took up the chant: 'Bus Them Back to Africa.' She looked scared. They took up the chant 'Here We Go, Southie' and sang patriotic songs."

Hicks had started a group called ROAR, which stood for Restore Our Alienated Rights, and ROAR signs were everywhere in South Boston, right there with "Resist" and "Never." And as the weeks kept falling off the calendar it was more of the same, the tension, the hate, the sense that everyone was walking along some delicate fault line. Throughout South Boston, especially in the housing projects, there were continual skirmishes between kids and police, kids throwing rocks, the police chasing them, the new cat and mouse, as if all that had taken on a life of its own.

"I would have loved to throw Molotov cocktails myself, along with the adults," wrote Michael Patrick MacDonald in *All Souls*, "but I was only a kid and the cops would probably catch me and beat me at the beach. So I just fantasized about killing them all. They were the enemy, the giant oppressor, like Goliath. And the people of South Boston were like David. Except that David won in the end, and we knew we were going to lose this one. But that made us even more like the Irish, who were always fighting in the songs even if they had to lose and die a glorious death."

But it wasn't just about race, as tortured as that was.

It was also about social class, about which Irish had made it out to the suburbs and which had been left behind, the "two toilet" Irish and the "one toilet" Irish. And it was about resentment, too, a classic case of the haves and the have-nots. One of the great ironies of the decision to pair South Boston and Roxbury in the first phase of busing was that it took two of the poorest neighborhoods of the city, two neighborhoods that had a high percentage of welfare families and single mothers, and used them as the test case; two neighborhoods that, race aside, had more in common with each other than they did with any of the suburbs that ringed Boston.

For the more that busing dragged on, and the more social upheaval it caused, the question became, where were the suburbs in all this?

Ultimately, that's what ended up bothering the people of the neighborhoods more than anything else, the sense that their neighborhoods had been assaulted, their lives uprooted, their kids used as social experiments, while the suburbs got a free pass. The sense that their lives were now being controlled by others.

"It was the right intentions and the wrong plan," Ray Flynn would later say, the same Ray Flynn who would one day become the mayor of Boston.

Flynn, first elected as a state rep in 1970, was as South Boston as the memorial on Dorchester Heights, with a face that could have come right out of County Cork. His father worked on the docks. His mother worked as a domestic. He was the second of four sons, and began selling the *Record-American* outside of Fenway Park when he was nine years old. The *Record* was a tabloid, it cost three cents, and it contained the daily number, which though illegal was extremely popular, people betting it with the innumerable bookies strewn throughout the city's neighborhoods. People would give Flynn a nickel. And on a good day he might go home with twelve to fourteen dollars, needed money, for that was when Flynn's father was in the hospital for five years, and times weren't easy.

One day Flynn was selling the *Record* outside the Hotel Somerset in the Back Bay, not far from the ballpark, the hotel where Ted Williams lived. The Yankees were in town, and they used to stay at the Somerset back then, and he was getting au-

tographs of the Yankee players as they came through the lobby
and out the front door. He had a Bic pen that cost two cents in
those days, and just as he went to get the autograph of the great
Joe DiMaggio, his pen stopped writing.

"Use this one," said Yankee second baseman Jerry Coleman,
giving him a pen that he had gotten for being the defensive
player of the year.

But before he could get DiMaggio to sign a taxi pulled up. It
was about eleven o'clock in the morning, and it was raining, and
as DiMaggio got in the backseat to meet someone, Flynn got in,
too. The cab pulled away and was going down Commonwealth
Avenue when Flynn realized the other person in the cab was Ted
Williams.

"Who's this?" Williams asked DiMaggio.

DiMaggio shrugged. "I don't know," he said.

So Williams stopped the cab and gave Flynn three dollars to
take a cab home.

Flynn was such a huge Williams fan in those days that every
time the *Record* columnist Dave Egan, called "the Colonel,"
would rip Williams, which he was famous for doing, Flynn would
rip the column out of the paper before he sold it to anyone.

At about the same time Flynn became one of the ball boys
for the Celtics. Not only was it a dream job for a kid who loved
sports, it also gave him an introduction to the famed Celtics
coach Red Auerbach, who would become one of his mentors.
By the time he was at South Boston High School he was a great
shooter, the kind of kid who hit jumpers as easily as other kids
changed television channels, and the ramifications of this ability were starting to expand Flynn's world. He became the only

white player on a black team based in Roxbury called the Bruins. And he had people telling him that he was good enough to
play basketball in college.

"Until then I thought I'd be a dockworker like my father
was," he said. "College? We didn't even have a car."

It was the late fifties, and one of the people he got to know
through basketball was the *Globe* writer Jack Barry, who knew
Joe Mullaney, the coach at Providence College, and one thing
led to another. So in the fall of '59 Flynn went off to college.
Providence College was in the process of supplanting Holy
Cross as the best college basketball team in New England, and
Flynn was right in the middle of it, becoming the MVP of the
1963 National Invitation Tournament in Madison Square Garden, at a time when that tournament had incredible cachet in
college basketball. And after Providence College had won the
tournament Flynn was interviewed on national television by
Curt Gowdy, the longtime broadcaster for the Red Sox, who had
done the game on national television.

Flynn hadn't wanted to be interviewed, didn't feel comfortable talking to the press then, but had been talked into it by
the *Globe* sportswriter Will McDonough, whom he knew from
South Boston.

"Your native Boston must be all proud of you," Gowdy said.

"No, no," Flynn said. "I'm not from Boston. I'm from South
Boston."

Two years later Flynn was in training camp with the Celtics, and it must have seemed as if he had spent his life prepar-
ing for this moment, the former ball boy who was going to get
a chance to play for the Boston Celtics. He had worked summers at Auerbach's basketball camp. One summer Auerbach

had gotten him a job at the famed Kutsher's in the Catskills. Now he was fighting for the last roster spot, thinking he was going to make it.

Until Auerbach called him into his hotel room.

"I never forgot what he told me," said Flynn. "He said that nobody has ever worked any harder than you have. And that nobody deserves to play for the Boston Celtics any more than you do. But that the Celtics didn't get to be world champions by playing favorites, however much he liked me, and that I wasn't going to make it, that he was picking someone else over me. I was heartbroken. It was devastating. At the time it was like my whole life was shattered. All I ever wanted to do was play basketball. But you know what? It was a great lesson to learn. Not just about sports, but about life."

He worked as an assistant basketball coach at Stonehill for a year, and one day ran into Auerbach, who said to meet him that night at a Chinese restaurant in Cambridge to discuss Flynn's future, which was as up in the air as one of his jump shots, even if he was planning to soon get married. There were several men at the table that night, movers and shakers in their own right.

"Ray is like my own kid," Auerbach told the men, "and I'm not going to his wedding and see him there without a job."

Soon after Flynn got a job as a probation officer.

He also started a neighborhood basketball league with Kenny Hudson, who would go on to become the first black referee in the NBA. His job might have been as a probation officer, but his passion was sports and kids and he soon realized that Boston seemed to have very few opportunities. He was instrumental in getting a playground built in South Boston, he and a few others going to both the *Boston Globe* and Warren Buffet, who ran Gillette in those days, the company based in South Boston where, when asked where they worked, women would answer, "I sweat for Gillette." Both gave him money. But it seemed everything he tried to do was met with roadblocks, as though Boston was a maze and you'd better have some politician leading you through it.

Then in 1970 South Boston's John McCormack, the Speaker of the U.S. House of Representatives, retired, and the political dominos began changing. It was the opening for Flynn to run as a state rep from South Boston.

"There was no mention of busing when I ran," he said. "That wasn't my issue. My issue was helping kids."

Four years later he was right in the middle of it; it was unavoidable. Flynn was against busing. He believed in neighborhood schools, the right of the neighborhood to sustain its own identity. That had been the South Boston he knew, the nurturing place he had come of age in, shaped by selfless coaches, a community that tried to take care of its own, a world that revolved around family, church, sports, country, as if it was still the fifties and Boston was over the bridge, another country. The kind of neighborhood where the men who worked with his father on the docks had taken up a collection to send his father to New York and stay in a hotel to see his son play in Madison Square Garden.

But he didn't like the violence.

And he didn't like the racism.

Hadn't he once played on a team based in Roxbury where he'd been the only white player, hopping on the back of the "T" and going all over the city to places like Roxbury and Mattapan, places that now were mostly all black, and had never felt any fear? Hadn't he played on a college team that had several black players, including John Thompson, who would go on to become the famed coach of Georgetown? Hadn't one of his best friends on that team been a black kid from Cleveland named Jimmy Stone? Hadn't the team once been in Cincinnati and gone into a cafeteria where the black players weren't served, and he had gone to one of the priests, who was traveling with the team, and said that this wasn't right, that they were a team and teams did everything together, and the priest agreed and they had left? Hadn't he been there in the Boston Garden as a Celtics ball boy when the Celtics had black players, hadn't he grown up rooting for Russell? Hadn't his basketball career taught him at a young age to deal with blacks and see them as people, not simply stereotypes?

So for Flynn, busing became a minefield.

He was starting a political career at a time when there was only one issue in Boston, one issue that divided the city, one issue that had come to define his hometown. There was no way he could avoid it. So he marched in the demonstrations, and he spoke at the rallies, and he, unquestionably, was one of the antibusing leaders, right there with Louise Day Hicks and Albert "Dapper" O'Neil, and all of the other South Boston politicos, his face in the newspapers and on television, his name now known throughout the city. And if he was against busing, and believed in neighborhood schools, and resented being told by a federal judge how they should be run, and if he wanted to preserve the way of life he had come of age in in South Boston, the fact that his hometown had now been spread all over the world as synonymous with racism broke his heart.

"Many of my neighbors thought I was too soft," he said. "It was the only election I ever lost in my life, the one in '75."

CHAPTER SIX

Bucky Dent came to the plate in the third inning.

He was the light-hitting Yankee shortstop who didn't really fit into the raucous clubhouse culture of the Yankees. He had come over from the White Sox in a heralded deal the year before, and since he had grown up as a Yankee fan he was thrilled to have been traded, saw it as a childhood dream come true. He knew that Martin didn't have a lot of faith in him, as he was forever taking him out in late innings for a pinch hitter, and because of that Dent didn't have a lot of confidence in himself. He was dark haired, with all-American good looks, and had grown up in Florida, a small -town kid who had spent most of his adolescence thinking his aunt was his mother, until one day his mother blurted out the truth. He would be an adult before he discovered who his father was, or that his real last name was O'Dey.

He had missed thirty-five games with a hamstring problem, and felt like he was finally getting back to some rhythm as he stepped in against Torrez with one out in the top of the third, the same Mike Torrez he had played with the year before and had been friends with. Now he made the second out of the inning, lining out to Rice, who was playing right field because Dwight Evans had had problems with dizziness after being beaned in August.

Rivers then doubled down the right-field line, but was stranded on second when Torrez again struck out Munson.

Torrez had now pitched shutout ball through three innings.

He was from Topeka, Kansas, the son of parents who had emigrated from Mexico. He was six feet five, and six years earlier he had won sixteen games with the Montreal Expos. In 1975 he had won twenty games with the Orioles and the following year was sent to Oakland in a seven-player deal that sent Reggie Jackson to the Orioles. Last year, with the Yankees, he had had seven straight wins in July and August and then had thrown two complete-game victories in the World Series. He was called "Taco" by his teammates, thanks to Tiant, and he had been in big games before.

George Scott led off for Boston in the bottom of the third.

It had been a difficult season for the Boomer, so named because a teammate had said when he was a rookie in 1966, "Man, you put a boom on the ball." So Boomer it had become. The year before he had hit thirty-three home runs, but he was now thirty-four, and both age and his increasing weight had taken its toll. He always had had trouble with his weight, going back to the '67 season, when manager Dick Williams was constantly on him about his propensity to gain weight. Their relationship always had been strained, to the point that Williams had once said that talking to Scott "was like talking to cement." It was one of those comments that never got forgotten, would forever follow Scott around like some afternoon shadow, although later in his life Scott would say that Williams was the best manager he had ever played for.

Scott always had been colorful, complete with some gold teeth. He referred to his home runs as "taters," often spoke in the patois of the segregated South, usually saying something that sounded like "muffafucka" every third or fourth word. In many ways he'd been a racial pioneer with the Red Sox, a very good player certainly, but also someone who understood the realities in Boston, sensing from the beginning that he lived in two worlds.

In all the important ways he already had traveled so very far from the grim realities of his childhood in the Mississippi Delta. Mississippi had been the heart of darkness then, and the delta had the reputation as the poorest, most repressive part of the country. When he was growing up only 5 percent of blacks there were registered to vote, many living in glorified shacks with no running water. Scott's family was typical. His father had died when he was an infant, his mother worked a succession of menial jobs trying to keep food on the table for Scott and his two siblings. He had gone to a black high school three miles away, even though the white school was only a few blocks from his house. But Scott didn't grow up rebelling against the existing social order. He wasn't militant. He just wanted to play ball.

In the fall of '71 he'd been traded to Milwaukee, and four years later had tied Reggie Jackson for the American League home-run lead with thirty-six. The previous year he had been traded back to the Red Sox, where he responded with a big year, thirty-three "taters," and had been one of an amazing number of seven Sox players on the American League team for the All-Star Game. But that had been last year. This year had been a struggle, a portent of the future. Once he had been incredibly fluid and graceful at first base for a big man, as good a defensive first baseman as there was in the game, but now his weight had become an issue in the field, too. At one point in the season he had sat in front of his locker staring at his stomach, and saying, "I got Donlop Disease. My belly done lopped over my belt."

And as he had struggled, his batting average sliding, his power numbers down, seemingly unable to pull the ball on the left side anymore, the barbs and criticism started. Cliff Keane and Larry Claflin made watermelon and fried chicken references on their radio show when Scott's name came up, to the point that the *Globe* columnist Ray Fitzgerald had written that we didn't need any more watermelon jokes. Scott always had been a fan favorite, but all that had started to change during the Sox's swoon. It all had seemed sad, for Scott had been a very good player, and now he was in the twilight, the end in sight.

This time, though, Scott delivered, tattooing a pitch deep off the center-field wall for a double. Jack Brohamer, the twenty-eight-year-old utility infielder who was playing third base instead of Hobson, who had bone chips in his elbow, sacrificed Scott to third. But Burleson then grounded to Nettles at third, stranding Scott, and Jerry Remy flied out to left to end the inning.

Torrez coasted through the top half of the fourth, even though Piniella had led off the inning with an infield single. He had now pitched four scoreless innings and had only given up two hits.

More important, he still led 1–0.

That was the score as the game headed into the fifth inning.

Torrez walked Roy White to open the inning, but nothing came of it, and then the Sox went in order and the game now moved to the top of the sixth inning, still an old-fashioned pitcher's duel in a ballpark known as a hitter's park. But even if Guidry knew he didn't have his best stuff, surely not the kind of stuff he'd had when he'd shut out the Sox twice in September, he was pitching effectively. That was the other great thing about Guidry. He was not just a pitcher who was great because he had great stuff. He had learned how to pitch, too, had come to know that the true art of pitching was being able to keep your team in the game when you didn't have your best stuff. So he knew that was his job today, to keep the Yankees in the game as long as he could, because he also knew he wasn't going to be there the entire game.

Torrez, on the other hand, was pitching the game of his dreams. He was throwing well, had the Yankees off balance and out of their rhythm, was doing just what the Red Sox and their fans had hoped he could do. Truth be told, the fans didn't have a lot of confidence in Torrez. Yes, he had won sixteen games, but he hadn't been as dominating as he was supposed to have been, not for all the money the Sox were paying him, and had gone 0–6 in the time when the Sox had been floundering, failing in eight straight starts. They had confidence in Tiant, of course. They also had confidence in Eckersley, who had won twenty games in his first season in Boston. But Torrez? Not really. He had to earn their trust.

And so far he was doing so.

He did it again in the top of the sixth.

By now the shadows had been starting to spread across the field as Torrez struck out Munson for the third straight time.

Then after Piniella flew out to Fred Lynn in deep center, Jackson grounded to Remy at second, and Torrez had now gotten through six innings without giving up a run.

Rick Burleson opened up the Red Sox half of the sixth inning with a double to left. In the Yankees' bullpen Goose Gossage got up and began to get loose, while Remy stepped into the batter's box.

He was the only Massachusetts kid on the roster, having grown up in Somerset, a town about fifty miles south of Boston. He had broken into the major leagues with the California Angels as a scrappy little second baseman in 1975, had been traded to Boston the previous December, coming back to the team he had grown up rooting for as a kid, the prodigal son in cleats, someone who used to go to Fenway a handful of times as a kid every summer, taken there by his father and grandfather. He was an upgrade over Denny Doyle at second base, as he was a better hitter and had more speed.

When he had first arrived he had felt the tangible pressure of being a local kid playing in Boston, as though every mistake had been magnified, at least in his own mind. He also had been well aware that he was joining what seemed to be an all-star team, what with Yaz, Fisk, Rice, Lynn, Tiant. He knew, though, that he brought them speed, something there wasn't a plethora of on the Red Sox, even with all their talent. He knew he made the team better.

He sacrificed Burleson to third, and Rice came to the plate.

"MVP . . . MVP . . . MVP," chanted the frenzied crowd.

Rice responded with a single to center and the Sox now led 2–0 as Fenway went wild.

Yastrzemski now stepped in, and it was becoming apparent

that Guidry was tiring, no longer the same Guidry who had dominated the American League throughout the summer. Would this
be the inning that blew the game open, the Sox already with a
two-run lead and the heart of the order coming to the plate?

The pressure was all on Guidry and the Yankees now, the
game already in the sixth inning, the Yankees already down to
their last nine outs. Now Guidry was facing Yaz, who already had
homered off him, the Yaz whose legend in Fenway Park was almost a living thing. The old ballyard was full of deafening noise
and anticipation. Everyone believed in Yaz. He was the link to
the '67 season that had changed everything in Boston, the season that had brought the passion back to Fenway Park. But this
time Yaz bounced to Chambliss at first base, as Rice went down
to second.

This brought Carlton Fisk to the plate to another thunderous cheer. Fisk was already a Red Sox icon. As every Sox fan
knew by now, Fisk had grown up in a small town on the New
Hampshire–Vermont border, not exactly the environment most
great catchers came from. He was not the kind of kid who grew
up playing in innumerable games, not in northern New England, where the winters were long, the springs were almost
nonexistent, and the summers seemed to disappear as quickly
as a shadow. He was big, and he was strong, and he looked like
a catcher would look if you were going to mold one out of clay.
He had been the Sox's first-round pick in January of 1967 when
he was at the University of New Hampshire. Five years later he
was the starting catcher in Boston, complete with the nickname
of "Pudge," which he had carried with him since his childhood,
although it now seemed an anomaly, having nothing to do with
the man he had become.

In a sense, he was as New England as the White Mountains: proud, resolute, no nonsense, with a touch of arrogance sprinkled in. Fisk danced to his own drummer, did things his way. Even as a rookie he was the boss behind the plate, even with veteran pitchers, even the ones who didn't like the slow pace he used behind the plate, the game being run on Fisk Time. He was not outwardly emotional, didn't say a whole lot, so he wasn't a leader in any conventional way, wasn't one to give rah-rah speeches. But he had the respect of everyone in the clubhouse.

He was the Rookie of the Year in '72, and from the beginning he competed with Munson as the best catcher in the American League, almost as if it had been inevitable. Two talented young catchers, Boston and New York, Red Sox and Yankees. But it was three years earlier, in the sixth game of the '75 World Series, that he had his defining moment as a professional athlete. He would go on to play for almost two decades, eventually ending up in the Hall of Fame, but it was his home run in the twelfth inning of the sixth game that was his freeze-frame moment. The television image of Fisk leaping down the first-base line, gesturing with his arms to have the ball stay fair, became one of the most recognizable scenes in the history of New England sports, one of those images that went on to have a life of its own. It would forever define Fisk, that one home run that seemed to come right out of adolescent fiction, a home run that became such an important part of Red Sox history.

But there would be no heroics now.

Fisk was intentionally walked.

Guidry would now pitch to Fred Lynn with runners on first and second with two outs. And if he wasn't having the year he'd had three years ago when he entered the major leagues like he owned them, back when he'd been both the Rookie of the Year and the MVP of the league, Lynn was still an amazing talent, a center fielder who could run and make diving catches on the outfield grass, a left-handed hitter who had both power and the ability to hit for average. In one game as a rookie in Tiger Stadium he had three home runs and an amazing ten RBIs. Back then it seemed as if Lynn might be a talent for the ages, as if there was nothing he seemingly couldn't do on a baseball field.

In many ways he was the prototypical California kid, forever coming into the clubhouse in cutoffs and T-shirts, acting as if he didn't have a care in the world. It was like he'd been born to hit in Fenway Park, someone who could pull the ball with power, but also could go to left field and flick doubles off the wall. When he had first come up he'd been a dead pull hitter, for there had been a short right-field fence at USC that had been geared to him. But he quickly learned to hit the wall at Fenway, and once in batting practice had hit ten straight balls over the wall, and came to believe that in batting practice he could hit a pitch over the wall just about any time he wanted to, both with an inside-out swing and by going the other way with an outside pitch.

He had grown up playing a lot of sports, had come to believe that he had benefited as a baseball player by all of them. He played center field like a defensive back, patrolling his territory. He had excellent footwork from always guarding the best player in basketball. Football also had taught him how to get hit, so he was forever crashing into fences in pursuit of fly balls, a kind of recklessness that came from once having been a defensive back and routinely throwing his body at people.

He had been recruited to the University of Southern California as a defensive back, so he had a toughness about him, even if he didn't wear it as a calling card. He had played baseball at USC for Rod Dedeaux, the legendary coach who also had had Bill Lee, and he had been shaped by both Dedeaux and USC's great success to expect good things to happen. Twice he had been a college All-American. So he hadn't been overwhelmed by his great rookie year in '75. He already had played in a World Series, as if he had been groomed for them.

"I always expected to do well," he said. "We were the best college team in the country at USC, and hardly ever lost, so I was used to winning. When Fisk hit his home run in the sixth game in '75 and we were going to get to go to a seventh game I figured, that's it, we've got them."

He believed that this team was better than the '75 team had been, that they were the best team in baseball, and that they would win this game and go on to win the World Series. He had hit .298 in this, his fourth, season, and if it wasn't what he'd done as a rookie, he was a player with great gifts for the game, an extremely graceful player. Now he smoked a line drive headed for the corner in right field. The crowd had erupted at the crack of the bat, and at first glance it seemed like a sure double, the kind of hit that would score two runs and give the Red Sox a 4–0 lead and also probably get Guidry out of the game, and force the Yankees to go to their middle relief. But Piniella, even though he seemed to stumble, and had his head almost turned around, as though to ward off the glaring sun, somehow managed to make the catch.

Piniella was an emotional player with a good bat, never someone known for his defensive exploits. He didn't run very well, and he never had been particularly graceful, even in his earlier years. He was now in his mid-thirties, nearing the end of his career, someone who was always being told that he was only going to play against left-handed pitchers, only to always seem to find his way into the lineup, because he could hit line drives and was one of those guys who were considered winners, their performance better than their natural ability. He was forever throwing his batting helmet at a wall in the dugout after an unsuccessful time at-bat, to the point that one day Lemon snapped at him, "Goddam it, there's no reason to throw your helmet. It doesn't do any good. I'm getting tired of watching helmets flying by my head."

That had been the day Lemon had had one of his rare team meetings, chewing out Rivers for not having been in the on-deck circle, a traditional baseball sacrilege. The meeting had only lasted a couple of minutes, Lemon blowing off a little steam, certainly nothing significant to a team that had been used to Martin's meltdowns, and he had ended it in typical Lemon fashion. He'd been in the process of walking away when he'd turned back and said, "And one more thing, I don't want to see any more helmets whizzing by my head."

Everyone laughed, and then Lemon laughed, too.

It had only been a small moment, but it illustrated the completely different styles of Lemon and Martin. Lemon had made his point and moved on, while Martin undoubtedly would have been looking to fight somebody. Was it the reason why the Yankees had come back to catch the Sox? Well, not the only one, given that they had gotten healthy. But it was a big part, no question about it, as Lemon had made it all about the players.

Piniella was from Tampa, had become very friendly with Steinbrenner, who had made Tampa his winter home, and unofficially came to be known around the Yankees as Steinbrenner's surrogate son. He loved the racetrack, as did Steinbrenner, another way in which the two had bonded. He also loved the verbal jousting of the clubhouse, could take it as well as dish it out, was one of the boys. Eventually, he would go on to manage in the big leagues, the Yankees among others, and be known for his fiery style. But on this afternoon he had just made a crucial play, even if he hadn't won all the style points. Afterward, he would say that he knew Guidry didn't have his best stuff, thus Sox hitters would be more inclined to get around on him and pull the ball. This was the reason why he had seemed to be so out of position in Lynn's at-bat. Lynn would counter with the fact that he never pulled Guidry and there was no reason for Piniella to be playing him that close to the line, regardless of how he thought Guidry had been throwing. Even years later Lynn would cling to his belief that Piniella had been out of position, regardless of what he said.

Whatever the reason, Piniella had played Lynn much closer to the right-field line than he probably should have, and thus was able to rob Lynn of a surefire hit. And as the sixth inning closed it might have been the play of the game, a play that would come back to haunt the Red Sox as surely as some old ghost.

Still, the Sox led 2–0 as the shadows continued to spread across the field and the Fenway crowd was beginning to think that maybe this year was going to be different, that this was going to finally be their redemption, that this was their moment, this was their time.

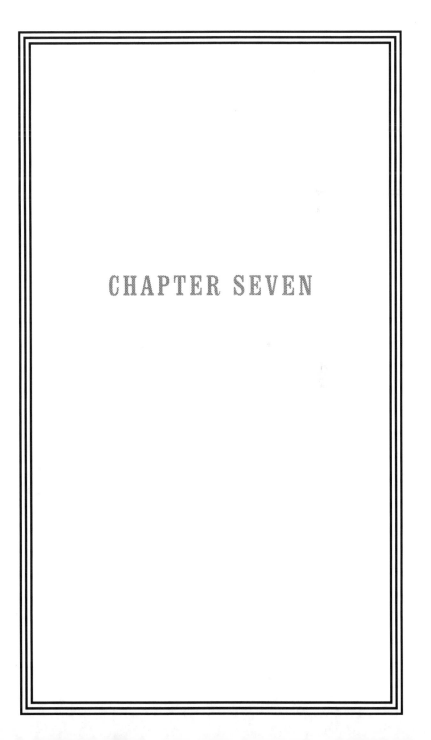

CHAPTER SEVEN

Round two of Boston's busing nightmare began on September 8, 1975, in the tough working-class neighborhood of Charlestown, outside a high school in the shadow of the Bunker Hill Monument.

This was Phase II of Garrity's plan, and on the first day of the new school year it seemed like "déjà vu all over again," as the former Yankee great Yogi Berra used to say.

Early that morning, before school was scheduled to begin, helicopters swept over the area. In Monument Square, hundreds of police lined the sidewalks around the 221-foot-high monument, a granite obelisk that had been erected in 1843 to honor the Battle of Bunker Hill, the first major battle between the British and Patriot forces in the Revolutionary War. This was where a group of bedraggled colonial soldiers had fought courageously against the vaunted and experienced British redcoats in June of 1775 in one of the most famous battles of the Revolutionary War, the setting for one of the most famous lines in American history: "Don't fire until you see the whites of their eyes." This had been said for the simple reason that bullets were scarce for the colonial soldiers, who were both poorly trained and ill equipped. The British were trying to occupy Breed's Hill, which overlooked Boston Harbor, a site thought to have great strategic importance. The local soldiers had been vastly outnumbered, but that bedraggled bunch managed to repel two major assaults by the British, and while the colonists lost the battle, nearly half the British forces were either killed or injured. More important, their courageous stand made the British question its commitment in Boston, and this, too, had kept the rebellion going.

It was a neighborhood that had been represented in the Eleventh District of the United States Congress by John "Honey Fitz" Fitzgerald, longtime colorful mayor James Michael Curley, John F. Kennedy, and now Tip O'Neill, a neighborhood whose roots always were political in the best Boston tradition, full of patronage and tribal loyalties. It had been where JFK had first run for political office in 1946. He had been twenty-nine then, had spent very little of his life in Boston. His official residence was a Beacon Hill hotel called the Bellevue. He had already lived a life very far from the gritty Charlestown, even if his grandfather had once represented the district, and everything about him, from his education to his speech to his patrician demeanor, set him apart. And when he first came to campaign in Charlestown he was criticized for being a political carpetbagger, having nothing to do with Charlestown.

If anything, that was the thing that hurt him most of all, for as J. Anthony Lukas wrote in *Common Ground*, Boston's Irish were notoriously resentful of the " 'two toilet' Irish who had betrayed their heritage by moving to the suburbs and sending their sons to Harvard."

But, as the story goes, Kennedy went to speak at a meeting at an American Legion Hall to a group of mothers who had lost sons in the war. They called themselves Gold Star Mothers, and at one point Kennedy looked out over them and said, "I think I know how you feel because my mother is a Gold Star Mother, too," a reference to his older brother, Joe, who had been shot down over Germany.

Kennedy went on to lose in Charlestown, but not by much, and went to Congress. Two years later he won overwhelmingly there, and would do so in every one of his subsequent elections. When Ted Kennedy ran for his brother's old Senate seat in 1962, amidst arguments he was nowhere near ready for the job, Charlestown gave him 86.8 percent of its vote.

But on that September morning in 1975 there was the sense that Charlestown was being cast adrift. There were police in blue uniforms. There were police in light blue shirts and helmets. There were police in riot helmets with Plexiglas visors. There were snipers on the nearby rooftops. And there were scores of media, everything from reporters to photographers and TV cameramen. It all seemed like a movie set.

The high school, also on a hill like in South Boston, was an old gray building that was in the northwest corner of Monument Square, and also like South Boston, it was the symbolic center of the community.

It was not the only similarity between Charlestown and South Boston, these two neighborhoods that would become the battlegrounds of busing in Boston. Charlestown also was on a peninsula, bordered by the two rivers, the Mystic and the

Charles. It was in the northern part of the city and had been founded as early as 1628. It was rich in history, and was the location from which Paul Revere had begun his famous ride to alert the townsfolk that the British were coming before the battles in suburban Lexington and Concord.

It was in the northern section of Boston, one square mile of narrow streets, tenements, housing projects, and bars, with an ugly elevated highway that went through it, and a tribal attitude that didn't take kindly to either change or outsiders. It, too, was mostly Irish, the legacy of the potato famine in Ireland in the 1840s that had sent scores of immigrants to Boston. Once, Charlestown had revolved around the Boston navy yard, which was along the waterfront, a bustling place that had three shifts and was Charlestown's lifeblood, back when the story was that Charlestown had more bars per capita than any other town in the country. But the early seventies had seen the navy yard close, and that, combined with the lousy economy and runaway inflation, had changed "the Town," as it was affectionately called. It had become poorer, more desperate, more on edge. There was a high percentage of people on welfare, the projects were full of single mothers with too many kids, only about 15 percent of the high school graduates went on to college, and the perception was that Charlestown was just another old, tired Boston neighborhood full of the Irish who had been left behind, a smaller South Boston.

And now the busing had begun.

The first day went relatively peacefully, given the police presence, and compared to the events at South Boston High School the year before. There was a makeshift dummy of a black person that had been thrown off the roof of a nearby housing project, to the delight of the cheering crowd below, then burned, as the mob shouted, "Burn, nigger, burn." In the afternoon roughly three hundred people, most of them teenagers, had marched up Breed's Hill toward the monument chanting, "Here we go, Charlestown, here we go," overturning a few cars and setting fire to another.

It was the next day, though, that was more telling. By mid-morning about four hundred mothers, some holding infants and some pushing strollers, had started up the street led by a small child carrying an American flag. Many of them were from the local subset of ROAR called "Powder Keg," because, as one said, "we have a short fuse." They sang "The Battle Hymn of the Republic" and chanted Hail Marys. They went by an elementary school and headed toward Monument Square and Charlestown High School. As they neared the school a police line blocked the street. Behind it, there were scores of police with batons. They were told that they had to stay at least one hundred yards away from the school, that that was the law.

They objected.

"I'm telling you now, you can't go any further," said one of the police superintendents.

At this point, many of the women sank to their knees and started praying.

"Our Father, who art in Heaven," they sang out. "Hallowed be thy name."

Two police wagons and some police on motorcycles surrounded the mothers.

This went on for almost an hour, the women sitting in the street, the police surrounding them, as the police tried to decide what to do. The last thing they needed was to be filmed dragging mothers out of the street.

But what to do?

Eventually, some of the older women and some with small children took up the police offer of marching down the side of the street that was farthest away from the high school, at which point they could go to the nearby training field where some of the antibusing rallies already had taken place.

The others refused.

They started to sing "We Shall Overcome," but it sputtered out. Instead, they began marching toward the line of police. The police were under orders to simply hold their ground, but all too quickly it became a confrontation. Scuffles broke out. The women were quickly pushed back. There was screaming and some of the mothers fell to the ground, and then some of the Townie men who had been on the periphery tried to come to their aid, and the police grabbed them, and everything escalated. It had taken only five minutes or so to calm everything down, but it had been ugly, another grisly scene in the city, as if a dispatch from a war.

That September the celebrated *New York Daily News* columnist Jimmy Breslin came to Boston to write about the crisis for the *Boston Globe*. Breslin was forty-eight, at the height of his fame, known for his street-smart slices of New York, and his ability to cut through the pretense with a style all his own, one that captured the rhythms of both New York's boroughs and the city itself. His career had been made fourteen years earlier, when he had written a column on the man who had dug President Kennedy's grave in the days after his assassination in Dallas. In the late sixties he had run for president of the city council of New York City, on the same ticket that had the writer Norman Mailer running for mayor, and he had been all over the news a year before when David Berkowitz, New York City's "Son of Sam" killer, had written letters to Breslin at the *New York Daily News*, letters the *Daily News* had printed, which had only increased Breslin's celebrity.

Breslin started out his career as a sportswriter in New York, but when he came to Boston it was not to write about the red-hot Red Sox, but about busing. His presence in Boston was one more example of the *Globe*'s desire to be seen as more than just a regional paper, with the largest circulation in New England. They wanted a paper that was seen as a player on the national stage, if not exactly the *New York Times* or the *Washington Post*, then at least the next rung down the national ladder, a newspaper of significance, not just one with a big circulation.

"In the Battle Royal here in Boston, the victor is awarded the same prize as the loser—possession of a place like Charlestown High School," Breslin wrote. "Maybe a quarter of the school's graduates get to a college. But on they fight, South Boston, Charlestown, Roxbury. And not once does anyone stop clawing for long enough to see that all they accomplished is to make things easier for the eternal opponent—the people with money and power—who pull even farther and farther ahead each day."

Breslin understood that the real issue was not so much race as poverty, not so much race as limited opportunity. He understood that for the people who lived in the suburbs and the wealthier parts of Boston, this had become someone else's fight, something that had little to do with them, save for the fact that it sent out the image of Boston as a racist city.

Breslin understood that the reaction to busing was about class as much as it was about race, about who had made it out and who had been left behind, the "two toilet" Irish and the "one toilet Irish." It was about the *Boston Globe*, which was seen by many in the neighborhoods to be pandering to the monied people in the suburbs and leaving them behind. It was about the belief that they had been betrayed by their politicians, the ones they had voted for, given both their hopes and their hearts to, the ones who were supposed to be representing them.

Hadn't they helped launch Jack Kennedy so many years ago?

Hadn't they helped put Teddy Kennedy in the Senate?

Weren't they the ones who had held the signs and stood in the rain to vote and were for America right or wrong, while all the hippies were burning the flag and blacks were protesting and everyone was smoking dope and trying to change all the rules?

So that was a part of it, too, and you could see it in the faces of the people confronting the cops, the ones who stood up at meetings and wanted someone to listen, could see the anger and the rage, as if they knew that the ground they had always walked on was shifting beneath their feet and all they could do was shout their frustration into the wind. All these people who were realizing that the country they had known, the one they had fought for, the one they loved, was changing right in front of their eyes.

The Red Sox went to the World Series in October of 1975 for the first time in eight years, a welcome diversion from the city's problems. It had been a great team, full of many of the players that were now in this game with the Yankees, and in this divided city they were a balm.

They also were a study in race relations, at least in the sense that they got along. Reggie Smith was gone, had been traded to St. Louis two years earlier. Rice was a rookie, and the last thing he was going to comment on was Boston's racial crisis. And maybe the most popular player on the team was Tiant, who had grown up in Cuba.

That was the great irony. Here was Boston going through busing hell and arguably the most popular athlete in Boston was a black Cuban, who was all but adored by both the Fenway crowds and the Boston press, because how could anyone not like Luis Tiant? But whatever Tiant thought about busing and what was happening in his adopted city was kept hidden somewhere in his jokes, his carefree personality, and the charisma he brought with him to the pitcher's mound.

Not that he wasn't aware of what was going on.

He had seen racism all his life. He had seen it as a child in Cuba. He had seen it as a young man in the minor leagues in the South in the sixties, where there were still places he couldn't go, no matter what the law might have said. He had seen it in every country he'd ever been in, had come to believe that it was simply human nature not to trust people different than you, that it was simply the way things were. And for all his jokes and all his humor, he had come to look at the world through world-weary eyes.

"I was prepared for what was happening in Boson," he said.

In many ways, Tiant dealt with race by not dealing with it. He was a baseball player, he was living in a new country, speaking a new language, and he felt it wasn't his place to speak out. And if he was aware of the racial history of the Red Sox, he always liked Tom Yawkey, who always was great with him.

"I never got hung up with black and white," he said. "I didn't care. If I liked you I liked you, it didn't matter what color you were. And I prefer dealing with racist people rather than people who treated you nice to your face, and then spoke behind your back. And the fans in Boston were the best. They always showed me respect. And I pitched my game, I did what I had to do. And the buses? That was a crazy thing. But I didn't want to complain and tell people what to do."

Rice was similar.

He had been only a rookie. He didn't think it was his place to make a lot of pronouncements. He also had grown up in a place where racism and prejudice were simply the way things were, the South Carolina of his childhood. He also had dealt with busing, as in the famous story of him having gone to the white high school his senior year while his sister remained at the black school, for the simple reason that "I was a better athlete."

He also had found a certain irony in what was happening in Boston, as here he was in this big Northern city that was supposed to be so progressive, and yet back in the South it was as though they already had been through it, were steps ahead. Not for him to talk about it then. He knew better.

The only player who had spoken out on the subject had been Lee, and that had happened in June, in a postgame tirade in the Red Sox clubhouse. The Sox had been blasted 11–2 by the Indians and a swarm of writers had been peppering Yastrzemski, one asking him how the Sox could possibly recover from such a humiliating beating. At one point, Yastrzemski ducked into the trainer's room, in an attempt to get away from all the questions, when Lee, trying to create a diversion, threw a trash can across the room.

"This is a horseshit city, a racist city, with horseshit fans and horseshit writers," he said angrily. "The fans boo Yaz when he's playing his heart out, and they boo Fisk, who always gives his all. They are all afraid we're going to lose their precious little pennant. If the writers and fans want to quit on us, fine. Then they're quitters. But what can you expect? The only one with guts in this town is Judge Arthur Garrity."

Rest assured there were a lot of people who almost choked on their cornflakes when they read that quote in the newspapers the next morning.

But that was Bill Lee.

"I got a lot of hate mail on that incident," Lee would later write in his book, *The Wrong Stuff.* "Like, I thought you were an asshole, but now I know it."

He also got one from City Councilman Albert "Dapper" O'Neil, an ardent antibusing advocate from South Boston, who was one of the key figures at many of the South Boston rallies.

"The letter was typed on paper bearing his official letterhead," Lee wrote. "The typing ran all over the page, the punctuation marks were misplaced. The letter accused me of being ignorant, cast severe doubts on my ability as a pitcher and questioned my manhood. It ended with the postscript asking me if I had the guts to reply. I did. I wrote, 'Dear Mr. O'Neil, I think you should know that some moron has stolen your stationery, and is writing letters to me on it.'"

Hate mail wasn't the only backlash. One night, shortly afterward, some members of the notorious Winter Hill Gang, one of the cornerstones of the Boston mob, showed up at his house in Stoughton, a small town south of the city. He was living there with his wife and two young kids, and all of a sudden there were guys at the door saying they were going to kill him.

"We eventually ended up going out for pizza and getting drunk together," Lee said, "but it was scary there for a while."

He was in his sixth year with the Red Sox by then, had already become the baseball carnival act, a role he says developed soon after he learned he wasn't going to please all the people all the time. But he had known from the beginning that in the world of a major-league clubhouse he was very different. He had gone to USC, came from an educated family, had been going for a master's degree while in the minor leagues, writing a thesis on the "fall of southeast Asia" in 1970, reading books on Vietnam by the likes of David Halberstam and Neil Sheehan. To him, with too few exceptions, most ballplayers were "cigarette smoking, dumb-as-a-post guys who were like canaries in a mineshaft."

He had gone to high school in northern California in the early sixties, had once seen Jim Morrison and the Doors at Fillmore West, the famed San Francisco rock club, where, he wrote in his book, "just being there got you high." So by the time he got through college he was very familiar with marijuana and the accoutrements of the burgeoning counterculture. In his first couple of years in Boston this was fairly submerged. He was young, he had a young family, and he was trying to stay in the big leagues. Then he walked into spring training with a "Lick Dick in '72" T-shirt and manager Eddie Kasko went apoplectic.

But he soon learned that his teammates cared little for what he said. They were too immersed in their own careers, their own lives. And if Lee was "the Spaceman," well, that was all right, too, as long as he kept getting hitters out. It was certainly true that baseball was its own world, insular and narrow, a life that went from game to game, with little time for too many other interests. It was the nature of the sport, and there was pressure on players to both believe in and follow the unwritten rules. Players who were different, who challenged the status quo, were suspect. Unless they put up great numbers, of course. Then they were tolerated. And Lee battled when he went to the mound, and in the end, that's what mattered most to his teammates, not the fact that he often said things that made them shake their heads.

And it was in no one's interest to be public over what was happening all around them in the city in which they played, what was all over the papers and on the TV news at night. Yes, Yastrzemski had done some public-service announcements, essentially saying that people in Boston could make anything work. But to the players, busing was something that didn't affect them. Most everyone lived in the suburbs. No one had any children affected by busing.

"Boston in the early seventies wasn't easy," said Lynn. "But it was beyond my field of vision then."

So what was happening in Fenway Park and what was happening in the city's neighborhoods almost seemed to exist in parallel universes during the '75 World Series. That had been the theme of another one of the columns Breslin had written in his brief stay in Boston, one about some black women in a housing project in Roxbury whose daily struggle had nothing to do with all the bright lights and national media who were in town for the World Series, women for whom the World Series could have been taking place on the dark side of the moon for all they cared.

By the autumn of '78 it was less so.

And if there were no doubt still black women in Roxbury whose daily struggle had nothing to do with the national media in town to cover the playoff game between the Red Sox and the

Yankees, still a minority community whose allegiance was not to the Red Sox, there also was the sense that the volume was being turned down in Boston, that maybe the worst actually was over, and this city might be able to start to heal.

The Red Sox would go on to lose the '75 World Series in the seventh game, but there was no shame in that. The Reds were a great team, and the Red Sox had extended them right to the end. Even more important, the summer had rekindled the incredible interest in the team, the sense that every game was an event, even before the playoffs had begun. And the World Series had been the time when the *Boston Globe* cemented itself as having one of the best sports sections in the country. With the national media in town, the *Globe* put out a special baseball section every day, in addition to their normal sports pages. And the rising star was Peter Gammons, who used the platform of the series to become a national baseball writer.

He was thirty that year, a Massachusetts native from the small town of Groton, where his father was a minister. He had gone to the University of North Carolina and had begun at the *Globe* as part of the young brigade of reporters who had joined the paper and were beginning to change it, part of editor Thomas Winship's vision to make it a great paper. Many of the new reporters were products of the sixties and they brought that with them to the *Globe* as surely as they brought their journalism degrees. They tended to be bright, countercultural, antiestablishment, and to a newspaper business that still seemed rooted in the who-what-when-and-where style of *The Front Page* they were like a gust of wind blowing through a dusty old corridor.

Gammons certainly was.

His light hair was longish in the style of the day, and he sprinkled his stories with youth culture and music references, had an almost encyclopedic knowledge of baseball and the people who had played it, and he became a must-read. He began a baseball Sunday notes column that was like opening a safe and taking a peek inside the game, full of rumored trades, minor leaguers of interest, and other baseball esoterica that hadn't been on the sports page before, a printed blog decades before anyone would ever hear the word. First it would become his signature. Later, it would become the template for nearly every sports page in the country.

He began covering the Red Sox for the *Globe* in 1971, essentially as the backup for Cliff Keane, but had already been there for three years after leaving the University of North Carolina when offered a job at the *Globe*. He began the Sunday notes column in 1972 and soon began making his reputation, not only for his knowledge but for his impressionistic, free-form style.

Or consider this wrap-up for the '75 Red Sox season:

"We have postponed autumn long enough now. There are storm windows to put in, wood to chop for the whistling months ahead. The floorboards are getting awfully cold in the morning, the cider sweet. Where Lynn dove and El Tiante stood will be frozen soon, and while it is now 43 years for Thomas A. Yawkey and 57 for New England, the fugue that was the 1975 baseball season will play in our heads until next we meet at the Fens again."

But it was in the '75 World Series that he made his bones, especially his story after Fisk's game-six heroics, which gave Gammons his shining moment, brought Gammons to the attention of the national baseball media in ways that were impossible to ignore.

"Then all of a sudden the ball was suspended out there in the black of morning like the Mystic River Bridge," he wrote in the next day's *Globe*.

He went on to write that Fisk had broke for first, then stopped and watched. He later remembered none of the clumsy hula dance the NBA made famous, only that "it seemed the weight of Christmas morning." And that "in Raymond, New Hampshire, a minister ran across to his church, grabbed the rope, and began ringing the church bell."

It was distinctive writing, both colorful and elegiac, and it had come on an extremely tight deadline, sportswriting at its best, the kind of writing that had come to define the *Globe*. It had the humorous, offbeat columns of Ray Fitzgerald, who had been at the *Globe* for thirteen years and once had played baseball at Notre Dame. It had the hard-hitting Will McDonough, the South Boston native, who covered the Patriots and was as plugged into Boston sports and the people who played them as anyone there was, already the *Globe*'s institutional memory, with the best sources in town. There was Bob Ryan, the Gammons of basketball, who brought the same energy and personalized style to the Celtics. And there was Montville, a great young columnist with his own distinctive voice. There was Larry Whiteside, the first black sportswriter at a major paper in Boston, hired to cover the Red Sox in 1973. They had the erudite John Powers.

All of whom would go on to widespread success in their profession: Gammons with *Sports Illustrated*, books, and as ESPN's baseball insider; McDonough as a sideline analyst for network

NFL games, and becoming such an institution in Boston that his wake in 2003 was held in the Fleet Center; Ryan with books and being named to the Basketball Hall of Fame for his long-standing excellent reportage; Montville at both *Sports Illustrated* and as the author of bestselling sports books. It was an incredible staff, and it was given the reins to essentially reinvent the American sports page.

Much of the staff had been hired by Ernie Roberts, who had worked in public relations at Dartmouth before becoming the *Globe*'s sports editor in 1966. He not only appreciated good writing, he had an eye for it, and as the *Globe* set out to infuse the paper with young talent, as part of editor Tom Winship's vision to turn the *Globe* into a national paper, Roberts set out to transform the sports staff.

"Until then the sports guys were just around," said Montville, who came to the *Globe* from the *New Haven Journal* in 1968 when he was twenty-four. "I think Cliff Keane had been in the advertising department before he came to sports. But Ernie Roberts set out to acquire talent. He went out and got Ray Fitzgerald from Springfield, where he had been a great high school athlete and his father had played minor-league baseball. Both Gammons and Ryan had been interns. Joe Concannon had worked at both Holy Cross and Harvard. John Powers had both gone to Harvard and worked in the sports information office there. So there was a whole influx of young guys."

There was no question that the *Globe* recognized how important sports were, and they set out to spare no expense in covering it. Winship, whose father had been the editor before him, fancied himself a Boston version of the *Washington Post*'s Ben Bradlee, with his bow ties, suspenders, and patrician background, and though he wasn't necessarily a big sports fan, he understood its significance.

A few years later Dave Smith was brought in from Miami to serve as Roberts's assistant.

"He was the nuts and bolts guy," Montville said, "the one who ran it."

And when Monday Night Football first went on the air, becoming an instant phenomenon, with Frank Gifford, Don Meredith, and Howard Cosell all but becoming household names, Smith instantly saw its cultural significance. That first year he sent Montville to cover every game, no matter where it was.

"I would cover the Patriots on Sunday and get on a plane the next morning and go to the city where Monday Night Football was," he said.

Montville had come to Boston in 1968, didn't know anything about the city. He was engaged at the time, first living in a rooming house on Beacon Hill, and his first impression of the city was that it was very different from the New Haven of his youth. In New Haven he had gone to a grammar school that was 60 percent black, and one of the great high school basketball teams of his childhood had been the so-called "Wonder Five" of Hillhouse High School, a team that had started three whites and two blacks. This was the world he was used to, and he soon learned Boston was different.

"There was a rotary on the way to work," he said, "and one way went to Columbia Point, which was black, one way went to South Boston, and one way went to the *Globe*. That pretty much seemed to define the city. Three roads off the rotary and they all went to different worlds."

But the *Globe* was a wonderful place to work if you were a

young writer. They let their writers go, embraced both their talent and their styles, however idiosyncratic they might be. They weren't heavily edited, like the writers at *Time* and *Newsweek* were, to the point that every story often sounded the same. The *Globe* sportswriters were encouraged to have their own voices, a philosophy that stemmed more from the alternative papers than large metropolitan newspapers back then. Part of this, certainly, was because the sports department in newspapers were traditionally referred to as the "toy department," thus were often free of many of the stylistic guidelines that governed other parts of the paper. And the other part was that the editors both appreciated talent and provided an environment where it could be developed. Which is how Gammons developed his distinctive notes columns.

"They probably asked him to write a column and he came up with a page," Montville said. "Both Gammons and Ryan were similar. They both were incredibly passionate in what they did, had an opinion on everything, and knew everybody in their respective sports. They were bloggers thirty years before anyone ever heard of the term."

For the rest of the school year there would be racial hostility in Charlestown, incident after incident, some making the newspapers, others that did not, for the unofficial word in Boston journalism was to try to keep busing and violence off the front page as much as possible, as the city's reputation had been so damaged.

In January there was a sit-in at the high school, and demonstrations in nearby East Boston High School for two days, even blocking the Callahan Tunnel, the one that went from Boston to East Boston and Logan Airport, for a while, even if busing hadn't even come to East Boston yet. In February 1976, the year of the country's bicentennial, the violence in Charlestown intensified, as scores of kids outside the Bunker Hill project threw rocks at police cars, which sent six officers to the hospital. Every night for about a week there were more thrown rocks, more Molotov cocktails, more police barricades, more violence, more stories in the newspapers, more images on TV, all adding to the perception that Boston was a racist city, full of hate and violence, the place that had become the new battleground for America's racial politics.

Nor were things any better in South Boston, even though they were in the second year. The city itself was on edge. The Brookline birthplace of JFK had been trashed, complete with a sign that read BUS TEDDY. There were still so many racial incidents inside South Boston High School that there was talk that the city was thinking of closing the school down. There also was the high absenteeism that there'd been the year before, to the point that one day the teacher Ione Malloy had a total of just twenty-two students all day. There were still the endless marches and demonstrations, often of mothers with their rosary beads and their Our Fathers, often led by Louise Day Hicks. And every time it seemed that things were starting to quiet down, another yellow school bus would get stoned, or there would be another clash between gangs of kids and the police, or another racial melee inside the school, and it would all start again, as if it were still the first day of busing, everything new and unsettled. Midway through the year the school was placed in receivership, and would now essentially be run by Judge Garrity. In February, there was a "fathers only" rally in South Boston that ended with seventy police and forty marchers injured.

So things limped along, a city under siege.

And all the while there was the increasing sense that not only wasn't this working, it was never going to work. It seemed that every day there was another story in the papers, or on Boston television, about more trouble, a laundry list of demonstrations, signs of protest, stories about the stonings of cars, scuffles with the police, who essentially were treated like an army of occupation, especially the city's Tactical Patrol Force, the elite antiriot squad that came to be hated for their storm-trooper tactics. This had become part of the city's daily life, always there, part of what Boston had become.

That spring there was a bomb scare at Hyde Park High School, a school in the southern section of the city that had once been overwhelmingly white, and once outside the black kids and the white kids threw rocks at each other. That had been just ten days after Senators Kennedy and Ed Brooke, who had been the first black senator since Reconstruction, had led a march from Boston Common to City Hall, through so much of the city's history, a march that was called a "Procession for Peace."

But peace was nowhere to be found.

And the antibusing forces had found a new leader.

Her name was Elvira Palladino, but she was known as "Pixie," and if Louise Day Hicks was matronly and almost staid, with her hats and her bright outfits, often called "the Iron Maiden" behind her back, Palladino was her alter ego. She was from East Boston, had become the head of the local chapter of ROAR, and was the daughter of a shoemaker. She quickly became known for both her street language and her propensity to say whatever was on her mind. That, and her dislike for Ted Kennedy and the other political leaders, whom she believed had sold out the neighborhoods, whom she derisively called the beautiful people. To her, being antibusing wasn't just a cause; it was personal. She had a strong sense of class consciousness, and she liked nothing better than to get in the face of the powerful and give them her two cents. If most of the antibusing leaders were politicians, used to speaking in public, Pixie seemed to have sprung from the group of mothers, the faceless who were always at the demonstrations, with their chants and their prayers and their signs, trying to cling to a world that was already behind them.

There was nothing subtle about Palladino.

Her daughter would one day say, "She got arrested so much, it would be nothing to hear, 'Mom got arrested again.'"

Palladino had campaigned against the Racial Imbalance Act in the late sixties, when she had aligned herself with Hicks. She began making a name for herself in those years before busing when tensions were running high, and as the story goes, once stood up in the gallery of the State House on the day the Racial Imbalance Act passed, and yelled out, "Sleep well, you creep." She also became infamous for tormenting Kennedy whenever he made an appearance in Boston. In one such appearance in neighboring Quincy, she and some supporters forced him to seek refuge in an MBTA station under police protection as Pixie and her group threw rocks at him and let the air out of the tires of his black limousine.

In 1975 she was elected to the school committee, only the second Italian-American in history to do so. By this time she, too, had her slice of fame, was admired for her pugnacious style, like the time she supposedly gave the Italian "kiss of death" sign to a politician, and for the sense that she wouldn't back down. For a while she and Hicks were closely aligned, to the point that Palladino would refer to them as "Hicksie and Pixie," but they were such disparate personalities, the daughter of a judge and the daughter of a shoemaker, and for all their shared ideals, they were so different, too.

"We left Boston because of busing," said Howard Bryant, the author of *Shut Out*, the book on race and the Red Sox, and the former columnist at the *Boston Herald* who now works at ESPN.

Bryant spent his childhood in Dorchester, in a house owned by his uncle off Blue Hill Avenue near Franklin Park. As a young kid he was part of METCO, the program that bused a small number of black kids into schools in the suburbs. He went to Newton, the leafy town on the west of Boston where Boston College is located.

"I wanted to stay there," he said. "The grass was green. There were no broken bottles. There were no winos across the street. It was nice."

His neighborhood was all black, with a small smattering of Latinos sprinkled in. It also was a neighborhood where all the older people hated the Red Sox, to the degree that Bryant says he didn't even know where Fenway was when he was a kid. Or as his uncle was fond of saying, "Why would I ever go there? I wouldn't feel safe there."

It was the early seventies and no one was immune to its horrors, not even a young kid who was bused every morning to a suburban school where the grass was green and there were no winos across the street. He had cousins who were bused to Hyde Park High School, where there had been endless problems.

"There was a lot of talk about white flight then," Bryant said, "but there was black flight, too. Every black family with any means at all was trying to get out, too. I remember my family always arguing about busing."

His mother's side of the family wanted to leave for some clean, well-lighted place, some place that was safe and where education was stressed. His father's side of the family? They wanted to stay in the neighborhood. They believed in black identity, continuing the struggle that had started in the sixties, one for civil rights and black pride. But Bryant's sister, two years older, was jumped and beaten one day, and after that his parents essentially said enough was enough. They moved to Plymouth, a South Shore town about fifty miles south. Bryant was nine years old.

"I was terrified of two things as a kid," he said. "The Ku Klux Klan and busing."

Bryant would grow up in Plymouth, go to high school there, often would be in classes where he was the only black, sometimes feeling like a freak. He even learned to talk about the Red Sox there, as if he had to travel fifty miles from Boston to have the Sox be part of the conversation. In many ways the move served him well. It got him into college, at Temple in Philadelphia, then into the newspaper business. It got him a professional life, one quite different from the one his cousins, who had stayed behind in Boston, have had, where the old neighborhood deteriorated, beset with drugs and gangs and all the other ills of urban life. It got him the chance to come back to Boston as a columnist for the *Boston Herald*. And it got him the chance to write a book in 2002 on the Red Sox and race, to examine in depth a story that only had been told in bits and pieces before, a book essential to fully understanding the history of the Red Sox, this team his family never were fans of. The team his family felt always had been one more plantation, one more place where blacks had not been treated equally.

Yet there's also been the sense that he's paid a psychic price for the move, too, that his family felt detached from the black experience. Or as his grandfather once said to him, "We don't care for the Red Sox around here, because the Red Sox never had any niggers. Never have, never will. You think about that."

But Boston was always home. It was where his family was from, where his parents had gone to high school. It was where his earliest memories were, his roots.

"I have a love-hate relationship with Boston and that was based on race," Bryant said. "There's no way around it."

He also remembers something his uncle once said, his uncle who had grown up in Boston, gone to school with whites in the sixties, thought that things hadn't been all that bad between the races then, only to see it all blow up.

"I never realized how much they hated us," he said.

Fenway Park, the country's oldest existing ballpark, shown in 1914, two years after it was built. The Boston Red Sox have been tenants from 1912 to the present.

Cigarette vendors outside Fenway Park during World War I.

A view of Fenway Park in the 1970s, looking from left field into home plate with the press box on top.

Baseball Hall of Famer Carl Yastrzemski, who played his entire twenty-three-year career for the Boston Red Sox after making his Major League debut on April 11, 1961.

Power-hitting left fielder Jim Rice, who played for the Boston Red Sox from 1974 to 1989. In 1978, Rice won the Most Valuable Player award.

All photos on this page: Courtesy of the Boston Red Sox

Hall of Fame pitcher Dennis Eckersley joined the Boston Red Sox in 1978 and that same year pitched a career-high twenty winning games.

Louise Day Hicks, a Boston politician and lawyer, who led the campaign against busing to achieve court-ordered school desegregation in the 1970s.

George Scott Jr., nicknamed Boomer, who came from Greenville, Mississippi, to become one of the first black Red Sox stars.

"Neighborhood schools for neighborhood children" was the rallying cry for antibusing protesters in Boston, many of whom were mothers like the ones pictured here.

A protester during the height of Boston's turmoil over forced busing, which polarized the city throughout the 1970s.

Rallies by Restore Our Alienated Rights, or ROAR, a group founded by Louise Day Hicks to protest court-ordered busing, often turned violent and gave Boston the reputation of being a racist city.

Kevin White, Boston's mayor from 1968 through 1984, twice defeated Louise Day Hicks for the mayor's post, but saw his national political ambitions crippled by the busing crisis.

Named Red Sox manager in 1976, Don Zimmer personified old-school baseball and made several controversial decisions during the team's '78 season.

BETTER NOT TO BE EDUCATED
THAN NOT TO BE FREE

Luis Tiant, born in Cuba, played for the Boston Red Sox from 1971 to 1978 and was one of the most popular Red Sox pitchers ever.

A youthful Senator Ted Kennedy, who was vilified by antibusing forces in the '70s, in a meeting with Louise Day Hicks (*top center*).

Youngsters such as these often took to the streets with their parents during the turmoil over forced busing, creating a staggering rate of absenteeism in Boston's public schools.

Protesters in "Southie" during Boston's busing crisis, which largely affected the city's poorer neighborhoods such as South Boston, Roxbury, and Charlestown.

Star Yankee outfielder Reggie Jackson, known for charisma and controversy, after hitting a home run during the October 2 playoff game.

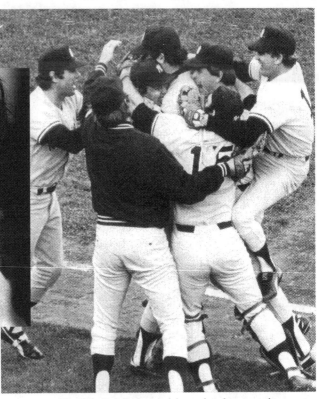

Red Sox icon Carl Yastzremski, who popped up to end the '78 playoff game, wears his defeat after the biggest loss of his life.

The New York Yankees celebrate their history-making win over the Boston Red Sox, a key moment in the long-running rivalry between the two ball clubs.

Red Sox catcher Carlton Fisk shakes hands with Yankees' owner George Steinbrenner in the Red Sox locker room following the game.

CHAPTER EIGHT

orrez had only thrown sixty-six pitches when he came out to start the seventh inning.

To him that was nothing. He felt strong and confident, and now he was just nine outs away from beating the Yankees and winning.

Nettles was the first hitter, always a dangerous one, and he gave Torrez a big break when he swung on the second pitch and lifted a routine fly ball to Rice in right. Torrez wasn't so fortunate with Chambliss, the second Yankee hitter of the inning, who always had been one of the most underrated Yankees, primarily because he tended to be quiet and unassuming, and on a Yankee team that was the antithesis of that, he tended to get lost in the tumult that could be the Yankee clubhouse.

He had been the Rookie of the Year in the American League in 1971, after spending a year at UCLA, and had been traded to the Yankees in 1974, where he quickly fit in. He would win a Gold Glove at the end of the year for his play at first base, and if he could be overshadowed on the Yankees, since he didn't have the kind of personality and star power that could get him on the back pages of the New York tabloids, he always knocked in runs.

He also had one of the all-time great quotes about Reggie Jackson, which had occurred one night in a hotel bar in Detroit when Jackson, tears streaming down his face, had said that "if I were white I'd rule the world."

"Reggie, do you know what you'd be if you were white? Just another damn white boy," Chambliss shot back. "Be glad you're black and getting all the publicity you do, getting away with all the shit you do."

Chambliss slapped a single into left field, for only the Yankees' third hit of the game.

And when Roy White singled to center things had suddenly changed. Now the Yankees had runners on first and second with only one out, and were only down 2–0, as once again the tension began to ratchet up in Fenway Park. It was now the late innings, baseball's crunch time. This was the Yankees' first real chance to get something going, as if everything else to this point had simply been prelude.

The weak-hitting Brian Doyle was due up next, but Lemon elected to hit for him, sending the left-handed-hitting Jim Spencer to the plate instead. He was only hitting .228, but he had good power, certainly was more of a home-run threat than the banjo-hitting Doyle. Zimmer quickly came out to the mound, joined by Fisk. He asked Torrez how he felt. Torrez said he felt fine. Zimmer told him to be careful with Spencer, for he knew Spencer had the potential to knock one out.

Torrez got him on an excellent fastball, one Spencer responded a little late to, and he flew out to Yastrzemski in left.

Enter Bucky Dent.

Into the moment of his baseball life.

The moment he would always be remembered for, his slice of baseball immortality.

Even if he didn't know it as he stepped into the batter's box on this wonderful fall day in Boston.

Dent had hit only four home runs all year, clearly was not the kind of home-run threat Spencer had been. He also had been having a mediocre September, not much of a factor in the Yankees' great run to this playoff game. He knew that if Martin still had been managing he undoubtedly would have been pinch-hit for, but he also knew that since Spencer had pinch-hit for Doyle, the Yankees were running out of middle infielders. So he would bat.

He had been using one of Mickey Rivers's bats, anything to change his luck. It was a little shorter and a little lighter than the ones he had been using, and he figured that might make him a little quicker to the ball.

The crowd was silent, waiting.

On Torrez's second pitch, a fastball high and inside to the crouching Dent, Dent fouled the ball straight down off the in-step of his left foot, hitting it with such impact it bounced fifteen feet in the air. He then moved out of the batter's box, toward the direction of the Yankee dugout, put one end of his bat on the ground and leaned against it and began rubbing his ankle, as the Yankee trainer ran out of the dugout to tend to him.

The game stopped.

Torrez stayed on the mound, tossing the ball into his glove. Fisk was talking to the umpire. The Yankee trainer was spraying Dent's ankle with a freezing compound.

A few minutes passed.

While all this was going on Mickey Rivers, who as the Yankee leadoff hitter was in the on-deck circle, noticed that the bat Dent was using had a hairline crack in it. He realized that one of the bats he'd cast aside after batting practice had obviously been picked up by Dent.

"Homey, that's the wrong bat," Rivers said to Dent. "That one's got a crack in it."

So Rivers handed another bat to the Yankee batboy and told him to give it to Dent.

"Tell him there are a lot of hits in it," Rivers said.

Dent stepped back into the batter's box, took a couple of practice swings. The drama had begun again, as if coming back from a brief timeout.

Torrez threw Dent another fastball.

Years later, he would say that he wished Dent had never fouled the ball off his foot, that he had had great concentration going throughout the entire game and that brief interlude had caused him to lose some of it, that those couple of minutes Dent was getting his ankle attended to had taken him just a bit out of his rhythm.

He also would say that it hadn't been a bad pitch, but that he didn't get it where he had wanted to. The plan had been to throw Dent a fastball inside and get him to back off the plate, then come back with a slider on the outside corner. But instead of staying inside, the fastball tailed back over the plate. What had started out to be a "waste" pitch now had become the biggest pitch of Torrez's career.

He would also say later that he didn't really throw that pitch, as much as guide it, and it caught too much of the plate.

"Bucky had a tendency to go into the bucket a little bit," he said, "and it got right in his wheelhouse."

It started out as nothing special, just a routine fly ball to left from a number-nine hitter without a lot of pop in his back, someone who was a contact hitter, not someone known for driving the ball. He hadn't hit a home run in two months.

When the ball left Dent's bat it first appeared that Yastrzemski was going to have no trouble catching it. One of Yastrzemski's little idiosyncrasies in left field was that if he knew the ball was going over Fenway's Green Monster he wouldn't even turn around, would simply stay in his outfield position, eyes straight ahead, as the ball flew over his head and over the wall behind him. It was something that always bothered some of the Red Sox pitchers, the feeling that Yastrzemski was somehow showing them up, his little way of saying what a horrible pitch that had been. This time it was the opposite, looked like Yastrzemski was going to be able to catch it.

Torrez certainly thought so.

He saw Yastrzemski pat his glove, and he knew that when Yaz patted his glove the ball was catchable. I'm out of the inning, he thought. Remy, playing second base, saw Yaz pound his glove and he, too, thought it was going to be caught. So did Fisk behind the plate. So did Zimmer watching from the corner of the dugout. Then Yastrzemski kept backing up, and then he was at the base of the wall, and Torrez couldn't believe what he was seeing, and then he thought maybe it was just going to hit the wall and Yaz, who was so good playing balls off it, would hold White on third and they would still be ahead 2–1.

That's what all the Red Sox now thought, because they had seen innumerable fly balls that would have been simply routine in other ballparks go off the wall in Fenway, and now it was looking like this was going to be another one, a cheapie that ended up a double, a Fenway special.

Yastrzemski was now at the base of the wall, now thinking it was going to go off the wall and how he might be able to throw out White at third, or if not that, then hold Dent to a single, because he'd been playing balls off the wall since 1961, and no one knew it better than he did.

But it didn't hit the wall.

Later, Torrez would say that as he had looked out at the flag he saw that it was blowing out, the sudden realization that the wind had changed, the kind of wind that sends routine fly balls to left field into the screen on top of the wall. Yastrzemski seemed to lean back against the wall, then he bent both knees and fell forward, as though he was going to collapse, before he righted himself.

Fenway was completely silent, had turned into a baseball version of a wake, as Dent followed both Chambliss and White to home plate. When the ball had left Dent's bat he'd been hoping that the ball had a chance to make the wall, so he had sprinted to first base, and as he rounded the bag he still didn't know where the ball was going to land. Then he saw the second-base umpire circling with his hand that it was a home run, and everything changed.

He had always dreamed of hitting a home run to win a game. Wasn't that every little kid's dream? Hit a home run to win the big game? Wasn't that the fodder sandlot dreams are made of? But he had never done it, not at any level of baseball.

Until now.

Chambliss and White were waiting for him at the plate, of

course, and as Dent approached home plate he did a little jump and landed on it with both feet. And then there was the mob scene of Yankee players who had run out of the dugout to hug him and jump around in wild celebration. A small group of Yankee wives and officials, sitting near the Yankee dugout, were also celebrating, but everywhere else Fenway was like a tomb. The unthinkable had happened, on a home run by Bucky Dent, no less.

The Yankees were now ahead 3–2.

And Mickey Rivers was up, the top of the Yankee order, and all of a sudden Torrez walked him, and any momentum the Sox had now seemed as gone as Labor Day.

On the mound, Torrez tried to compose himself. He was still pitching well, he told himself, only down a run, still very much in this game. He felt good, always had been able to throw a lot of innings. He was giving himself a pep talk, saying how he now had to get Munson, whom he already had struck out three times, how he had to get his concentration back and bear down, when he saw Zimmer walking toward him, amidst a cascade of boos, and signaling to right field and the Red Sox bullpen, where reliever Bob Stanley had been warming up.

He didn't want to come out. Wasn't he still throwing well? Didn't he still feel good? Wasn't this only a one-run game? Then why was Zimmer going to take him out?

He was not happy on the mound when Zimmer came to get the ball, the symbolic gesture that a pitcher is out of the game. But what could he do? He began walking to the dugout as the crowd applauded. He had pitched well, better than anyone probably had a right to expect. Had pitched very well, until he had thrown one bad pitch that had tailed back over the plate when it wasn't supposed to, and Dent had made him pay a very big price for his mistake.

He went down the dugout steps and fired both his cap and glove at the bench.

Mike Torrez's role in this passion play was over.

But the game wasn't.

Stanley was in just his second season as a Red Sox relief pitcher. He threw a hard sinker and had had a good season, part of the troika of relief pitchers that also included Bill Campbell and Dick Drago. Now his job was to silence the Yankees and give the Sox bats a chance to go ahead, as they would have three innings left to try and do so.

But Rivers stole second on Stanley's first pitch to Munson, and then scored when Munson doubled to center, giving the Yankees a 4–2 lead.

The momentum had definitely changed.

Butch Hobson led off for the Red Sox against Guidry in the bottom of the seventh inning.

He was from Alabama, had been a backup quarterback for Bear Bryant at the University of Alabama, and if Paul Newman had played baseball he would have been Butch Hobson, who quickly became one of the team's heartthrobs. He had hit thirty home runs the year before, his first with the Red Sox, but the bone chips in his elbow had essentially sabotaged his season. His forty-three errors had been the most of anyone in the American League, and his throwing from third base had become so inconsistent that he had asked to be taken out of the lineup near the end of the season, as he no longer was able to throw the ball from third base to the pitcher without any pain, never mind to first base. He knew that his throwing was hurting the team.

Zimmer loved him, for he played the game like the football player he once had been, hard-nosed, asking no quarter. In fact, Zimmer's reluctance to move Hobson off third base, when it had become apparent that every throw from third base had become an adventure, had been one of the things he'd been vilified for on talk radio.

Now, in the lineup as the designated hitter, Hobson went down looking as Guidry threw a fastball on the outside corner of the plate.

Then George Scott singled to right, and that was enough for Bob Lemon. He came out of the Yankee dugout and signaled to the Yankee bullpen in right field.

Guidry was done, even though Munson told Lemon that Guidry was still throwing well, and didn't want to come out.

"You're done, Meat," Lemon said, asking for the ball.

Later, Lemon would say that he wasn't going to let Guidry lose the game, that Guidry had had such an amazing season it was not going to end here in this playoff game with a loss. It also had been part of his strategy going into the game. Guidry was pitching on only three days' rest, and when Lemon sensed him starting to tire he was going to go to Goose Gossage. Managing to Lemon was simple: go with your best. And he figured that he had the best starter in the game, and the best reliever, and he was going to use them both. If he were going to lose it was going to be with his two best guys.

So it was time for Richard "Goose" Gossage, the Yankees' star reliever, the one who had been signed as a free agent after the '77 season, leaving the Pittsburgh Pirates, even though the

Yankees already had left-handed Sparky Lyle, who had won the Cy Young Award the year before. Gossage was six feet three, threw a fastball in the high nineties, and with his bushy mustache and wild mane of hair sticking out from his cap combined with the way he glared at hitters, he was an imposing figure on the mound. No one dug in too deep against Goose Gossage.

He had grown up in Colorado, developed his distinctive pitching style as a teenager throwing in his backyard with his older brother, who called him a sissy and told him to throw harder. That had been the start of his flailing style, all arms and legs that seemed to come right at a hitter. That, and a ball that seemed to all but explode at hitters.

As a young pitcher he had been taught an off-speed pitch by a pitching coach who once had been part of the old Boston Braves in the late forties, where he'd teamed with the great Warren Spahn, the old line being "Spahn and Sain and two days of rain." The off-speed pitch, combined with his 99-mph fastball, and a little bit of fear factor among hitters, made Gossage a great relief pitcher.

The other huge influence in his development came from the slugger Dick Allen and had taken place in spring training with the White Sox when Allen decided to step in against the young flamethrower whose ball was making the catcher's mitt pop. Allen told Gossage that he had one of the best arms he'd ever seen, and told him to throw his fastball right at a hitter's front elbow. Allen told him that was the pitch that was so difficult for hitters to get the barrel of the bat on the ball. Gossage said that he feared he might hit someone in the head with that pitch.

"What's wrong with that?" said Allen. "Plus, every guy in that dugout is watching."

That was the start of no one digging in too deep against Goose Gossage.

In retrospect, Gossage's adjustment to the Yankees had been more difficult than anyone would have expected.

He expected that he and Lyle would share the job. That hadn't happened. Making his arrival more awkward was the fact that Lyle, the team's prankster, was adored by both his teammates and the fans, and had won the Cy Young Award the year before. If Gossage hadn't realized this when he had signed with the Yankees, he learned soon enough. On the day of the Yankees' home opener, as a world championship banner from the year before had been hoisted in the rafters by former Yankee greats Mickey Mantle and Roger Maris, he had been booed as the Yankee roster had been introduced.

Goose Gossage?

Who needed Goose Gossage?

He had not pitched well in his first few appearances on the road, and the Yankee fans were giving him an introduction to the realities of playing in New York. In his first game as a Yankee he had given up a game-winning home run, and then gave up a game-winning hit in his second appearance.

His struggles continued for roughly six weeks. He was trying too hard, which led to overthrowing, which only made everything worse. It got so bad that when the Toyota Celica would come to transport him from the bullpen to the pitcher's mound, nearby fans would throw things at it, everything from beer to peanuts to hot dogs. By the time the car arrived near the dugout, its front window would be covered with condiments.

Interestingly, his new Yankee teammates dealt with his difficult adjustment very differently. They teased him about it, made fun of it. Once, Munson met him at the mound and said, "Okay, Goose, how are you going to lose this one?"

Another time, when he came into the game with the bases loaded, Rivers had turned around in a sprinter's stance, as though just waiting to go running after some long drive.

Then there was the time Rivers threw himself on the hood of the Toyota that had come to pick up Gossage in the bullpen, telling an umpire, who had come out to see what was going on, "Please, Mr. Umpire. We don't want Goose to come in. We wants to win this game. We don't wants to lose."

This was the Yankees way, by making fun of everything, their way of alleviating the pressure, as if nothing was sacred, certainly not something taking place on a baseball field.

Yet it had taken one more embarrassing moment before he finally began to find his groove in New York. After making a bad throw to first to lose a game in Toronto, he went into the clubhouse, crawled into his locker, curled up in the fetal position, and began crying. It all seemed too much. Too much pressure. No success. His confidence was shattered. For the only time in his career he wanted to quit and go back home to Colorado. Until Catfish Hunter touched him on the shoulder. When he looked up he saw Munson, Jackson, Piniella, and Nettles.

"Get up, Goose," Hunter said. "Get dressed. We're all going out to dinner and you're going with us. You're down now, but you're going to come out of it."

That had been the beginning.

He had ended the year with ten wins, twenty-seven saves, and an ERA of 2.01. Maybe more important, he had ended the year as one of those guys out of the bullpen whom no one wanted to face.

The first batter he faced was Bob Bailey, nicknamed "Beatle," a journeyman who had bounced around the National League for years, and rest assured there had been no trumpets blaring when he'd arrived in Boston the year before, as little more than outfield insurance and a bat off the bench. Zimmer had said that Bailey was the kind of guy who would win some games for the Sox as a pinch hitter, but that had mostly been wishful thinking. This would have been the perfect time for Carbo, but he had been sold to Cleveland in July, jettisoned for no apparent reason other than the purge of the Buffalo Heads, so now Bailey was at the plate. He was at the end of his career and he had to face the hard-throwing Gossage in the shadows of Fenway Park. It almost didn't seem fair.

It wasn't.

Gossage threw him four straight fastballs. The last one Bailey watched for strike three.

Then Gossage got Burleson to ground out to Dent at short and the Yankees were out of the seventh, leading 4–2, the shadows growing longer across Fenway Park.

CHAPTER NINE

ighteen months after it had begun there was an incident that would come to define busing in Boston, an incident so egregious and so symbolic that it, once again, put the city on the national news and reinforced its image as a racist city. It happened on April 5, 1976, and it began with another demonstration, this time at the downtown City Hall Plaza, where both City Hall and the federal building were.

It was called a boycott of classes, and it was another in the long list of demonstrations designed to put pressure on both Judge Garrity and the politicians. Some students from both South Boston High School and Charlestown High School first had met with Louise Day Hicks, who had brought them into the empty council chamber. She had received them warmly, and had them recite the Pledge of Allegiance. There is a picture from that morning, taken by a photographer from the *Herald American*, and it shows a group of kids, complete with the longish hair of the times, with their right hands over their hearts. One of them is holding a large American flag in his left hand.

For that was the other reality about the protestors: they saw themselves as patriots, part of a long list of Americans who had to fight for their rights. This wasn't the counterculture of the late sixties with its flag burning and its anti-American rhetoric. These were people who all but wrapped themselves in the flag, people who saw their struggle as similar to that of those ragged bands of colonists who once had fought the redcoats in Charlestown and had been with Washington at the fort on top of the hill in South Boston as the British ships had sat out in the harbor. They saw themselves as the defenders of liberty as well as their neighborhood schools.

There were roughly two hundred white kids in City Hall Plaza that morning, lured there by flyers and leaflets and word of mouth, and to quote from the book *The Soiling of Old Glory*, "They attended for every reason, and for no reason at all: they despised forced busing, they hated blacks, they feared change, they followed their parents' lead, they welcomed days off from school, they felt like they were part of a group."

As fate would have it, there was a group of black students there for a tour that morning, and the two groups yelled and threw some food at each other. Then the group of white students marched into the plaza and into history.

It was just three months away from the Bicentennial, the nation's two-hundred-year birthday party, big doings in a city so rich in history as Boston, the "cradle of liberty." There was going to be an appearance of the Tall Ships in Boston Harbor and a concert on the Esplanade by the Boston Pops, massive fireworks, and all the trappings of a city so steeped in its history celebrating America's birthday. Boston had big plans for the Bicentennial. On this morning many of the students had entered the plaza with flags and bicentennial banners to go along with the antibusing signs that were about as familiar now as demonstrations and Yastrzemski's face.

His name was Theodore Landsmark, and if ever there was a case of being the wrong man at the wrong time it was Landsmark. He had been to an exclusive New England prep school, and he had been to Yale at the same time George Bush had been there, one of only sixteen black students in his freshman class. He had marched for civil rights in the South, had worked for Michael Dukakis at a prestigious Boston law firm, and now worked for the Contractors Association. Which was why he was in City Hall Plaza, on his way to a morning meeting about minority hiring.

But the kids in the plaza knew none of that, of course. To them, Landsmark was invisible, just another faceless black guy, a symbol of everything they had grown to hate.

So it didn't matter that Landsmark had nothing to do with the rally, or that he was wearing a three-piece suit. Didn't matter that it was only his third year in Boston, and that his roots were somewhere else. Didn't matter that he had no idea that there had been a demonstration planned for City Hall Plaza that morning.

The protestors saw him and that was enough. Someone yelled, "Get the nigger," someone else tried to trip him, and others jumped in front of him and began punching and kicking him. Then a seventeen-year-old kid from South Boston, who had dropped out of school because of busing, and who had taken his family's flag with him that morning, and was fueled by an anger that had been building up for nearly two years now, an anger that had all but raised him, thrust the American flag at Landsmark.

The entire incident probably lasted fifteen seconds, maybe twenty, and Landsmark was quickly helped afterward by the police and by a deputy mayor who helped take him to a hospital. He was treated there for contusions and a broken nose, and after a big bandage was placed on his face, he was released.

How could this have happened to a man in a three-piece suit walking across City Hall Plaza in the middle of the day?

"I couldn't put my Yale degree in front of me to protect myself," Landsmark told a writer. "The thing that is most troubling is that it happened not because I was somebody but because I was anybody . . . I was just a nigger they were trying to kill."

Only this time it went out for everyone to see.

A photographer for the *Herald American* was in City Hall Plaza that morning on little more than a whim, and the fact that he hadn't had an assignment that morning. His name was Stanley Forman. He was from nearby Revere, and had begun working at the *Record-American* ten years ago, a paper that had morphed into the *Herald American* three years earlier. He had a reputation for chasing down news, one of those photographers of legend who all but lived with a police scanner and was forever getting out of bed in the middle of the night to follow breaking news, someone well regarded in his profession. Three years earlier he had taken another incredible picture, one of a woman and a child in a free fall out of a burning building on Marlborough Street, that had solidified his reputation, a picture that had circulated around the world. Now he was about to take another. When he saw the incident start to develop he immediately started taking as many pictures as quickly as he could shoot them.

The next morning Forman's photograph was on the front page of the *Herald American*, in the center of the page, underneath the lead story that said in big black type "Howard Hughes Dead." The photograph, underneath a caption that read "Youths beat black lawyer at City Hall," dominated the middle part of the paper, and showed a kid with a large American flag apparently about to spear a black man in a light three-piece suit whose back is being held by an unidentified man. In the background are a bunch of other kids who seem to be advancing on the black man.

Underneath that picture is another one, about half as big, that shows the black man on all fours on the ground as a white kid with bushy hair and wearing a white shirt is about to kick him. To the right of that picture is a small story entitled "Mayor Decries Attack."

The story also ran on the front page of the *Boston Globe*, although not so prominently. The *Globe* also led with the news that the famed financier Howard Hughes had died, using the headline HOWARD HUGHES DIES ON AMBULANCE JET TO HOUSTON. The other main story was about how thousands had participated in a daylong riot in Peking, and a column by the sportswriter Will McDonough, on the fact that the New England Patriots had just traded away quarterback Jim Plunkett to the San Francisco 49ers, ran down the left side of the front page.

A photograph of the attack was near the bottom of the front page. It showed Landsmark, his hands up, as if to protect his face, being pulled from the back by three males. The American flag is not in the picture, and the headline read BLACK MAN BEATEN BY YOUNG BUSING PROTESTORS.

And it wasn't just big news in Boston.

The picture of a white kid assaulting a black man with the American flag went out across the country. It was on ABC television with Harry Reasoner. It was on the front page of many newspapers in the country, including the *Washington Post*, the *Chicago Tribune*, and the *San Francisco Chronicle*. It also was displayed in many papers around the world. Once again, Boston was in the national news because of a tragic racial incident.

The incident brought cries of indignation from both legislators and politicians. Kevin White, who had witnessed it from his office in City Hall, called it "racism, pure and simple," said it hadn't been about busing at all. Governor Dukakis decried mob violence, and later the next day several black leaders gathered in City Hall Plaza, not far from where the attack had taken place, and called for the Massachusetts attorney general to investigate the role of both the city council and the school committee for inciting violence in the young people in the city. And, almost as an exclamation point on the mood of the city, the pastor of the Ebenezer Baptist Church said that "war has been declared on black folk in Boston."

Once again, busing in Boston had become a national story, and the image of angry white kids pledging allegiance to the flag and then attacking a black man in a public place seemed to transcend the incident itself, resurrecting all the hatred. The *Globe* was bombarded with letters to the editor criticizing it for sensationalizing white-on-black crime, while downplaying black-on-white crime, once again beating the old drum that the *Globe*'s editorial pages were run by liberal men who lived in the suburbs and tried to tell the people in the neighborhoods how to think, how to run their lives.

Or as Billy Bulger, the state rep from Southie, liked to say, "To telephone the *Globe*'s 'Urban Team' after dark you had to dial 1 first."

The *Globe*, in turn, blamed the violence and racial hatred on the failure of leadership in the home, in the schools, in the community, and by public officials. One editorial read, "Uncontrolled street violence in Boston has made headlines across the country for the past two years. It is impossible to overestimate the damage it is doing to the spirit of the city, the psyche of its citizens, and its reputation across the nation and throughout the world."

Then there was the powerful voice of columnist Mike Barnicle, the *Globe*'s version of Jimmy Breslin. Barnicle was of Irish heritage, a man who had grown up in central Massachusetts, gone to Boston University, had worked in Washington for Bobby Kennedy, had been in the Robert Redford movie *The Candidate*, and both understood and captured the rhythms of Boston as well as anyone.

In one column he debunked the South Boston belief that busing was not about race.

"When you take a close look at what happened," he wrote, "it wasn't really about busing at all. It was about race, about the basics, about calling people 'niggers,' and laughing as they hit the ground, noses broken and clothes splattered with blood. Theodore Landsmark was hit by a long steel pole flying the red, white and blue flag of the United States of America. He was hit by the flag exactly eight years to the week after Martin Luther King had a flag draped over him. We've come a long way."

And the violence wasn't over.

Two weeks after Landsmark had been attacked in City Hall

Plaza a white man was driving in Roxbury when some black kids started throwing rocks at his car. One of them broke the windshield and hit him in the head. The car crashed into another vehicle, at which point some of the black kids dragged thirty-four-year-old Richard Poleet out of his car and began beating him, both with fists and rocks. When he was taken to Boston City Hospital he had a fractured skull, facial injuries, and internal bleeding, injuries he eventually would die from.

The rhetoric started all over again, both from community leaders and in newspaper editorials. It was now nineteen months after busing had begun in Boston and things seemed worse than ever, to the point that the idea of a black person walking through South Boston, or a white person walking through Roxbury, would be akin to a suicide mission. This was now more than just some demonstrators carrying signs and yelling at school buses carrying black children, more than inflammatory rhetoric and marches through the streets, even more than stoning buses and racial incidents in the schools. This was flat-out hatred.

And just three days after the attack on Poleet, amidst plans for an antiviolence march planned for the streets of Boston the next day, a bomb went off at the Suffolk County Courthouse, injuring nearly two dozen people.

"These are troubled times for the City of Boston," Dukakis said in a live television broadcast.

The next day a crowd reported to be as many as fifty thousand marched in a massive parade denouncing violence through downtown that ended at City Hall Plaza, a march that included both Senators Kennedy and Brooke, Mayor White and Governor Dukakis. It was later reported to be a mostly white, middle-class crowd, but there were blacks, too, and at the end the crowd sang "God Bless America."

Two people who didn't march were the black leader Mel King, a state representative, and Louise Day Hicks.

Mel King was forty-eight, and had been both a community organizer and community activist since the early fifties. He was six feet five, had a shaved head, and sometimes appeared in public in dashikis. Complete with a definite presence. Eight years earlier he had been one of the leaders trying to stop the demolition of neighborhoods by the Boston Redevelopment Organization, and one of his most successful ventures was organizing a sit-in at the corner of Dartmouth and Columbus streets in the South End, which was called "Tent City." Despite attempts by the police to break it up, up to four hundred people lived there for almost four days, attracting thousands of people. There were tents and wooden shanties. There was music and bongo drums. Bill Russell, who had an interest in a nearby South End neighborhood, provided food. And in the end, King and his followers won, housing eventually going up there instead of the parking lot that had been planned.

King had emerged as arguably the most visible leader of the black community, and for almost two decades now had been in the forefront of the struggle for racial justice in Boston. He did not march in the parade through the streets of Boston, but instead stood in front of the State House on Beacon Street in a blue jumpsuit and mauve hat and said that while he thought the march was a good thing, "when the prayer meeting is over, I think we ought to go see the mayor and say, 'What are we going to do now?'"

Hicks was more strident.

"The only march that will mean anything will be on Judge Garrity's courtroom," she said.

The fear was that the city was going to erupt into a race war, that this was where all the demonstrations and all the incidents, all the rhetoric and all the hate, was leading; the fear that busing had taken the veneer off the neighborhoods and revealed the deep divisions, the sense that the two races in Boston now peered at each other over a distance as great as the Continental Divide.

For here it was nineteen months after busing had begun and things certainly weren't any better. If anything, they were worse. There were still racial incidents in the schools. There were still demonstrations in the neighborhoods. There was still the daily tension, the feeling that at any time anything could happen. Absenteeism was still very high at South Boston High School, where there was the constant feeling that the school simply didn't work, that busing had helped no one, and made no one happy, and that both the black students and the white students were seeing their dreams dying on some altar of change that no one seemed to want, little more than pawns on some giant chessboard in Judge Garrity's office, experiments in social engineering, their fates decided by men who lived in other places.

Maybe most of all, there was the sense that the neighborhoods had been all but abandoned by the legislators and politicians, that their problems were not the problems that anyone cared about, that they were portrayed in the media as narrow-minded and provincial at best, racist at worst, as if that judgment had been cast in stone. That had become one of the timeless complaints as the months went by and nothing seemed to change, the sense that no matter how many times they wrapped themselves in the flag and said that they were patriots in the best sense of the word, fighting against the federal judge's decree the same way their forefathers had once fought the British, they were condemned in the media.

They also had been influenced by the tumult of the sixties, even if many of them undoubtedly wouldn't have admitted it. The sixties had done more than just send shock waves through the country, with its protests and its assaults on traditional values. They also had changed the way people viewed both government and institutions, and authority, too. If those seeds had been planted in the sixties, they flowered in the seventies. Watergate, the rise of feminism and the women's movement, the black power movement, drug use among the young, gas lines, runaway inflation; all had combined to stage an assault on the body politic. All had fundamentally changed the country, making it a very different place than it had been in the fifties.

Maybe it was this simple: It was harder to tell people what to do, whether that was teachers, parents, religious leaders, politicians, baseball managers, even the government itself.

All those things were in play in Boston as busing and its ramifications tore through the city like some unrelenting hurricane. The popularity of both Louise Day Hicks and Pixie Palladino spoke to that. Not only were they women, they also were both mothers. But it was their ability to articulate and express the anger and frustration among working-class people, the ones who once had been the solid supporters of the establishment less than a decade before, that made them leaders, however unlikely that might have seemed.

In a sense, though, they weren't talking about some vision of a better future. Their vision was backward. They wanted to go back to what Boston had been, to what America had been, back before the unrest of the sixties had set in motion forces that could no longer be contained.

In retrospect, the Landsmark incident in City Hall Plaza became a turning point.

It had been so shocking, so ugly, portrayed Boston in such a negative light that there was the increasing sense that people were tired of it.

This from *All Souls*:

"What a vicious son of a bitch," Ma said, looking at the picture of a Southie neighbor from down the road on the front page of the *Herald*. . . . Ma said she'd just about had it. "Busing is a horror," she said, "but this is no way to fight it. People like that are making us all look bad." . . . One day you'd be clapping and cheering the inspirational words of Louise Day Hicks and Senator Billy Bulger, and the next day you'd see the blood on the news, black and white people's blood."

The following fall school opened with more calm, fewer incidents. At least in the papers and on the TV news.

Yet the Boston schools were still very far from working, especially at South Boston High School, where all too often it was as if nothing had changed at all. In May of '77 a stick of dynamite was discovered in the parking lot of the school. An Associated Press picture showed a dozen or so police in the middle of the street. In front of them in paint were the words "Go Home Jerome You Failed," a reference to Jerome Wynegar, who had been brought in by Judge Garrity to run South Boston High School. There were so many absences that spring that school began list-

ing the names of those present on what always had been known
as the "absence list" because it was shorter. There were constant racial incidents. And on the last day of school no students
showed up.

Graduation that spring was held downtown in the Hynes
Auditorium, and it came complete with motorcycle patrols, five
mounted police horses, more cops along the sides of the auditorium, and teachers, administrators, and fifty-five aides inside. At
one point three female graduates whisked off their graduation
robes to reveal shamrocks, as people in the crowed applauded,
and two others later did the same thing, revealing "Southie" and
"Southie is my home."

But in the city elections in the fall both Hicks and Palladino
would be defeated, Hicks in her city council race and Palladino
in her bid for another term on the school committee. As would
John Kerrigan, an ardent antibuser who once had told a black
reporter, "You're just one generation away from swinging from
trees."

Why did they all get beat?

There were several theories, everything from the fact that
Hicks had made a secret deal with Kevin White where she would
keep ROAR neutral in elections in return for some patronage
jobs for her family, to the fact that she always had been a one-
trick-pony candidate and that pony had left the barn. Whatever
the reasons, their losses were symbolic of the public affirmation
that their influence was waning, that they had been all about
keeping busing out of the neighborhoods and they had failed to
do so. And if Palladino would come back in '79 and get elected
again, never again would she have the same influence.

Maybe it was this simple: It had gone on too long. The protests. The demonstrations. The speeches. The words tossed back and forth like a baseball between the players in the outfield warming up before an inning.

The leading vote getter had been a woman named Kathleen Sullivan, a moderate who was opposed to busing but believed that the school committee had to follow the law, whether it agreed with it or not. In the same election a man named John O'Bryant also was elected to the school committee, becoming the first black to be elected to the committee in seventy-six years, although there was speculation that a significant portion of the electorate had assumed he was Irish.

Reelected as a state representative was Ray Flynn, whose career had accelerated during the busing crisis. He might have first been elected in 1971 essentially on a platform to help kids, but his opposition to busing put him in the limelight. Unlike some of the other antibusing leaders, his message had been more against the police presence in South Boston and the way the media had covered the neighborhood. He had never had the stridency of Louise Day Hicks, his rhetoric was more under-stated, and for whatever reason his popularity kept growing as some of the others' lessened.

The overriding message?

Boston had had enough.

Maybe it had been the aftermath of the Landsmark incident in City Hall Plaza a year and a half earlier, the ugly incident that had bothered many people who opposed busing, as though what had started out as simply trying to protect the neighborhood school and defend the home turf had escalated into a black man being attacked with an America flag on a morning in the middle of downtown Boston. There was the sense that something had

changed, there had been a seismic shift in the public consciousness, as though people wanted to turn down the noise, especially the incredible violence, which now went back and forth
with no end in sight, and no promise of resolution, just more of
the same. As if Boston had become some American version of
Northern Ireland, a city that no longer seemed safe, a city that
had come apart, Humpty Dumpty lying on the ground in pieces,
waiting for all the king's horses and all the king's men to put it
back together again.

CHAPTER TEN

Reggie Jackson had had a quiet game.

He'd had the drive to left field in the first inning that had looked for an instant as though it might go out, the soft breeze holding it up enough for Yastrzemski to have caught it at the base of the wall. But he had yet to make the big dramatic statement, the kind he had made his reputation on, like the year before when he had hit three home runs in the sixth game of the World Series against the Dodgers. That was the Reggie of legend, coming up big at the big time, and the Yankees were almost used to it by now. The World Series. The Game of the Week on television. The bigger the stage the more he seemed to deliver. This was at the core of his star power, not his batting average, or even his home-run totals, but the fact that he not only relished the spotlight but performed so well in the middle of it. Even the teammates that considered him a star in his own movie, and could get tired of his obvious need to constantly be the center of attention, acknowledged that he came through when it counted the most, that he seemed to concentrate more in the big moments, become more focused.

Now it was the top of the eighth inning, the shadows spreading across the field, the Yankees leading 4–2, and Jackson was leading off the inning. Bob Stanley was pitching. Stanley was big and burly, nicknamed "Steamer," and his best pitch was a hard sinker. He had grown up in New Jersey and was in his second year with the Red Sox, and had been an excellent 15–2 as a reliever, so good that Zimmer would say afterward that Stanley might have been his most effective pitcher much of the year. But Jackson loved hard stuff, the lower the better, and on Stanley's third pitch to him he hit a shot to center field that he knew was gone as soon as he hit it, momentarily staring at it heading for the center-field bleachers like an artist staring at his creation on the canvas before him. It was his twenty-seventh home run of the season, and his most important.

Fenway seemed as silent as a cemetery at three in the morning. After Jackson crossed home plate and was greeted by Graig Nettles, who had been in the on-deck circle, he headed over to shake the hand of Steinbrenner, who was sitting in a box near the Yankee dugout along the third-base line.

In many ways they were kindred spirits, Jackson and Steinbrenner, both driven, insecure, forever needing the roar of the crowd or the back of the New York tabloids to reaffirm their worth, forever needing to win again and again. They were both made for New York and the big stage, for not only had they both become larger than life, they both needed to be larger than life. They had both become almost fictional characters, with their flaws and excesses right there with their strengths, men admired, but never truly loved; men who always seemed to feel that they had something to prove, that their fame was fragile and could be taken away from them in a heartbeat, Steinbrenner for not having his Yankees win, Jackson becoming just another player with an under .300 batting average.

Steinbrenner's flaws would become more public later, his dictatorial style, his infatuation with stars, his lack of patience, his belief that his money could buy anything, even world championships, the way it had bought his rise from a guy from Cleveland who owned a shipping company into one of the most recognizable names in American sports. But both the flaws and his assertion that he was the undisputed boss had been there from the beginning.

Like the time Piniella had first joined the Yankees in 1974 and was at spring training, and here was this guy he didn't recognize telling players to "Put those caps on. Look like Yankees."

"Who the hell is that guy?" Piniella asked Munson.

"That is the principal owner of the Yankees, George M. Steinbrenner the Third," Munson said dryly.

Piniella looked closely at Steinbrenner. He saw the pressed pants. He saw the laundered shirt. He saw the shined shoes. He saw how Steinbrenner seemed to be almost obsessed about neatness. And since he liked to go days without shaving, he knew they would clash, that it was inevitable.

"Lou, you can't dress with hair that long," Steinbrenner said one day.

"Why not?" countered Piniella. "What does long hair have to do with my ability to play?"

"It's a matter of discipline," Steinbrenner said. "I won't have it."

"If our Lord Jesus Christ came back down with his long hair you wouldn't let him play on this team," said Piniella.

"Come with me," Steinbrenner said.

They walked across the street to a motel that had a pool.

"If you can walk across the water in that pool, Lou, you don't have to get a haircut."

Piniella got a haircut.

Steinbrenner didn't know a whole lot about baseball in those early years, bringing a football mentality to it, seemingly obsessed with "having balls" and playing hard. Jim Spencer, the reserve outfielder, would say that Steinbrenner "didn't understand that this was a major-league team, not Purdue." But he knew how to run a business.

"I can get on the back pages of the *News* and *Post* anytime I want," he once told Piniella. "All I have to do is holler a little bit. They love it. It sells newspapers. That's what they're interested in. It's a business. If I don't raise a little hell, I don't sell tickets for us. Always remember, Lou, baseball is a business."

But he had rescued the Yankees from the morass of the late sixties, willing to spend money, restoring the Yankees to the top of the baseball world again. He already had been banned from baseball for a year, the result of his conviction on making illegal contributions to the Nixon campaign in 1972, and already was a controversial figure, not the kind of traditional owner who stayed in the background but the kind of CEO who would come after him in corporate America, CEO as star. But his public squabble with Martin had hurt him in New York. Martin was the fan favorite, the visible link to the storied past, the little guy who would never back down, as if he carried all of New York's grit and attitude with him every time he went out to get in some umpire's face, kicking his feet in the dirt, the veins in his neck in bas relief. This was the Billy Martin of legend, and the fans couldn't get enough of it.

Steinbrenner?

Steinbrenner was the boss, with all the negative connotations that came with that, a ship owner from Cleveland, no less.

Jackson was another who intuitively understood the power of the media to shape perception. It no doubt had been one of the reasons why he wanted to play in New York, being uncannily prescient with his onetime remark that if he played there they'd name a candy bar after him. He also was a product of his time, a black player who had been raised in a Philadelphia suburb and who had been around whites all his life, someone who had gone to the University of Arizona. This wasn't George Scott, who had come of age in the segregated South and carried that baggage with him. This was an articulate black man in a new America, one who not only had benefited from the civil rights movement in the sixties but also wanted the perks that the black baseball pioneers in the fifties and sixties had struggled for.

It was not Jackson's race that bothered so many of Jackson's teammates. It was his insecurities, his insatiable need for attention, his need to always be seen as a superstar and never just one of the guys. Baseball clubhouses can be fragile ecosystems, with their own cultures, and from the time he'd first arrived with the Yankees in spring training in '77 Jackson had never understood that. The "straw that stirs the drink" foolishness in *Sport* magazine that June, the remark that had so bothered Munson, had been the most obvious example. But it was more than that. It was the time he was quoted referring to himself as "the magnitude of me," his seemingly endless desire for publicity, his public posture that he was the epicenter of the Yankees. Or his propensity to say one thing to writers and another to his teammates, then wonder why his teammates didn't like that.

Maybe Piniella had expressed it best, once summing up the differences between Jackson and Catfish Hunter, the Yankees' other high-profile acquisition, who had joined the Yankees in 1974 when a loophole had gotten him out of his contract with the A's, back when Hunter had been the hottest pitcher in the game. That had been Steinbrenner's symbolic shot across the bow to the rest of the baseball world that he would do what it took to win, that it wasn't just self-serving quotes on the back pages of the tabloids.

"Catfish could take the kidding and Reggie couldn't," Piniella said. "Everybody laughed with Catfish. Everyone laughed at Reggie. Catfish came in and said I'm going to help the club. Reggie came in and said I'm going to carry the club. Catfish knew how to get along with people. Reggie didn't want to bother."

Eventually, Piniella would come to understand that beneath all the bravado Jackson was terribly insecure and wanted to be liked, just didn't know how to go about it.

Now his home run had given the Yankees a 5–2 lead, Mr. October once again.

It also had meant the end for Stanley as the Red Sox pitcher. Zimmer replaced him with the left-handed Andy Hassler, a journeyman reliever who had been acquired in July from Kansas City to help out in the bullpen. He did his job. He got Nettles, Chambliss, and White and the Sox were out of the inning.

But they were running out of time.

Remy was the first batter in the bottom of the eighth, and maybe no one could have made up his story. For he was the little kid whose childhood had been measured in trips to Fenway Park, all those little kids who flock to Fenway every year with their gloves and their big dreams, all those little kids who grow up thinking that one day they are going to play in Fenway Park for the Red Sox, all those dreams that eventually get sacrificed on the altar of childhood. He had grown up in Somerset, Massachusetts, a small town tucked in the southeastern corner of the state, near the Rhode Island border, and every year he would go to a handful of games in Fenway Park with his father and grandfather. He had even been there on that last weekend of the regular season in '67 when the Sox had beaten the Twins. But he never had been one of those teenage wunderkinds, one of those kids who seemed in some express lane to the big leagues.

Not even close.

He was small and wiry, and had grown up in an area where high school baseball teams probably play about sixteen or so games a year, and even some of them get called off because of bad weather. He hadn't even started as a sophomore in high school, but by his senior year he had been an All-Scholastic player in Massachusetts. But that hadn't been enough to change his life. He wanted to go play baseball at nearby Providence College, but he didn't get in. So he went to St. Leo's, a small school in Florida. But he was soon homesick and came back to Somerset two weeks later, enrolling at another small school, Roger Williams in Rhode Island. He was chosen in one of the later rounds of the winter draft by the California Angels, reporting to spring training in the spring of 1971.

"It was all so new," he said. "Flying across the country for the first time. Being one of hundreds of players."

He soon figured that he wasn't going to make it, that he

was too far behind those other kids who had grown up in warm-weather areas and played in many more games. He probably wouldn't have, if not for a man named Kenny Meyers, who had both signed him and was the Angels' minor-league hitting instructor. Meyers liked Remy because Remy could run, and he figured the Angels could teach him the rest. So Remy was sent to a lowly minor-league team in Idaho Falls, and he wasn't there long before he was ready to come home.

"My father convinced me to stay," he said.

The team in Idaho was comprised of players the organization had no real faith in, but Remy played well and began his ascent through the Angels' farm system. By the time he got to Double A his manager told him he could be a major leaguer, and in many ways that made all the difference, because he started to believe, too. No longer was he just an undersized kid from New England who didn't really think he could ever actually make it. In spring training in 1975 he caught the eye of the Angels manager Dick Williams, the man who had been the Red Sox manager during that magical '67 season that had so captivated Remy as a kid, and he beat out the veteran Denny Doyle for the second-base job.

But even though he had established himself with the Angels before being traded to the Red Sox for the pitcher Don Aase after the '77 season, coming back to his hometown team brought its own kind of pressure. To him, every mistake was magnified. And joining the Red Sox was like joining an All-Star team, complete with Yaz, his onetime childhood idol. So when the Sox got off to their big lead it wasn't like he was shocked or anything, for he knew how talented the team was. Yet, when the Yankees had started playing better he hadn't been surprised either. He knew how talented they were, that it was just a matter of them getting healthy.

And he liked playing for Zimmer, even though the players knew Zimmer didn't like pitchers. But if you were an everyday player he was easy to play for, the same lineup every day, just go out and play, no need to always be looking over your shoulder. Zimmer was a manager shaped by his times, and the times back then taught that you played your best players until they simply could not play anymore, the reason why he had played Fisk an amazing 154 of the 162 games, and had kept playing Hobson long after it was apparent he could no longer throw.

But Remy had been "scared to death" this morning. He had never played in anything remotely close to a game of this importance, this magnitude. He and his wife lived in a condominium complex in suburban Lexington called Drummer Boy Green, the same place Fisk and Lynn lived, and all three had driven in together, all with their suitcases, for if they won they were flying out to Kansas City after the game.

He doubled down the right-field line, and the Red Sox had another life.

Now Rice was at the plate, the best hitter in the American League, on his way to the MVP award for the season that would turn out to be the best in his fifteen-year career. He could be fooled on a pitch and still do great damage, for everyone who either played with or against him always commented on his amazing strength, the fact that when he hit the ball it was like it seemed to have been shot out of a cannon. Some players had weight-room strength. Rice had innate strength. He got a good swing on a Gossage pitch, but it was a little late and the ball went out to right field, once again toward Piniella, who had to battle the late afternoon sun. Piniella, who had been shading Rice to pull, once again had to run to make the catch. But it certainly was an easier play than he had made on Lynn in the sixth inning and Rice was out, and Yastrzemski was up with Remy still on second. Yaz singled up the middle for a base hit, scoring Remy. Once again, Yastrzemski had come through, as he'd done so many times in his career.

It was now 5–3, with Fisk at the plate, another one of the Sox icons, known for his resolve and his iron will, just like Yastrzemski.

Gossage was feeling the pressure. It was the biggest game of his life, and later he would say that he was trying to throw the ball too hard, and that was robbing him of his rhythm. He had been nervous the night before. He was nervous now. He also was very aware that Fisk had both the right-handed power to hit one into the screen and the sense of the dramatic, too, his classic World Series home run three years before forever on his résumé. Fisk was not a great hitter as much as a dangerous one. The count went to three and two, and remained that after two foul balls past third base. On the next pitch Fisk lined a single to center, Yastrzemski stopping at second.

That brought Lynn to the plate, the same Lynn who had been robbed by Piniella earlier in the game. This time, he hit Gossage's second pitch over Dent's head at shortstop into left field, scoring Yaz.

It was now 5–4.

The Sox down only a single run.

Runners on first and second.

Only one out.

Gossage struggling.

Hobson up.

Fenway in more pandemonium.

Were the Red Sox going to come back and take control of this game? Were all the years of frustration and broken dreams about to end, against the dreaded Yankees, no less? Were the nearly thirty-three thousand crammed into Fenway Park watching sweet redemption, payback for all the years that the Yankees had always seemed to lord it over them?

With the great Guidry already out of the game, and Gossage nowhere near as lights-out dominant as he had been, Sox fans had every right to hope. The Sox had come back from a 5–2 deficit, had come back from the dead the way they had come back in September, and why couldn't they do it one more time?

But Hobson, a little late on a fastball like Rice had been, flew out to right field, another fly ball that Piniella struggled with before catching it for the second out, and bringing Scott to the plate.

He already had two hits in the game, and Scott in the batter's box still had a definite presence, even in this year that foreshadowed the end of his career, the year in which the erosion of his skills seemed all but outlined in neon, his batting average a lowly .230. He could have eradicated all that with one more big hit, one more time when the Fenway crowd chanted "Boomer," the love swirling all around him, one more page from the old days. One more big hit that would have put the Sox ahead, changed the game around. But it was not to be. Gossage threw fastballs and Scott simply could not handle them, striking out swinging.

———

The Red Sox had been poised at the end of the '75 World Series to do great things. Virtually everyone in baseball thought so. They had talent throughout the lineup, two great young hitters in Lynn and Rice, the iconic Yastrzemski, as good a catcher as there was in the game in Fisk, and talented young players like Evans in right field, Burleson at short, and the sweet-swinging Cecil Cooper at first. They had just played in one of the all-time great World Series, and had taken the Cincinnati Reds, the great "Big Red Machine," to a seventh game. They believed it was their time to finally win, that they simply had too much talent not to.

There was also some urgency, too.

Yawkey was very sick, had been for a while, was increasingly frail and gaunt, even if few people knew just how bad he was. He was still all but wrapped in secrecy, surrounded by his handful of palace guards that kept the world out, still so private that he could walk through Fenway on game day and few fans would even know who he was. Hadn't that been the great story when Bernie Carbo had joined the Sox and was sitting in the clubhouse on one of his first days with the club and had seen an old man and, mistaking him for one of the clubhouse attendants, had given him twenty dollars and asked him to go get him a couple of cheeseburgers and some fries? How was Carbo supposed to know that the old man in the nondescript clothes in the clubhouse had been Tom Yawkey?

During the '75 Series there had been sentiment to finally win for Tom Yawkey, for he had owned the team for forty-two years, and didn't he deserve a world title, one chance to finish at the top of the heap, his reward for all the years, and all the money spent, and all the love he had given this team? There were generations of fans in New England who had never known any other owner of the Red Sox. He was the one constant as the names changed from Jimmie Foxx to Ted Williams, and from Yaz to Jim Rice, the one constant as everything had changed, and he had become the sentimental favorite to finally win a World Series.

It hadn't happened, of course, and on July 9, 1976, Yawkey died of leukemia in New England Baptist Hospital. On the night he died the flag in center field was lowered to half-mast, and when the Sox took the field for a game, John Kiley, the longtime organist, did not play the customary "Take Me Out to the Ball Game." He played nothing. An era had ended, and there was an outpouring of both tributes and affection. The *Boston Herald* called Yawkey "baseball's best friend," and his philanthropy and his legendary largesse with the players through the years was recognized. It would be later that his legacy would become more complicated, both the questions of racism and the criticism that his paternalistic style had inhibited the Red Sox from becoming mentioned in ways they hadn't been when he had died.

A few days later the new Basic Agreement between the players and owners went into effect, and the Sox re-signed Fisk, Lynn, and Burleson. But something irreparable had changed, as if the game had crossed some Maginot Line. Yawkey had felt betrayed by the new economic climate in the game, the specter of players easily becoming free agents, and the Sox had gone into the off-season after the World Series with the contract status of Fisk, Lynn, and Burleson unsettled, and the potential bitterness that came with that, something that rarely happened in the Yawkey era.

The '76 season had been the start of free agency, the result of Curt Flood's challenge to baseball's reserve clause, the one that said players essentially were owned by their teams until they were traded, released, or sold. Flood had refused to report to the Philadelphia Phillies after being traded by the St. Louis Cardinals in 1969, and the case had dragged on for years before it finally made its way to the Supreme Court, which essentially said it wasn't going to rule against the way Major League Baseball always had done things, and sent the case back to the lower courts.

Catfish Hunter had become a free agent on a technicality in 1974 after the flamboyant Oakland A's owner Charlie Finley had been late in paying his insurance coverage. But the courts declared the pitchers Andy Messersmith and Dave McNally free agents, and allowed them to pursue offers from other teams. More important, the new reserve clause called for players whose contracts were up to play out an option year, declare themselves free agents, and thus be up for bid. Baseball had changed, regardless of all the howling that emanated from front offices throughout the game, the party line being that free agency would ruin baseball.

In many ways 1976 was the season that never was for the Red Sox, whether that was because of the hangover from the Word Series, Yawkey's death, the loss of Lee after the brawl in Yankee Stadium, the general collapse of pitching, or all of the above. They were never really in the race, eventually finishing third, fifteen and a half games behind the Yankees. Then with five games left in the season manager Darrell Johnson, who Lee had said the year before "keeps falling out of trees and landing on his feet," was fired. The new manager was Zimmer, who had been Johnson's third-base coach.

But it was in the postseason that things got interesting, the establishing of baseball's new world order. The Yankees signed the star free-agent pitcher Don Gullet, and less than two weeks later signed Jackson. They might as well have put up a banner across Times Square.

Or as Steinbrenner would later say, "I didn't invent the system, but I used it."

So the Red Sox, now owned by the Yawkey Trust, which was managed by Yawkey's widow, Jean, and had two other partners in former backup catcher Haywood Sullivan and former Celtics trainer Buddy LeRoux, had a choice: either join the arms race or get left behind. That off-season, they dove into the free-agent pool, signing the reliever Bill Campbell for five years for just over a million dollars, big money for the time. They also traded Cecil Cooper to Milwaukee, bringing back Scott and Carbo.

The Red Sox had been very good in '77. Rice hit thirty-nine home runs. Scott hit thirty-three. Hobson hit thirty. Yastrzemski had twenty-eight. Fisk had twenty-six. Lynn, Evans, and Carbo all had at least fourteen. It was a prodigious power display, and there were times when the Sox seemed like the best team on the planet, balls flying over fences and into the grandstands as if it were some sort of audition for the old fifties television show *Home Run Derby*.

This was a Red Sox team of legend, the short wall a siren song, the kind of team that had become so emblematic of the Red Sox through the years, big bats but not enough pitching, a team constructed for the three-run home run. The pitching staff was inconsistent at best, made worse by Zimmer's constant tinkering. One of the theories was Zimmer didn't like pitchers because he once had been beaned by one. Whatever the reason, his tenure as the Red Sox manager was marked by his inability to get along with many of them. He believed that Lee had never been the same pitcher since having been thrown to the ground by Nettles in the Yankee Stadium brawl the year before. He believed that Lee, Rick Wise, and Ferguson Jenkins were mean-spirited. And he had come to dislike Lee intensely, a personal feud that was always in the clubhouse like a bad odor.

The Sox had been in first place in late August, but in mid -September they got swept by a Yankee team that would go on to win one hundred games, and finished two and a half games back, tied with Baltimore.

But it had been a difficult year, too, and part of that was the times.

It no longer was 1967, when first-year manager Dick Williams had gone to spring training and told his team that they had to wear sports coats or suits on the road, no sweaters, and no one objected. He also had told them that they couldn't wear dungarees, Levi's, or chino pants on the road, and that he expected them not to "dress sloppy" when the club was at home either, adding, "We'll leave the Bermuda shorts for the Beach Boys." Not only was it eleven years later and a different culture, with different fashions and different attitudes, but Zimmer was also dealing with the drug culture, specifically "the Buffalo Heads." There had been the time during a late-season game with Baltimore when he couldn't find Ferguson Jenkins, who was supposed to be in the bullpen but supposedly was sleeping off a hangover in a TV truck. Lee would later write in his book that he and several others, on a trip to New York, had gone to Xenon, one of the hot discos, describing women who were dressed as coneheads, "their bodies had been painted silver and that's all they wore."

Suffice it to say that Zimmer hadn't been part of the entourage.

Zimmer believed the Buffalo Heads were poison, were constantly undermining him, even if many in the media saw them as essentially harmless. Then again, that seemed split down generational lines, too, the older writers siding with Zimmer, the younger ones often viewing him as some old baseball lifer who had lost touch with the young players. Being a manager was becoming increasingly more difficult, no longer simply a matter of when you took the pitcher out.

And Zimmer was out on the end of the plank, too.

Not only was he now booed every time he came out of the dugout, seen as the reason for the squandering of the fourteen-game lead. Not only was he crucified on the nightly talk shows, his every decision examined as if it were some lab specimen under a microscope. It was so bad on the Sunday night *Sports Huddle*, hosted by Eddie Andelman, that callers were forbidden to refer to Zimmer by name, had to call him Chiang Kai-shek instead.

Zimmer had elected to get rid of Carbo in July, and the perception was that it was because he was Lee's buddy and another Buffalo Head, even though Carbo had been one of the heroes of the '75 World Series with his huge pinch-hit home run in game six that ultimately had given Fisk the chance for his heroics. Upon hearing the news Lee cleaned out his locker and angrily declared to the media that getting rid of Carbo had just cost the Red Sox the pennant. He then stayed away for twenty-four hours, and when he came back any relationship with Zimmer he had had, however strained, was over. After a few unimpressive starts Zimmer took him out of the rotation. That decision already had hurt Zimmer in the four-game massacre by the Yankees in September, when Zimmer had spurned Lee in favor of Bobby Sprowl, a call-up from Triple A Pawtucket, even though Lee's lifetime record against the Yankees was very good. Sprowl got chased early, and as Zimmer's detractors were quick to point out, if the Sox had won that game they already would have won the pennant, and they would be on their way to Kansas City, not going into the ninth inning down 5–4.

It's a variation of the same argument Torrez would make years later—namely, that if Zimmer had kept Lee in the rotation and Lee had won just half of his starts there never would have been a playoff game against the Yankees. The Sox would have easily won the division.

So winning this was a huge perception game for Zimmer, a chance to silence all the critics and all the boo birds, a chance to be the architect of a great win, a game that would have solidified him as a manager. Just as it was a huge perception game for this Red Sox team. And not just because it was against the Yankees, and all the history and passion that came with that, or that it would put them in the postseason for the first time in three years. It also was the validation on the promise of '75, the sense that this particular group of players finally had found what was always supposed to have been theirs.

CHAPTER ELEVEN

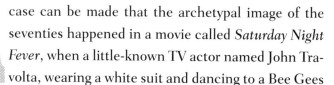 case can be made that the archetypal image of the seventies happened in a movie called *Saturday Night Fever*, when a little-known TV actor named John Travolta, wearing a white suit and dancing to a Bee Gees disco song, threw his right hand high over his head. It was all there, the glitter, the hedonism, the blatant sexuality, the pounding, unrelenting beat; all there in the new cultural headquarters, the discotheque.

Travolta played a guy named Tony Manero, who worked at a nowhere job in a paint store, still lived at home, and waited for the weekends, when he went to the clubs and immersed himself in some fantasy life, light-years away from the reality of the paint store. This was all happening to a Bee Gees sound track that was all over the radio, seemingly every kid in America singing "Stayin' Alive" in the shower, with lyrics that said "I've been kicked around since I was born." In a culture that was beginning to seem tired, disco hit the country like a cultural pandemic.

From January to May of '78 the Bee Gees dominated the singles and album charts, and at one point the *Saturday Night Fever* album was selling a million copies a week. In April, the Blues Brothers made their first appearance on *Saturday Night Live*, and two months after that the punk group the Dead Kennedys formed.

The counterculture of the sixties, with its peace signs and search for consciousness, its protest marches and message songs?

Gone, baby, gone.

This was about dancin' and stylin', this was about loud music and getting high and doing just about everything you could to forget about that nowhere job at the paint store.

"The whole scene was a response to the sixties," Michael Gomes says in *The Bronx Is Burning*. "Instead of changing the world we wanted to create our own little world."

Tom Wolfe, the New York magazine writer who found his fame with a style as flamboyant as the times he was writing about, labeled the seventies the "Me Decade." That was right on target. It wasn't just coincidence that one of the most popular books of the decade was *Jonathan Livingston Seagull*, the story about a lonely seagull searching for meaning, the one who refuses to fly with the pack, but breaks out on his own, flying by himself. It had been written by Richard Bach, a book as thin as a New York model, but it captured the essence of the times in ways that few other things did. This wasn't about communal living, about sharing. This was the opposite of that. This was about flying solo.

It also wasn't just coincidence that many of the hit movies, from *Chinatown* to *Taxi Driver* to *The Godfather* and *The God-*

father Part II, seemed to have corruption at their core, the sense that both society and institutions were rotting from the inside, that the only thing left was the integrity of the individual and his journey through the minefield of a system that no longer worked. Either that, or the tension that came from two eras in collision, the one that had defined the America that used to be and the one it was becoming.

The television show that seemed to capture this best was *All in the Family*, which debuted on CBS in January 1971 and soon became one of the most important and influential shows in the history of American television. It was based on a sixties British television show called *Till Death Do Us Part*, and featured a blue-collar bigot named Archie Bunker, who lived in a brick row house in Astoria, Queens, with his "dingbat" wife, Edith, his daughter, Gloria, and her hippie husband, Michael, a long-haired college student who symbolized the changing America that Archie had come to loathe. Their verbal battles were a microcosm of the country's cultural battles.

At its heart, the show was a clash of the two Americas, the traditional one that had been under attack by the counterculture in the sixties and the new one that was being formed by young people in the seventies. To Archie, played by Carroll O'Connor, the social gains of "the spades," "the spics," and "the hebes" were coming not only at his expense but at the expense of the white working class, and each time he would go into one of his rants, it was like listening to the last gasp of someone who knew the foundation upon which he had built his life was moving beneath him.

The show was not only groundbreaking for Archie's racial and ethnic epithets, but also for taking the issues that were swirling through the country and putting them on national television. It remained a hit until 1979, and then continued for four more years as *Archie Bunker's Place*, and Archie Bunker became a sort of American archetype, the blue-collar redneck trying to cling to the world he used to know, even as it was changing in his own house. No television show captured the era better, not only for the collision of eras it portrayed but as a snapshot of what was happening in so many families across the country.

Most of all, though, the seventies were about the exploration of self, a turning inward after all the social consciousness of the sixties, all its sense of sharing and talk of building a better world.

The sixties had been about trying to build a better world.

The seventies were about building a better me.

They also were about the rules changing.

Hair length on men no longer was an issue, as the archetype of the American man changed from the macho movie image of John Wayne to the softer one of Alan Alda. What had started in the counterculture of the sixties, seen by the established culture then almost as something illicit, a symbol of rebellion, had now become mainstream. As was the women's movement itself. No longer was it perceived as just some radical feminist movement on the so-called lunatic fringe. Now it was the housewife down the street talking about women's liberation, no longer wanting to be June Cleaver and the other idealized housewives from some fifties sitcom. Or else it was women looking for the same sexual freedom men had always sought, maybe best exemplified in one of the huge bestsellers of the decade, *Fear of Flying* by Erica Jong, whose heroine yearns for the "zipless fuck," her expression for anonymous sex. The decade also saw the inauguration of Title IX, the federal legislation that enabled women to have the same educational and athletic opportunities as men did, while the rise of affirmative action changed the look of college campuses. Rock music, once seen as merely the province of the young, now was an accepted part of the larger culture, routinely used in national television commercials to sell all kinds of products. And at the most obvious level fashions became more and more outrageous, the traditional blue suit stuffed away in some old footlocker, as outdated as Richard Nixon.

Can you say leisure suit?

Maybe nothing spoke of the seventies more than the leisure suit, with its wide lapels, its garish pretense, its attempt to combine a casual lifestyle with what purported to be fashion. If nothing else, though, it spoke of something different, a new era.

Everywhere you looked it was as if the old, familiar standards of civility were under attack, as Americans seemed to be reinventing themselves. The divorce rate skyrocketed. Young men and women routinely lived together. And a new movement seemed to spring up every month, whether EST, or transcendental meditation, or biofeedback, or anything that spoke of something different, something other than the white-bread, suburban, Ozzie and Harriet world of the fifties that the counterculture of the sixties had rebelled against. Now the signs of that rebellion had been mainstreamed, including drugs like marijuana and cocaine, which no longer were just the province of the young, or the rebellious, or people trying to distance themselves from establishment America. They, too, were now part of the culture in ways they never had been before.

It was the decade that gave us Evel Knievel, the daredevil

motorcycle jumper, with his sequins and his iconoclastic style; the Sonny and Cher television show, which was recycled hippies for middle America; the rise of the Sunbelt, and the sense that the old industrial cities of the Northeast and Midwest were all about the past tense. It gave us such musicians as David Bowie and such groups as the Village People, with their eyeliner and their costumes, and the sense that it was all a show, the more decadent and the more outrageous the better, another spit in the eye of established values. Yet it also was the decade that saw the beginning of the music industry being controlled by large corporations, which began to see the financial potential of what, only a few years earlier, had been considered the counterculture.

The seventies also saw the rise of ethnic culture, with the enormous popularity of the *Godfather* movies and the *Roots* miniseries, the most watched television series in history. And maybe nowhere was this more on display than on television. Shows like *The Jeffersons* and *Chico and the Man* reflected this. So did the movies, where actors such as Al Pacino, Robert De Niro, and Dustin Hoffman, men who a generation earlier more likely would have been known as character actors, were redefining what major stars both looked like and sounded like.

The times they had a-changed.

No longer was the melting pot the ideal, the notion that all the different ethnic groups went into the stew and what emerged was something called an American. That always had been the American story, the sense that people from all over the world came here and became assimilated, learning English, learning this country's history and beliefs, and then passing them down to their children, who were Americans in the true sense of the word, the old world their parents had left behind little more than faded family pictures in some old personal album. Now every ethnic group seemed to come with a hyphen, their heritage celebrated, making them different from everyone else. America had become more factionalized in ways it hadn't seemed to be before, an amalgamation of individual parts, clamoring for larger pieces of the national pie. Women. Blacks. Gays. They all wanted more. More rights. More acceptance. More affirmation. More. As if everyone had a cause, and they weren't afraid to trumpet it. The rise of identity politics.

The *Newsweek* columnist Meg Greenfield called the American cultural landscape "an ethnic ballet, an affirmative-action program gone mad."

And it all seemed to be dancing to a disco beat, this heavily stylized music that had sprung up from the underground clubs in New York City, a fusion of black, Latin, and gay culture. It also was urban culture, and that in itself made it different than the youth culture of the sixties, whose center tended to be college campuses.

One of the most popular discos in Boston was located on the street that ran behind Fenway's famed left-field wall. The building, which had been there since the beginning of the century, had had many uses, but in 1969 it became a psychedelic club called the Ark. Later, it morphed into a music club called the Boston Tea Party, managed by Don Law, whose father had once produced music for Southern black musicians and would go on to become one of the biggest concert promoters in the country. Many of rock's biggest acts played the Boston Tea Party, among them the Grateful Dead, Led Zeppelin, The Who, Bob Dylan. By the middle of the decade the location had changed identities again, this time as a disco, with two of its owners being Steve

Rubell and Ian Schrager. In 1977, the two of them would take this model and bring it to Manhattan, where it would become Studio 54, the disco club that arguably came to best define both the glitter and decadence of the disco era, complete with a prop outside of the Man on the Moon shoveling a coke spoon under his nose, and women hanging upside down on trapezes inside, just in case anyone had missed the theme.

The Boston club was now called 15 Lansdowne. It had several levels and strobe lights and mirrored balls over the dance floor and black and silver décor everywhere. It was dark and shadowy, and everywhere there was the promise of sex, as if Caligula had designed it all in between Roman orgies. It had frenetic dance music that never stopped, so the entire atmosphere was an explosion of the senses, its own little universe in the shadow of Fenway Park, a sneak preview of some hedonistic apocalypse.

"There were drugs all over the place, joints and lines of coke everywhere," said Carlo Brogna, who worked there one summer while going to Harvard, when the uniform for male waiters was tight satiny basketball shorts and a tank top. "Sometimes you would get joints for tips, so by the end of the night I'd be going home with a hundred bucks and three joints."

The club was only about a pop-up away from Kenmore Square, just down the street from Boston University, and late at night the area could have passed for an Edward Hopper painting, with its all-night eateries and bars. One of the most popular was Lucifer's, a big singles club, and across the street was the Rathskeller, which everyone called "the Rat," and often hired guys from South Boston to be bouncers. It was deep in the basement of a dingy building, one of those no-pretense places that made a dive look good, but it was one of the most popular music clubs in Boston. The Rat was the antithesis of 15 Lansdowne, so in a sense the two clubs that were so close to each other were the yin and yang of the Boston club scene, and revealed the richness of it. Disco was in 15 Lansdowne, the burgeoning punk movement was at the Rat, with everyone from the Talking Heads to the Ramones, the punk group from New York, playing there, and in the middle was Lucifer's, a monument to the new sexual freedom.

And as disco, and the culture that surrounded it, became more and more mainstream, punk became the antidote. Punk was an attempt to get back to the roots, strip away all the glitter and all the packaging and get back to the heart of rock music, back when it was supposed to mean something, stand for something, back before disco had robbed it of its soul. That was the thinking, anyway. If disco was intended to obliterate reality, punk embraced all the grungy aspects of it, appealing to college kids and disaffected youth. And in Boston in the seventies, in the midst of a city with a huge youth culture, it was all there, disco, punk, rock, and just about anything else you were looking for.

Kenmore Square was not the only entertainment area in the city, of course.

There was the "Combat Zone" downtown on Washington Street, the city's monument to sleaze, with clubs like the Teddy Bare Lounge and the Intermission Lounge, the Pilgrim Theatre and the Two O'Clock Lounge. It had sprung up in the early sixties, after Scollay Square had been demolished to build Government Center and other urban renewal projects, and featured strippers, go-go dancers, peep shows, X-rated movie theaters, nude dancers, and all other features of the so-called adult entertainment business. In the mid-seventies it had been zoned for adult entertainment venues by Mayor White, and it developed its own unique culture, complete with strippers who became cult figures, with names like Princess Cheyenne and Misty Tropique. In 1974 it had been the scene of a political scandal when Wilbur Mills, chairman of the House Ways and Means Committee, appeared onstage with the stripper Fanne Foxe, who went by the stage name "the Argentine Firecracker."

The Combat Zone also had a slew of prostitutes, and the kind of gritty surroundings where many a drunken college kid no doubt went home without his wallet, but it had turned really ugly one night in 1976 when a Harvard football player was stabbed to death. The ensuing publicity focused on the crime in the area, bad publicity. Eventually, the surrounding property would become too valuable, and the pressure from adjoining Chinatown to clean up the area would begin its demise, but in the seventies the Combat Zone was as much a part of downtown as the theater district.

Boston had a huge youth culture, not only because of its innumerable colleges but also due to the number of graduates who stayed in the area and gave the city a certain hip image, making it the East Coast answer to San Francisco. It was what Fred Lynn had first liked about it, back there in August of '74, when he had been called up from Triple A Pawtucket and used to walk around Boston, getting to know his new city, all the kids that essentially were in his age group. It also was one of the key reasons why Lee was so popular, for not only was he a Red Sox player, he was one of them, with his antiestablishment rhetoric and counterculture leanings, their link to the Red Sox.

Largely because of the youth culture, Boston also had given

rise to two quality alternative papers: the *Boston Phoenix*, which had evolved out of an entertainment paper called *Boston After Dark*, and the *Real Paper*, which had evolved out of the sale of the *Cambridge Phoenix* to Stephen Mindich, who owned the paper that would become the *Boston Phoenix*. Both papers, which had started out as so-called underground papers in the sixties, became known for their strong investigative pieces and their hip coverage of the area's vibrant arts scene.

They were extremely popular with both young people and the innumerable antiestablishment types spread throughout the Boston-Cambridge area, many of whom had come of age in the sixties and still carried that aesthetic with them, as if it were a moveable feast. From their appearance to their lifestyle, and from their beliefs to their politics, they were obvious symbols of a new generation, and by their numbers alone they were a force. Both the *Phoenix* and the *Real Paper* were their anthems in ways that the *Globe* and the *Herald* could never be, except for their daily coverage of sports.

They also served as springboards for some major talents, giving young writers a chance to be read, room to grow, all in an atmosphere without a whole lot of structure, the perfect incubator for young writers to begin learning their craft. Mike Lupica, who would become one of the country's top sportswriters at the *New York Daily News*, and the author of many successful sports books, began at the *Phoenix* when he was still a student at Boston College. As did George Kimball, who would go on to become a longtime sportswriter at the *Boston Herald*, and Charles Pierce, who would go on to write for both the *Herald* and the *Globe* and also do books. As did Janet Maslin, who would go on to be a film critic for the *New York Times*, and Sidney Blumenthal, who became an adviser to President Clinton. Their rise to mainstream papers and magazines mirrored the changing of the country, as what once had been considered counterculture, underground if you will, became as mainstream as the morning newspaper.

The *Real Paper*'s alumni list includes the *Time* columnist and TV commentator Joe Klein, the *Newsweek* film critic David Anson, and Jon Landau, who was on the ground floor of American musical history.

It was 1974 and Landau had gone to a Harvard Square club to see a young singer, and this is what he wrote afterward:

"Tonight there is someone I can write of the way I used to write, without reservations of any kind. Last Thursday, at the Harvard Square Theatre, I saw my rock 'n' roll past flash before my eyes. And I saw something else: I saw rock and roll's future and its name is Bruce Springsteen. And on a night when I needed to feel young, he made me feel like I was hearing music for the first time.

"When his two-hour set ended I could only think, can anyone really be this good; can anyone say this much to me, can rock 'n' roll still speak with this kind of power and glory? And then I felt the sores on my thighs where I had been pounding my hands in time for the entire concert and I knew that the answer was yes.

"Springsteen does it all. He is a rock 'n' roll punk, a Latin street punk, a ballet dancer, an actor, a joker, bar band leader, hot-shit rhythm guitar leader, extraordinary singer, and a truly great rock 'n' roll composer. He leads a band like he's been doing it forever. I racked my brains but simply can't think of a white artist who does so many things so superbly."

The review went on the wires and jump-started Springsteen's

career, and Landau soon quit the writing business to become Springsteen's manager.

A year later Springsteen was on the cover of both *Time* and *Newsweek*, the kind of fame that must have seemed as far away as the moon that night in '73 when he had opened for Chicago in the Boston Garden, the biggest arena he had ever played in. It was the kind of fame that had become an albatross, for as he told the *Boston Globe*, "It really threw me off. I had no understanding at all of the media, of how or what to do or what effect it would have on me."

But in late September of '78, a week before the Sox-Yankee playoff game, he played to a sold-out crowd in the Boston Garden, the old arena on Causeway Street in the North End that was home to both the Celtics and the Bruins. It had been there since 1928, a cavernous old building across the street from elevated railroad tracks, in a neighborhood right out of film noir, with narrow congested streets, cafeterias, small shot-and-beer bars, barbershops and Sullivan's Tap, which had a bar as long as a city block, a part of Boston where, as Leigh Montville once wrote in *Sports Illustrated*, "Jimmy Cagney could have very easily tipped his hat to George Raft."

The Garden had hosted everything from the circus to midget auto races to indoor softball to the Ice Capades. Once, Notre Dame had even played a football game there. But it was not the ideal venue for a concert. The acoustics were bad. The building was too big. So Springsteen had been a little wary.

"I was really worried today when I came in here," he told Ernie Santosuosso of the *Boston Globe*. "I've never heard a good thing about the place."

He shouldn't have been.

The screaming crowd called him back for five encores, and the *Globe* account of the evening said how Boston has been a milestone in his career, dating back to Joe's Place and Oliver's in the early seventies. The article led the Sunday *Globe*'s "Living" section, a reaffirmation that Springsteen was no longer just a guy with a band, however popular, nor just a guy kids liked, but a cultural phenomenon, someone who had been discovered, if you will, in the pages of the *Real Paper* four years earlier.

One of the biggest sports names in Boston that year was Bill Rodgers, the man who had come to symbolize the country's fascination with running. A decade earlier the few people seen jogging on the streets were all but objects of ridicule. Not now. Joggers were everywhere, and Rodgers was one of its heroes. Rodgers had won the world-famous Boston Marathon in 1975, and two years later he and his brother Charlie opened the Bill Rodgers Running Center in Cleveland Circle. He had won the Boston Marathon again in the spring of '78, and after that the two brothers opened up another running store in Faneuil Hall, the old marketplace that had become a symbol of the New Boston, turned into boutiques and specialty shops.

On Saturday night, less than forty-eight hours before the game, Billy Joel had played to a sold-out Boston Garden, saying, "Good evening. Welcome to the Boston bus terminal," as the crowd went bonkers. As they did every time the twenty-nine-year-old seemingly took a break, or made a move onstage.

"This was adulation befitting a superstar," Steve Morse wrote in the next day's *Globe*, "and it made you forget that only last winter he was playing the Orpheum. Four hit singles later, here he was in the Garden, still a little pepperpot but now in the biggest arena in town."

At the movies that weekend you could get ready to see Gregory Peck and James Mason in *The Boys from Brazil*, the film adaptation of the bestseller by Ira Levin, which was going to open in three days at the Pi Alley theater downtown on Washington Street. Or Jack Nicholson in *Goin' South*, a movie he also directed, scheduled to open the following weekend at the Charles Cinema, or Terrence Malick's *Days of Heaven*, also set to open at the Charles Cinema. Or else Richard Dreyfuss as a cynical private eye in *The Big Fix*.

Or you could see foreign films at the Orson Welles in Cambridge, or smaller independent films in several places in Greater Boston.

Boston also had a lively music scene. From the days of the old Club 47 in Cambridge, where local girl Joan Baez got her start, there was the sense that the Boston area was the San Francisco of the East Coast, hip and young and irreverent, the place where new bands could get both get discovered and attract a following.

Another new potential star on the Boston horizon in '78 was Larry Bird, although no one really knew it then. He had been drafted by the Celtics, the sixth pick in the draft, though he elected to return to Indiana State for his senior year. The following March he would lead Indiana State to the Final Four, where he eventually would lose to Magic Johnson and Michigan State in the championship game, and become the most celebrated college player in the country, foreshadowing what he would later become as a professional player.

In a few years he would arguably be as good a basketball player as there was on the planet, on his way to becoming one of the most revered and beloved athletes in Boston history. He also would become the centerpiece of a great Celtics team that would by the very nature of their roster become a symbol of racist Boston, unofficially known as "white America's" team in their epic battles with the Lakers in the eighties. No matter that the Celtics had been the first team to start five blacks in the NBA, or had been the first team in the NBA to have a black coach. That was the perception, and the fact that three of their stars were white—Bird, Kevin McHale, and Danny Ainge—along with some white reserves, only reinforced it. As if it had all been by design, the right kind of team for Boston.

That was the story line throughout the eighties, however simplistic it might have been, the fundamental Celtics versus the showtime Lakers, the work ethic of Bird versus the flash of Magic Johnson, the grittiness of the Boston Garden versus the glitter of the Fabulous Forum in Los Angeles. That had been the theme, one that was constantly pounded in the national media, one that heavily influenced the national image of Boston as a racist city, an image burned into the national consciousness by all those nightly news reports and national magazine stories, the legacy of busing in Boston.

All that would come later, of course.

But in the fall of 1978 the story was beginning, the Celtics already owning the rights to Larry Bird.

The furor over busing seemed to be quieting down in the summer of '78.

It had been going on for over four years now with endless demonstrations and endless violence and the sense that the very fabric of the city had been so severely damaged. It had hurt the career of Mayor White, who had had national ambitions, a man who in 1972 had been an attractive candidate, the liberal mayor of one of the biggest cities in the country, a man who had come into office in 1967 as a conciliator, someone who could bridge the world of the downtown establishment with the world of the neighborhoods. That had been his original appeal.

He had been accessible in the neighborhoods in ways that John Collins, his predecessor, had not been, and in the early days of his tenure he was a frequent visitor to Roxbury and the black sections of Dorchester and Mattapan. He had been influenced by both the style of the Kennedys and their commitment to civil rights, and in those early years it was a common sight to see him in one of the black neighborhoods, coat off, tie loosened, the portrait of a mayor as man of the people. He established little City Halls in the neighborhoods, and was sensitive to the long-held perception that the mayor was little more than a rubber stamp for the downtown financiers, one that become widespread in the sixties as the downtown urban renewal projects and the expansion of Logan Airport into East Boston had decimated some old established neighborhoods.

He had come very close to being George McGovern's choice for vice presidential running mate in 1972, and seemed to be a man with an unlimited future, until the political realities of busing had ended all that. So as the seventies moved on. No doubt sensing that busing was an unwinnable issue, White seemed to retreat away from the issue more and more, focusing less on the problems in the neighborhoods and more on trying to build his legacy as one of the caretakers of the New Boston.

Two years earlier the Supreme Court had refused to hear appeals on Garrity's initial ruling, a decision that was a major defeat for the antibusing forces, leaving them with no place to turn. They had tried to overturn Garrity's ruling in the courts; they had failed. They had protested in front of his home in the suburbs. They had protested at City Hall. They had protested against the *Boston Globe*. They had gone through all the strategies the protestors of the sixties had used, and none of them had worked. And even if Hicks had said, "The people of Boston have been had," and Palladino said, "Now the people have no place to go," and lesser community leaders like James Kelly, who ran the South Boston Information Center and always seemed to be at Hicks's side, said, "As long as there is forced busing in the city, violence and racial confrontation are unavoidable," there was the growing sense by the summer of '78 that there was despair among the people who opposed busing. The ones with the means now had their kids in parochial schools, either that or they had moved out of the city and into the suburbs. Many kids in South Boston had simply dropped out of school altogether. Whatever the reason, the violence of two years earlier, the aftermath of Landsmark's beating in City Hall Plaza and the fears of a race war, had subsided, even if the anger and hostilities were still there, the city as racially segregated as it ever had been.

Maybe it was this simple: It had been going on for so long, there had been so many demonstrations and protest marches, so many signs and placards and "Resist" signs on buildings, and what had it gotten? Every day the school buses rolled through the streets of Boston. All too often there were racial incidents in the schools, as though they long ago had become facts of school life, right there with hall passes and study halls. Busing was still the law, and all of the protests against it hadn't changed that.

Judge Garrity was still in control of the Boston public schools and all of the antibusing rhetoric hadn't changed that either.

Both Hicks's and Palladino's influence had lessened, given their defeats in the city elections in the fall of '77 and the fact that they both had been one-issue politicians, on the side that had lost. They had been promising victory for too long now, and it hadn't happened. If both white flight and a huge dropout rate had severely affected the schools, when it came to policy nothing had changed since September of 1974, when the first buses had started rolling, save for the fact that innumerable kids, both white and black, had been put through hell.

"Three hundred students came in today and two hundred and ninety of them wanted to fight," said Jerome Wynegar, the man from the Midwest brought in by Judge Garrity to run South Boston High School, one day in the spring of 1977. "Usually the fights were over by noontime, but today they went right up to and including the last period of the day."

That was the reality, and it transcended all the rhetoric on both sides, all the good intentions, all the plans and study groups, all the hope that had been there back in September of '74 that things eventually would calm down. Things hadn't calmed down, but now there was a sense of resignation. Both Hicks and Palladino were essentially done as leaders. Hicks had had a remarkable run, one that had begun nearly fifteen years earlier when she first began making news on the school committee with her commitment to neighborhood rights, but in many ways the "Iron Maiden" had become yesterday's news, a symbol of another time. Almost a generation of kids had grown up and gone through the school system while she had been giving speeches in her coats and her hats and her lace-curtain Irish gentility, her face on the cover of *Newsweek*, her name known to everyone. But all that now seemed to be more and more in the past, as if the war was over, and there were no more troops to lead.

The '77–'78 school year had been relatively tranquil, at least compared to the three years that had come before. The massive demonstrations were mostly over, if not the disruptions inside the schools. But they no longer got the kind of media attention they once had, for the simple reason that racial incidents inside schools were no longer news, not in Boston, not anymore. Nor was the high absenteeism, or the number of kids who had dropped out, or the daily tensions, or any of the other things that had become daily realities in the schools. It was an old story and the media had moved on.

Desegregation and busing were a fact of life.

But Boston was not immune to the cultural zeitgeist.

"Everyone was going into downtown Boston now, to hit the clubs and dance to Chic, A Taste of Honey, Chaka Khan, and Taka Boom," wrote Michael Patrick MacDonald in *All Souls*. "The older teenagers snuck into the adult clubs, while we twelve-year-olds were sneaking into Illusions, the new disco for teenagers fourteen and up."

It was a scene awash in drugs, from the tiny red mescaline pills that sold for three dollars a pop to the marijuana that was everywhere. There were constant fights in the clubs, usually the result of drunkenness, and closing time usually meant more fights in Kenmore Square, where the light towers from Fenway seemed to stare down like the all-seeing Dr T. J. Eckleburg in *The Great Gatsby*.

"Mobs of drunk Southie kids would start beating on anyone

who came in their path on the way home, especially if there was anything odd about them," MacDonald wrote. "One guy was beaten because he was a 'faggot college student,' another guy got it because he was a 'rock 'n' roll pussy.'"

He went on to describe how the summer of '78 turned into a war between the Irish South Boston kids and the Italian East Boston kids, even if they were supposed to be blood brothers because of busing, where the most dangerous words of that summer became "Where you from?"

It was the year in which the serial killer Ted Bundy had been captured in Florida in February, and the Hollywood director Roman Polanski, who had directed Jack Nicholson in *Chinatown*, skipped bail and fled to France after pleading guilty to having sex with a thirteen-year-old girl. It was the year that Resorts International opened a casino in Atlantic City, the first one in the eastern United States, the year Anwar Sadat and Menachem Begin signed the Camp David Accords, the attempt to bring peace to the Middle East, and Dianne Feinstein became the mayor of San Francisco, the first woman mayor of a California city. It was the year that *Annie Hall* won the Oscar as the best movie of 1977, and that movies as disparate as *The Deer Hunter*, *Grease*, *An Unmarried Woman*, and *Animal House* were hits.

But by the middle of the afternoon on October 2, 1978, normal life in Boston and most of New England had ceased to exist, with everyone either watching TV, where the game was on national television as well as on Channel 38, the Red Sox's network, or else trying to get close to a radio. Prisoners at the downtown Charles Street jail watched from their cells, Catholic brothers watched in their monasteries, and trading at the

Boston Stock Exchange took place under the din of portable radios. As early as two o'clock, a half hour before the game was to
begin, shoppers had all but disappeared from downtown streets,
and even in the city's downtown Combat Zone, topless dancers
strutted before distracted crowds.

Even in the underground subway system the game wasn't
too far away.

"Last stop, all change," said one conductor as a train rolled
into Harvard station. "Sox are ahead one to nothing."

The passengers cheered.

Even at famed MIT in Cambridge, one of the citadels of ac-
ademic achievement and braininess, both students and faculty
gathered in front of the thousand television screens of the school's
in-house cable TV network, the first time in history anything other
than educational or intellectual fare had been shown.

And at the end of the fifth inning the *Boston Evening Globe*
hit the streets. Aside from a small strip across the bottom, the
entire front page was dominated by an action photo of Mickey
Rivers sliding into second base underneath a tag by Rick Burleson, and a huge headline that read RED SOX AHEAD. On top of
the headline was a line score, and to the right of the photo was a
bare-bones recap of the first five innings, underneath a headline
that read YAZ HOMERS IN 2D.

There was the sense that afternoon that nothing was more
important than the Red Sox and the Yankees in Fenway Park,
that the entire city had paused, at least for a few hours, on an
afternoon that had brought all the disparate parts of Boston together in a common cause.

Wasn't that the redemptive power of sports, at least in
theory?

They had the power to take us out of ourselves, if only for a little while. And this game seemed to be coming at the right time. School had been back in session for almost a month and there had been no major incidents. That, in itself, was a blessing for this city that had had four years of them, four years when the schools had seemed like battle zones. So the *Evening Globe* could splash the first five innings of the game across its front page, bigger than life itself, for it didn't have to cover another yellow school bus full of little black kids being stoned on its way into South Boston, didn't have to cover another all-out riot at Hyde Park High School, didn't have to cover another installment in what had seemed to be a long-running local war, the fabric of the city being torn away, piece by piece.

This was about a baseball game, a brief little respite from the real world, but it was more than that, too.

It was about the Red Sox, who had been playing in this city since 1901, had been one of the few constants as everything had changed around them in seventy-seven years of unimaginable history. It was about the Red Sox that had come to be as much Boston as anything else, right there with the Common, and the Old North Church, and Faneuil Hall, and the brownstones in the Back Bay. It was about the Red Sox, who had come to represent the beautiful losers, the franchise that hadn't won a World Series since 1918, and always seemed to be carrying some old curse on their backs, whether it was for selling Babe Ruth to the Yankees or was simply the old ghosts from the Puritan past, those gloomy forefathers with their long black coats and their obsession with sin. Or maybe it was the psychic price for being the last team in baseball to integrate. Or then again, maybe it was just that they never seemed to have enough pitching.

Whatever the reason, there had been something magical about this summer. The Red Sox in a pennant race always created a buzz throughout New England, the radio on in every store you went into, at the beach, everywhere, the Red Sox as community, the ultimate water fountain conversation, the players larger than life, as though everyone was rooting for them, the Red Sox one of the very few things that could bring people together. That was baseball's appeal, one of the few things that had the power to pull just about everyone together, one of the Holy Trinity of conversation starters in Boston, right there with the weather and how bad the politicians were.

And this wasn't '75, when the city had been directly in busing's crosshairs, back when the second phase had started in Charlestown and Southie was still like the Wild West, back when it seemed as if the city was going to simply implode, that no city could withstand the constant violence. The appearance in the World Series then had been an escape from all the turmoil, certainly, but there had been the definite feeling then that Boston was being torn apart, with no end in sight.

Now there was an end in sight.

Or at least there was reason to hope there was one.

So this game was something to feel good about, not as an antidote to the madness that had been going on three years earlier, but as an antidote to the malaise that had set in after the madness. For that malaise was almost tangible.

How could it not have been?

Here was this storied city that had been publicly humiliated, like some proud family who wakes up one day to see all its long-held secrets on the front page of the newspaper. Here was this city that liked to refer to itself as "the Athens of America" and had come to be viewed nationally as no different from some Southern city that also had been ripped apart by racism. Here was a city that always had prided itself on its history and its culture now being known as the city that had the worst school busing violence in American history.

Was there ever a city that needed, once again, to feel good about itself?

Was there ever a city that needed a cathartic moment, a big symbolic win, something to break through the malaise that had settled over this city for the past few years like summer fog?

Not then there wasn't.

So this brilliant autumn afternoon in '78, in this city that had endured so much pain, there was the sense that it might just be possible to care about the outcome of a baseball game and not have to feel guilty about it. The sense that it was possible.

And if it would be presumptuous to say that the Red Sox healed a bruised city in the summer of '78, it also would be inaccurate. There were almost no black faces in the stands. And as Howard Bryant would point out in his book on race and the Red Sox a quarter of a century later, that was more than economics. That was based on history, and memory, and the fact that old attitudes die hard. There was a sizeable part of the population who weren't going to root for the Red Sox, regardless of how good they were, or how big the game they were playing in.

But in a city so traumatized by its racial hell, there was a certain hope in the fact that the Red Sox were a model of integration, even if there were so few mentions of it. These were not the Red Sox of the fifties. Not with Jim Rice the best hitter on the team and heading for an MVP award and George Scott at first base, and Tiant arguably getting the biggest cheers of anyone. This was a team where black players played significant roles. It was also a team that was a daily example that whites and blacks could not only interact with one another but could thrive doing it.

What did it mean to the city?

That's difficult to quantify.

Busing had so irreparably changed the fabric of life in Boston, even to the people who didn't have kids in the schools, or live in one of the neighborhoods where it was taking place. Boston had become synonymous with racism, no different from so many of the Southern cities in the civil rights battles in the sixties, and those scars would be difficult to erase. Years later there would be black free agents who didn't want to come to the Red Sox because of the perception that Boston was a racist city. In 2002 *Boston Magazine* would run an article asking the question "Is Boston Racist?" The legacy of busing, and the wounds it left behind, would last for decades, forever a part of Boston history.

But in that summer of '78, as so many people in both Boston and the rest of New England followed the Red Sox, there's little question that they were a reprieve, something to take pride in, a part of Boston that was still good and full of cheers.

And even in embattled South Boston the Red Sox were a daily presence, all over the radio, all over the television.

"Everyone was always trying to get tickets," said Carol Shedd, who grew up across the street from the Old Colony project and was bused when she was in the eighth grade. "My father worked for the post office, and he always seemed able to get tickets. He seemed to know everybody. I would probably go to four or five games every year. My brothers would go, too. He was always trying to teach me to score, although I never really figured it out."

She remembers how everyone loved the Red Sox, and the fact that they had some black players was irrelevant, as though they didn't see a contradiction between rooting for Jim Rice and loving Luis Tiant, but not wanting their kids to go to school with black kids.

"They all liked Freddie Lynn more than Rice," she continued, "but they still rooted for Rice, too."

As though the Red Sox were the Red Sox, exempt from the realities of busing.

For there was no question that the Sox were a welcome escape in 1978, if not a sign that maybe the city had crossed some Maginot Line and the worst was over.

CHAPTER TWELVE

o here it was:

Bottom of the ninth.

The Sox down 5–4.

The Yankees had gotten a runner on base in the top of the ninth, but Dick Drago replaced Hassler and got Thurman Munson to bounce a ball into the hole, where Rick Burleson made a nifty play to cause the force at second.

Gossage was still on the mound for the Yankees, about to enter into his third inning.

It had not been a great performance by him, but he had a one-run lead and was only three outs away from winning the game and sending the Yankees to the playoffs in Kansas City and the Red Sox home for the winter.

The first Red Sox hitter was Dwight Evans, who had been beaned in late August and had been bothered by dizziness and headaches ever since, the reason why Rice was in right field for this game and Hobson was the designated hitter. He was in his sixth full season with the Sox, had been signed in 1969 by Joe Stephenson, the longtime Sox scout in Southern California, and had first been sent to Jamestown, New York, where there were so many players they didn't have enough uniforms, and he had to practice in dungarees and a sweatshirt. Three years later he joined the Sox in September, a big, rawboned kid with a great arm who was confident in right field from the beginning but struggled at the plate. He would get appreciably better as a hitter in the second half of his career, would play until 1990 for the Red Sox and would have a wonderful career, but on this late afternoon, when the shadows now covered most of the field, he was in the game, even though he hadn't played in a week.

So maybe it's not surprising that he flew out harmlessly to left.

One out.

But when Burleson walked on just five pitches, Gossage obviously close to spent, hope again ran through Fenway like a line drive into the gap as Remy came to the plate. People were on their feet, the noise deafening. Remy thought it was almost suffocating.

Remy knew that Gossage didn't have a lot left. He had doubled against him his last time up, and after Gossage threw two strikes to him he didn't think he had the same stuff he'd had in his last at-bat. After fouling off a pitch he hit a rope of a line drive into sun-splashed right field, the only piece of the park that still had sun. And once again, here was another ball coming at Piniella that he was having trouble seeing. In fact, this time he couldn't see it at all. All he knew was it was coming his way. He had seen it leave the bat, knew it was a line drive, but had no clue where it was going to land. After the game he would say that he hadn't seen the ball at all, had no idea where it was going to land. Over his head? In front of him? On his head? He had no idea.

Piniella was nothing if not crafty, though. He knew that if he started flailing around that Burleson would know he couldn't see the ball and would be racing toward second base thinking of third. So he pretended to be in control of the play. He backed up a couple of steps, pounded his glove a couple of times, as if waiting for the ball to land in it. The ploy worked. Burleson stopped halfway to second, waiting to see where the ball was going.

The ball bounced about ten feet in front of Piniella, and to the left, and as it did Piniella seemed to take a swipe at it and somehow it stuck in his glove. Luck. The ball had simply bounced into his glove. Afterward, many would say that it had been the play of the game, not only because the ball had somehow bounced into his glove but because Piniella's gamesmanship while he was struggling to see the ball had caused Burleson to slow down just enough, so that when the ball actually did bounce into Piniella's glove, Burleson had to stop at second base instead of continuing on to third. Going from first to third on a single to right is a staple of baseball strategy, especially with a runner with the speed of Burleson, and Piniella had prevented that. And if the ball had gotten by him Burleson would have scored the tying run and Remy undoubtedly would have gone to second.

But now the Sox had runners on first and second with only one out, and Rice and Yastrzemski were coming to the plate.

Fenway was in pandemonium.

Rice was at the plate, with the chance to put the exclamation point on a season that had seen him hit .316, with forty-six home runs and 139 RBIs, a season that would make him the MVP in the American League, establishing him as one of the true elite players in the game in only his fourth season. It was a classic baseball matchup, as old as the game itself, strength against strength, power pitcher against power hitter. He already had singled home a run, but hadn't made the one dramatic statement, his chance to put his imprint on this game, his chance to make up for missing the '75 World Series, his chance to become indelibly stamped in Red Sox history, like Yaz had done in '67 and Fisk had done in his '75 home run in the World Series. He had never had the defining moment that would give him his slice of Red Sox immortality.

This was that chance.

For one of the stark facts of sports is we remember the big moment while so many of the great seasons blur together, the facts ultimately forgotten. Yastrzemski's '67 season that had won the first pennant for the Sox in twenty-one years. Jackson's three home runs in the World Series the year before. The Giants' Bobby Thomson's epic home run in the playoff game that beat the Dodgers in 1951, forever remembered. At the end of the year Rice would be named the MVP of the season, an incredible honor certainly, but not what gets you talked about forever, not the kind of dramatic statement that always would be a part of New England lore.

He sent a drive to right center, out to where Piniella had been fighting the sun all afternoon, but this time Piniella saw it all the way, and it nestled into his glove right in front of the warning track. It had been a ball that seemed to have a chance to go out when it had left Rice's bat, as though aided along by the thunderous roar of the crowd, until it simply didn't have enough

legs. And in many ways it would come to define Rice's career
with the Red Sox, as unfair as that is. Great players come and
go, eventually slip away into the mists of time. Great moments
get remembered forever. This had been one of those chances.
But it hadn't happened.

Two outs.

Yaz coming to the plate.

As if direct from central casting.

Could anyone make this up?

It had all come down to Yastrzemski, this thirty-nine-year-
old man who had spent so much of his life here in Fenway Park,
here in this old ballyard that long ago had become his own personal field of dreams. He stepped into the batter's box and did
all his routine things to get ready, hitching up his pants, making
sure his helmet was secure, picking up some dirt and rubbing it
on the handle of his bat, planting his left foot, the bat held high
over his head, all the familiar things that Red Sox fans had seen
for seventeen years now, the fidgety things that were Yaz at the
plate.

Hadn't he been born for a situation like this?

Hadn't all those years as a kid hitting the endless balls his
father and uncles had thrown at him, back when his childhood
had seemed as if he were an apprentice in a baseball workshop,
prepared him for this?

Hadn't he been here so many times before in his long career,
like that last weekend in '67 against the Twins when he simply
had put his team on his back and carried them to their first
pennant in twenty-one years, big hit after big hit, until everyone
knew that if he were at the plate he would come through?

He also was the person every Red Sox fan from Eastport,

Maine, to Block Island, Rhode Island, the entire fan base that one day, who, so many years later, would come to be known as "Red Sox Nation," also wanted at the plate. Yaz. Number 8. The Captain. The one who always seemed to deliver, at least that's what the legend said. That was the legacy of '67, and it always would be there, inviolate, the Red Sox immortality that would get passed on down through the generations like a prized possession. He might be thirty-nine, and he might have only hit .277 for the season with only seventeen home runs, but he was still Yaz, still larger than life, and this was the kind of moment he had seemed to own so often in his career. He was Yaz, and he still had that aura about him, no matter what the numbers said.

He also knew, maybe better than anyone, the passing of time, the chances already squandered for that elusive world championship, the two seventh games lost in Fenway Park, so close. He was thirty-nine, and although still productive, he no longer was what he once had been. The word was you could get him out now on off-speed stuff, and he had spent much of the year with a succession of nagging injuries, the kind that come when you're thirty-nine and your body is starting to betray you, the kind that come when you're thirty-nine and you are inching closer to the finish line. How many more chances would there be?

But he wasn't nervous. Nor did he hear the crowd. He was off in some other realm, some personal place where it's just him and the pitcher, the essence of concentration, a place he'd been so many times before. He also wasn't thinking home run, or anything necessarily dramatic, because he knew better than that. There was a big hole between first and second base, and that's what he was thinking. Just hit a pitch through that hole and the game is tied. Just hit a pitch through that hole and keep this game going, keep this season going, keep the ability to dream going.

On the mound, Gossage was going through his own form of private hell.

The night before, trying to go to sleep in the Sheraton in the Prudential Center, he had a premonition that it was all going to come down the next day to him and Yastrzemski, as if to win the game he was going to have to take down the Boston icon to do it. That had been the scenario that had kept running through his head, robbing him of his sleep, him against Yaz, everything on the line. Later, he would say that he hadn't gone to sleep that night counting sheep. He had gone to sleep counting fastballs to Yaz.

And now here it was.

He was now in his third inning in the game and he hadn't felt good for any of them. He had been too nervous, too ramped up, trying to throw the ball a million miles an hour, even when he knew that that never worked, was always counterproductive. He had felt the pressure in ways he had never really felt it before, for this was the biggest game of his life, and he knew that right now it was all on him, winning this game, going to the playoffs, the chance for the Yankees to repeat as world champions, all of it.

And here was Yastrzemski at the plate with two men on in the bottom of the ninth, the atmosphere as charged as he had ever seen, in another classic matchup. Power pitcher against a man who was a great fastball hitter.

Moments before, watching Yastrzemski come to the plate, Gossage stepped off the mound and had a conversation with himself, trying to figure out why he was so nervous, and what he could do to try and calm himself down, essentially asking questions, then answering them, a personal point, counterpoint. His knees were shaking. His palms were sweaty. He felt like he couldn't breathe.

"Up until that point I was nervous and I was scared to death," he would later say. "My legs were banging together, so if someone had come out there to talk to me, I wouldn't even have known he was there. I was that nervous and that scared. I'd never come close to playing in a game of that magnitude."

So he gave himself a pep talk:

"Relax, Rick. You've always played the game for fun, so enjoy the moment. This is why you play the game. You've been playing all your life for a moment like this."

Later, he would say that in that instant he had a "moment of total clarity." For he had asked himself one question: What was the worst thing that could happen? And the answer obviously had been that Yaz would get a big hit and the Sox would win and he and the Yankees would lose. That was the worst thing.

And if it did happen?

Then what?

He would be back home in Colorado hunting for elk, life would go on.

And that was his moment of clarity, the realization that this was a baseball game, not life and death, and that whatever the outcome of this battle with Yastrzemski the universe would go on. And with that realization a calm came over him. Somehow he had put the game in perspective. Until then he had been pitching as if he were going to face a firing squad if he lost, as if he had the weight of the world on his big shoulders.

"It felt like the weight of the world had been lifted off my shoulders," he said. "Nervous butterflies fluttered away and I became my normal, focused self."

And the other thing he told himself?

If he were going to lose it was going to be with his best pitch, his strength. He was where he was in life because of his fastball, and he was going to go with fastballs now. No trickery. No attempt to fool anyone. No trying to get someone to hit a bad pitch. Just reach back and try to throw the ball by someone, the reason he was in the major leagues to begin with.

Fastballs.

He missed inside with the first one.

"I was in the on-deck circle," Fisk would later say, "just like I was when Yaz flew out to end the '75 series. You know, they should have just stopped the game right then, and said, 'Okay, that's it. The season is over. You're both world champs. We can't decide between you, and neither of you should have to lose."

It was as though Fisk sensed that however the at-bat played out, it would somehow be anticlimactic, that no ending could do justice to a playoff game of such tension, such dramatics. That here were two teams and it had come down to the 163rd game of the season, through a season that had begun in the spring and now was ending in the fall, through six months of games and six months of an emotional journey, and now it all was coming down to this one at-bat, Gossage against Yastrzemski.

A classic matchup that was now looking for an ending, a pennant race looking for resolution.

Gossage came back with another fastball that would turn out to be his best of the day. Later, Munson would say that the ball seemed to explode as it reached the player, like a high-priced engine finding another gear, and in doing so it came in on the hands of Yastrzemski, who already had started his swing, surprising him. The result was Yastrzemski undercut the pitch, popped it up in the direction of third base.

The first thing Graig Nettles, the Yankee third baseman, thought when he saw the ball coming in his direction, was "Why me?" He didn't necessarily like handling pop-ups anyway, and here was the biggest one of his life. He was almost on the third-base line, a few yards in back of the bag, and the ball was in the air, and then it was in his glove, and then it was over.

"I knew the season would be over as soon as Yastrzemski's pop-up came down," Fisk would later say. "It seemed like the ball stayed up there forever, like everything was cranked down into slow motion. . . . After the last out, I looked around and the crowd was stunned. Nobody moved."

Thurman Munson stood near home plate and waved his catcher's mask over his head. Piniella, his arms raised in triumph, came running in from right field. The Yankees in the dugout rushed out on the field, even Steinbrenner, who left his box near the visitors' dugout and rushed on the field to embrace Lemon. But they seemed out of place, like laughing at a wake.

When the ball had gone up in the air it was as though all the noise and all the hopes and all the passion was instantly gone, a silence.

"It was like someone had dropped a huge tent over Fenway Park," Piniella would say later. "You could hear a fan cough."

For the longest time it seemed like nobody in Fenway moved. Some people put their hands over their faces. A few cried. A few groaned. Most just stood there in silence.

The silence lasted for about forty-five seconds. Still, nobody moved. And then it was as if everyone remembered they had just witnessed an amazing playoff game and clapping began, much like the applause given to a virtuoso symphony performance. When the cheering ended, most of the fans stayed standing, and the slow exodus began. On the field were several mounted police, waiting for the charge onto the field that never came.

"When it ended it was like a chill was in the air," said Scott MacKay, the young Vermont reporter who had bought a ticket from a scalper and was high up in the bleachers. "It was like summer was over."

The fans had cheered, shouted, stomped their feet, and screamed throughout the three hours of a historic playoff game.

But in the end?

In the end there was only silence.

Ron Guidry had been lying on the training table in the visitors' clubhouse with an ice pack on his shoulder, his postgame ritual, when the game ended and he heard his celebrating teammates come up the ramp and into the clubhouse. It was pandemonium. The Yankees had done it, had come back from fourteen games back in July to win the American League East. Guidry came out of the trainer's room and hugged Gossage from behind, all but jumping on the larger man's neck.

"Thank you," he said.

Steinbrenner was holding court for the media just outside the Yankee shower room.

"This game had to be the greatest of all spectator sports," he was saying when Guidry came out of the shower.

"George," Guidry said. "Tell them about the time you told

me I'd never make it in this league. Go ahead, George, tell them about that."

Steinbrenner quickly said he never had told Guidry that, but that once in spring training a few years ago "I took Guidry aside and told him he had to have more guts if he wanted to win. I told him he had to have more courage. Now he has more than anyone. Today proves he's the greatest pitcher in baseball."

Guidry had been just one of the Yankee stars, of course, even on a day when he hadn't had his best stuff.

There had been Gossage, who had gotten the outs he had to get, even if at the end he seemed to be running on fumes. There had been Dent, for sure, the improbable hero, the one who would be the one most remembered for this game, even if his home run had come in the seventh inning, and it would take two more runs to win it for the Yankees. There had been Jackson, whose blast in the eighth would prove to be the difference, Mr. October once again. And there had been Piniella, whose two big plays in tough right field might have been the difference, the same Piniella who never had been known for his agility in the outfield, just the kind of guy who always seemed to find a way to beat you.

"Maybe they ought to have a wild card in baseball," he said, amidst the jubilant din. "So that both of the best teams in baseball can make the playoffs. It's a shame for one of these teams to have to go home. But you knew that we both couldn't win."

He went on to say that the Yankees always knew they could win, even when they were down and Torrez was pitching so well, that the four games they had won in Fenway in early September had given them incredible confidence. But there was no gloating, for the Yankees knew that there was no difference between the two teams, knew that they had both played 163 games, and it had come down to the last pitch, or maybe even a quarter of an inch, the quarter of an inch that made Yastrzemski pop the ball up rather than drive it somewhere, something that might have changed everything. As if the Yankees knew they had not so much won as survived.

"They should have given both teams a standing ovation," said Nettles. "It was a great game, and I'm happy the Yankees won. But the thing that makes me happiest is that we did it by beating Torrez. We owed him that. He's been badmouthing us all year. We didn't appreciate that. If it wasn't for us he wouldn't be in the position to sign a 2.7-million-dollar contract. Maybe this will teach him to keep his mouth shut."

It was funereal inside the Red Sox clubhouse.

Years later Tiant would say that it was his saddest day in baseball.

When the game had ended Zimmer had made the media wait until he spoke to his team, most of whom were crying, as was Zimmer. It was the first time he had ever done so in his baseball life. He told them that he was proud of them, that when everyone else had written them off they had kept believing. He told them they had nothing to be ashamed of, nothing to hang their heads for. Told them that sometimes things happen that you have absolutely no control over.

"This is something you just have to live with," he said. "It's baseball."

Now Yastrzemski was talking to about thirty or so writers who were standing around his locker, his eyes still rimmed with tears. He said it had been one of the greatest games he had ever played in. He said he wished he would have had the chance to play with this particular team his entire career. The writers would keep coming, wave after wave of them, and Yaz, ever the old pro, dealt with them like he knew that that, too, was part of the job. That went with being the captain, the guy who had first come to play in Boston before anyone had ever heard of either the Beatles or the Vietnam War, back when JFK had been in the White House asking people what they were going to do for their country. So he alternated between praising the Yankees and trying to be philosophical, with a voice that sometimes seemed to get thick with emotion. He had never been particularly great with the media. He didn't tell stories. He didn't come out with memorable one-liners, ones that would easily translate into sound bites. He dealt with the media the way he had made himself a great player: he grinded away at it.

"You have to wonder whether it was meant to be," he said, his voice trailing off.

But the questions kept coming.

"Gossage has the kind of fastball that has a lot of movement on it," he said, "and I started swinging and I tried to hold up and if I did we might still be here . . . still playing."

His voice trailed off.

"It's not the end of the world," he continued. "People are dying of cancer. People are dying all over the world outside of baseball. I'm not going to commit suicide. I'm going to think about 1979."

He had a cup of beer in his hand and the sadness was all but etched into his face.

"Captain," said Bob Stanley, extending his right hand. "A great year. I'm proud to play with you."

Soon afterward, Reggie Jackson came through a crowd of

people at the entrance to the clubhouse and approached Yastrzemski. "You're the best, Yaz, the best I've ever seen."

"Thanks, Reggie," Yastrzemski said, and then he poked his finger in Jackson's chest. "Win it all."

Jackson went around the room shaking the players' hands and telling them, "We both should be champions." And he wasn't the only Yankee in the Sox clubhouse. Steinbrenner came in, too, telling the Sox players, "We won, but you didn't lose."

Burleson was sitting to Yastrzemski's right, his head down.

"The shame of it," he said, as a TV camera lit up the area, "is that these two teams are so evenly matched, but when we wake up tomorrow morning we're not going to be able to play any more baseball games. This is going to be awful. Tomorrow, when I wake up in the morning it's going to be awful."

Yastrzemski smiled at him, then Ned Martin, the longtime broadcast voice of the Red Sox, walked over to him and shook Yastrzemski's hand. Martin was fifty-five, known for his erudite delivery and his frequent literary references, a man who once said about baseball that "you can still see something in about every game that you've never seen before. That's the beauty of baseball, I guess. It's never predictable, even though it never changes." He had started broadcasting Red Sox games in 1961, Yastrzemski's rookie year, and they had come of age together with the Red Sox.

"Yaz," he said, "I wanted you up there at that time. You're the only one I wanted up there."

"I wanted to be up there," Yastrzemski said.

His eyes welled up for a second, and then he turned and walked past Martin and into the trainer's room, a sanctuary away from all the questions and all the notepads. Afterward, it was reported that that's where he broke down, out of sight. He had had so many huge hits in his career, so many times he had come through, the moments that were the foundation his legend was based on. But he hadn't this time. This time a pitch had surprised him, running in on him at the last moment, and he had popped it up. And if he knew that no one blamed him, knew that it was just baseball, knew the game's arithmetic said that sometimes you won the battle, but the pitcher won more of them, it didn't make the hurt go away.

Shortly before, he had been hugged by Ken Harrelson, the former Sox player who now did color on the Sox television broadcasts alongside Dick Stockton.

"Old man, you're the best," Harrelson had said.

"And he is the best," Mike Barnicle would write the next day in the *Globe*. "He has always been the best, that premier kind of performer. The kind of talent you never get tired of seeing. He is Sinatra singing in a small smoky room. He is Picasso with a bat. He is age and time blended into the mellow autumn of his athletic years to the point where his presence alone is an inspiration to a team. He is No. 8. The Captain."

And, once again, he had come so very close.

Torrez was saying how he hadn't wanted to come out, that it had only been a 3–2 game and that he'd been pitching well.

"But that was the manager's decision," he said. "I guess that's the way he wanted to do it."

Lee was more direct, firing a diatribe at Zimmer. "He lost the pennant. We should have been home free. A man shouldn't bury veteran ballplayers. He shouldn't have buried me."

Zimmer, his eyes wet and looking straight ahead, sat before dozens of reporters.

"I've been in many photo finishes," he said, "but this is the toughest one."

At one point, he was asked about the constant criticism leveled at him.

"I've listened to it all summer," he said. "I listened to it when we were fourteen games in front. I did everything I felt I could. That doesn't mean every move satisfied you or the next guy."

The next day he would head home to Florida, leaving early, replaying the game over and over in his head, like some bad dream he couldn't shake. He would be by himself for the long ride, hours full of might-have-beens, a trip that must have seemed almost haunted. He was a baseball man, had lived his life inside the game, so no one had to tell him of the game's vagaries. Still, this had been the game that had hurt the most, a game that had changed in the seventh inning on one swing by Bucky Dent, of all people.

Years later, while a coach for the Yankees, in one of those strange twists of baseball fate, Zimmer would rent Dent's house in New Jersey. Everywhere he looked it seemed as if there were pictures of that at-bat on the walls. Zimmer turned all those pictures around.

But now he sat there in front of the reporters, his eyes wet, and tried to explain how much this one had hurt, of how close they had been, and how now it was over.

Left unsaid were the ramifications of that.

EPILOGUE

he Red Sox players thought there would be other chances, of course.

That had been the feeling in the clubhouse, even through the tears and regrets. They were a great team that had lost one of the great playoff games in baseball history, but the consolation was that they would have more opportunities to win, that there would be many other big games to play.

Or so they thought.

But it would take eight years to get back to the playoffs, and by then the names were Roger Clemens and Bruce Hurst, Wade Boggs and Tony Armas. The only two players left from '78 were Rice and Evans. By then Zimmer also would be long gone. Baseball is so often about the present tense, and eight years can be like dog years in baseball, a long time.

Little more than a month after the loss to the Yankees the Sox had offered Tiant a one-year extension, when he had wanted two. The Yankees offered him the two years and Tiant left, a move that Yastrzemski would later say "tore the heart and soul out of our team." In December, Lee was traded to Montreal for the journeyman infielder Stan Papi, a move that led fans to post signs around Boston asking, "Who's Stan Papi?" The Buffalo Heads were now officially gone.

An era had ended, even if no one knew it yet.

So maybe it's not surprising that the '79 season was a letdown in Boston, and a tragedy in New York. In early August Thurman Munson died in a plane crash. He always missed his wife and kids back home in Ohio, and in order to spend more time with them he had learned how to fly and had bought his own plane. He had even been known every once in a while to commute back and forth between New York and Ohio after games. He had been practicing takeoffs in Ohio when his plane hit a tree and burst into flames. The day after his death the Yankees paid tribute to him in a pregame ceremony in Yankee Stadium in which the eight other position players took the field, leaving the catcher's position vacant, the backup catcher Jerry Narron standing on the dugout steps during the ceremony. Terence Cardinal Cooke said a prayer, and Robert Merrill sang the National Anthem. When Munson's picture went up on the scoreboard many of the Yankee players cried.

The Yankees quickly announced that Munson's number 15 was being retired, and in September 1980 a plaque in his memory was placed in Monument Park inside Yankee Stadium.

The Yankees finished fourth in '79, and Billy Martin, who had replaced Lemon in June due to the team's slow start, was fired again after the season when he got into a fight with a marshmallow salesman in a hotel bar in Minnesota. It would not be the last time he would manage the Yankees, as he and

Steinbrenner began the baseball equivalent of a tortured relationship, two people who couldn't deal with each other but couldn't really leave either. He would be hired again to manage the Yankees in 1983, fired again, then hired again in 1985, fired again, then hired again in 1988, before getting fired again after another bar room fight. He would die in an automobile accident on Christmas Eve in 1989.

Both Rice and Lynn had great years for the Red Sox in '79, but Yastrzemski got hurt midway through the year, and the pitching fell apart. Why not? Lee won sixteen games for Montreal, and Tiant won thirteen for the Yankees. The Sox ended up third, a disappointing season, given what the year before had been.

And after that?

After that everything changed.

The Sox collapsed in 1980, as injuries ran through the clubhouse like the flu through an elementary school, and with five games to go in the year Zimmer was fired. It was inevitable. He had been vociferously booed for two years now, as if '78 was still his fault and no one had forgotten, and it came as no surprise to anyone when he was let go, not even Zimmer. He was a baseball man, and he knew how the game was played. Torrez also had been booed for the past two years, as if no one really remembered anymore that he had pitched well for six innings and had given up only three runs when he had left the game, the Sox only down a run. That had been forgotten. What was remembered was that he had given up the three-run homer to Dent, and that would haunt him in Boston until he was traded to the Mets in 1983.

But it was after the season that the culture of the Red Sox changed.

Money, which had never been an issue with the Red Sox under Tom Yawkey, now became one. The new Red Sox ownership began a time of financial retrenchment, finishing off the dismantlement of the '78 team that had begun two years before with the loss of both Tiant and Lee. In December, Burleson was traded to the Angels. Then in late December the front office apparently misread a clause in the Basic Agreement that governed the game and failed to tender a contract to both Fisk and Lynn by the given date, an error that gave both players the right to sign grievances that would make them free agents. The Sox quickly traded Lynn to California, while Fisk declared himself a free agent and signed with the White Sox.

There was speculation that Lynn wanted to go back home to California, even if years later he refuted that, saying that since he was a .350 hitter in Fenway Park and a .270 one everywhere else, he would have had to have been a fool to want to leave Boston.

But Fisk?

Fisk was a New England institution, the local kid who had made good. And now he was gone, along with the belief that Haywood Sullivan hadn't liked him, that it had become personal. One of the theories was that Fisk's uncertain contract status for a while there in '76 had changed him, made him more aware of the realities of the game. Never again would he simply be the kid from New England just happy to be playing for the Red Sox. There was a stubborn quality to Fisk, the same one that made him run a game behind the plate at his own pace, regardless of whether his pitchers liked it or not. Fisk moved to his own clock, and being made to look greedy and ungrateful by the Red Sox in '76 was something he never forgot.

Whatever the reason, Fisk's loss was a symbolic one, a dramatic reminder that things had changed, not only on the field but in the front office, too.

It would be six years before the Sox would get back to the kind of team they had been in '78, and by then Yastrzemski would be gone, too. He had retired in 1983, had played his entire twenty-three-year career with the Red Sox, had long ago became an almost mythical figure, the last link to that time before '67 when baseball in Boston had seemed so different, the bridge between Ted Williams and Jim Rice, one of the last symbolic remnants of the Tom Yawkey era. On his last day in Fenway he was honored in a pregame ceremony where he received a six-minute standing ovation and asked for a moment of silence for his mother and for Tom Yawkey.

"New England, I love you," he yelled out to the crowd.

Then he started slowly jogging around the perimeter of the stands, shaking as many hands as possible as he jogged by, slapping palms, as everyone in the ballpark stood and cheered, in this incredible impromptu display, especially coming from Yastrzemski. He always had seemed so under control, so driven, as if for all his success the game had never come easy for him, and he always had known he had to grind it out every step of the way.

Afterward, he said that he had wanted to show the emotions, as he had kept them blocked for twenty-three years.

Yaz was not the only Boston personality to walk away from the public stage in 1983. So did Kevin White, who had been mayor since 1967. His announcement that he would not run again had set off a political free-for-all. Initially, it was thought to be a three-man race between Mel King, one of the most visible black leaders in the city over the past two decades, the former radio personality David Finnegan, and Ray Flynn, the onetime college basketball star from South Boston. Finnegan, who was backed by the downtown business interests and spent twice as much on the campaign as Flynn and King combined, was perceived to be unbeatable. But he finished third in the primary.

So it came down to a runoff in the general election between King and Flynn, the black leader and the antibusing representative from South Boston, almost as if it were a microcosm of the tensions that had been in the city for over a decade. It was considered so significant that *Time* did a story, titled "Boston Wins in a Landslide," the gist being that in the primary nearly a third of King's votes had come from whites, and Flynn had been endorsed by the minister of one of the city's largest black churches, the hope that Boston was finally moving beyond the turmoil of the seventies. It seemed so symbolic that White had said of King's showing, "Man, am I glad to see that."

If at first glance it might be assumed that it was a nasty, contentious contest, it became just the opposite. King and Flynn were friendly; in fact, they had once played on the same Roxbury basketball team as kids, although not at the same time, King being older. Flynn tells the story of one of the debates, when he and King had been sitting together talking about mutual friends before it. And Flynn was running as a healer, someone who wanted to bring the neighborhoods together. Yes, he had been ardently antibusing, and, yes, he still believed in neighborhood schools, but he said he never had been a segregationist and he knew that the city had to move beyond the hate, that it was all but doomed if it failed to do so. He won with 80 percent of the white vote.

In his first years as mayor there's no question that Flynn

was different than White. He wasn't interested in any of the trappings of being mayor, the ceremonial style that White had always enjoyed. He continued to live in a wood-frame house in a South Boston blue-collar neighborhood with his wife and six kids. He once took in a homeless man and let him sleep on the couch at his home in South Boston. He put a black family, which had been burned out of their home, in a city-owned Beacon Hill mansion. He once was described as a "Paul Bunyan of a politician." No one doubted either his empathy or his lack of pretense.

His campaign promise had been to take Boston away from the downtown business establishment and give it back to the neighborhoods, and in a *People* magazine story about him he was described as having a "fervor, almost religious in nature, that sometimes makes him seem more like a visionary than a politician.

"More than almost any other major politician in America today, Flynn has about him the air of the believer," *People* wrote, "the little boy who actually listened to the homilies in church and has grown into a man who now thinks he can translate them into public policy."

There was a sense of incredible energy about him, as though he had taken the drive and work ethic that once had made him a college basketball star and brought it into the mayor's office. He was absolutely without pretense, and he seemed to move through the different strata of Boston as easily as he once had moved through opponents on the basketball courts of his youth. He would personally sign the hundreds of certificates that would go out to kids who had successfully completed a summer program. No detail seemed too small for him. No neighborhood meeting too insignificant. He seemed to have little interest in the downtown business establishment.

As soon as he took office Flynn had let it be known that his administration was not going to tolerate attacks on blacks. He was forever riding through the black neighborhoods, stopping to shoot baskets with kids in the park, shaking hands, always a presence. His overall message was fairness to everyone, and he not only reached out to minorities, he had a better record hiring them than White had had, the man who often had been derisively referred to as "Mayor Black."

The Boston public schools remained under Judge Garrity until 1985, at which point he gave control back to the school committee.

"The judge's withdrawal will symbolize an end to a time in Boston that everyone wants to put behind, and ends a chapter on a time that Bostonians want to forget," Flynn said.

It had been eleven years since busing had first begun, and by then there were few supporters of it, the consensus being that, however good the intentions might have been, it had been both rushed into and mishandled, creating innumerably more problems than it solved. Half of blacks surveyed in 1974 had said they liked busing, but most had changed their minds by 1982, down to just 14 percent. Or as Edward Logue, the head of the Boston Redevelopment Agency, said of Garrity, "Where there was unquestionably passive prejudice, he created active hate."

Shortly before he left office, White had said that he regretted the "excessiveness" in the way busing had been implemented, and that he wished he had put some pressure on Garrity to do it differently, specifically not to have paired South Boston and Roxbury together in the first phase. Virtually everywhere you looked you could find politicians trying to distance themselves from Garrity.

The schools were also different than they had been in the early seventies, had gone from 60 percent white in 1970 to 35 percent in 1980. Five years later an astounding 93 percent of the kids in the Boston public schools qualified for either free school lunches or lunches at a reduced rate. By the middle of the decade many of the schools were underperforming, and the question became: Why should my kid be bused into some other neighborhood to go to an inferior school?

In 1987, Flynn set out to desegregate public housing in the city, starting in South Boston, a move that was controversial at best in his hometown of Southie. The only wards he lost in that election were in South Boston, yet by '89 he had desegregated housing projects in both South Boston and Charlestown, moves that had been met with little resistance and no violence.

That also was the year, though, that a man named Charles Stuart claimed that a black man had killed his pregnant wife and shot him in the stomach in Roxbury's Mission Hill neighborhood, a case that once again inflamed racial tensions in the city. It was a high-profile case, and seemed to resurrect a lot of the old fears, until roughly four months later, after Stuart's brother claimed that Stuart had killed his wife and wounded himself. Flynn was credited with acting decisively to calm tensions, one more example of his sensitivity to race and its inherent potential to split the city. He was reelected in both '88 and '92, resigning in the middle of his third term after he was appointed by President Clinton to be the American ambassador to the Vatican.

Following that, he lost a bid for Congress in 1998, the seat that had been vacated by Robert Kennedy's son, Joe.

In August of 1999 Boston school officials finally decided to end using race as a factor in where kids go to school, twenty-five years after those first school buses had rolled into South Boston and turned Boston into "the Little Rock of the North." Facing pressure from a lawsuit by white parents and advocates of neighborhood schools, the school board had voted 5–2.

"It was pretty clear that using race in student assignments was not going to withstand court scrutiny," said the chairwoman of the school board. "We didn't think we had a viable case."

So it ended.

A month later Garrity died of cancer at seventy-nine.

It had been a quarter of a century since his judicial order had started busing, and by the time of his death there were few people on the record saying busing had been a good thing for Boston. Instead, it was almost universally denounced as a flawed plan by social engineers that had put theory ahead of children, and the belief, by both white and black parents, that no one had been served by it.

"Like many other great liberal judges, Garrity failed to apply the principle of 'equal protection without regard to race or gender' to white kids," a story in the *Los Angeles Times* said. "While we might miss Garrity's great mind, we may never be able to forgive him for his bias against white children."

The *Boston Globe* wrote that "images from the riots of 1974 still sear."

And in his state of the city address in 1999 Boston mayor Thomas Menino reiterated that the key thing was to give parents the choice of where to send their children to school.

"Parents should make that decision, not the politicians," he said.

On the day after Menino's statement not one person came to a school committee meeting to object.

Louise Day Hicks died in 2003 at the age of eighty-seven. Her passing was duly recognized, complete with a story in the *New York Times* recounting her career and her role in seventies Boston. She was still one of those names that resonated, one of those names that immediately conjured up a certain time and a certain place. After losing a council bid in '77, she filled a vacant seat for a year in '79, then lost again in 1981. After that, in poor health, she left politics, continuing to live in the house in City Point she had lived in her entire life. She was eulogized by Billy Bulger, the former president of the state senate, in the *New York Times* as someone willing to act upon her convictions, and no one could ever argue that. But by the time of her death she had been out of public life for over two decades, a name from the past, one that belonged to such a different time.

Or so it seemed.

Even South Boston had changed.

If the stereotype remained, the old Southie with shamrocks on the project walls, the old Southie of legend, the reality was somewhat different. The old South Boston might still turn out for St. Patrick's Day, with the parade and the green beer and music that resurrected images of the old sod, but by the turning of the century a study showed that 48 percent of the people living in South Boston had not been raised there. What did they know about busing? To them, it was all ancient history. The city was changing, and the neighborhoods with it. Gentrification was coming to South Boston and Charlestown, too. South

Boston because it was on the water, Charlestown for the old brownstones along Monument Square that had been rehabbed and sold to young professionals from somewhere else. To them busing was as much in the past as the battle at Bunker Hill, two things that had nothing to do with them.

That was, perhaps, best detailed in a small scene in the book *The Assist* by Neil Swidey that came out in 2007. The book was about a year with the Charlestown High School basketball team, and the differences between what Charlestown High School had been in 1975 and what it was today couldn't be more striking. Maybe the most symbolic being that its basketball team was all black, comprised of kids who arrived every day from around the city.

One day they went across the city to play at South Boston High School, in the same building that had been there in 1974, "a congested neighborhood of alphabet-lettered streets lined with three-decker tenements overlooking Dorchester Bay." The school was now roughly one hundred years old, the gym small and dark. There were no seats, so the spectators had to stand between the lines of the court and the nearby walls.

These Charlestown players didn't even call themselves "Townies" anymore, the name that Charlestown High School teams had been called forever. Then again, they hadn't even been born "when 'Townie' became shorthand for 'white and angry.' " They called themselves "Riders." To them, it sounded better.

The Charlestown coach was a man named Jack O'Brien, and he certainly knew the history of these two schools, and as he looked out at the scene in the South Boston High School gym he thought about how unthinkable it would have been thirty years earlier.

As Swidey writes:

"On this afternoon, besides one bench-warmer for Southie, the squads for both teams were entirely black. In fact, besides that kid, and the coaches for both teams, there wasn't another white face in the gym."

"There are pockets of old South Boston left," said Carol Shedd, "but it's pretty Yuppified. A lot of the old people can't afford to live there anymore."

Shedd was in the eighth grade in 1974. She was the youngest of six kids and she lived in the Lower End, across the street from the Old Colony projects. On the first day of school, on the first morning of busing, her mother walked her to the bus stop, past people protesting busing coming to South Boston. She was ticketed to be bused to the John W. McCormack Middle School in nearby Columbia Point in Dorchester, and she was the only one who got on the bus.

"My family was liberal," she said. "My parents were from Boston, but they hadn't grown up in South Boston."

But she had spent her first few years living in a housing project, had grown up singing all the Southie songs, like "We're from Southie and no one could be prouder, and if you can't hear it we'll yell a little louder."

Her eighth-grade class was mostly black, but she says, in retrospect, that she liked her teachers, both the white ones and the black ones, and never had any trouble. To her, it was an adventure of sorts, and if it was a little rough in the beginning, she soon got used to it. The worst part to her was that she never saw her school friends outside of school, for when school was over they lived in two different worlds. But she had black friends. That, in itself, was a sign that things were changing.

"Busing wasn't traumatic for me," she said, "but my brother had a different experience. He went to Southie High, got involved in a gang fight, and was more caught up in the whole South Boston thing."

The next year she went to a charter school in Copley Square, took the train there every morning, eventually getting a scholarship to Boston University. And she came to see that in South Boston then there was a denial of all the problems, the poverty, the alcoholism, the sense that everyone was crammed into this little corner of the world, with few exits.

She remembers South Boston then as a dangerous place. But there were incidents all over the city, downtown, too, and it was not uncommon to see fights. And that to go downtown and say you were from South Boston was a potentially loaded situation.

"I remember when I went to high school in Copley I was embarrassed to say I was from South Boston," Shedd said. "So many of the people there had embarrassed and degraded themselves, holding on to something that was impossible to hold on to. I would say, 'I'm from South Boston, but I'm not like that.' But I had two parents, and my mother was a very strong figure. I can see her taking me to the bus stop that first morning in her trench coat, and standing waiting with me for the bus to come."

Another one who saw the buses come was Bob Sales, then a reporter for the *Globe*, but a man who worked for several newspapers in his Boston journalistic career, including a nearly ten-year stint as the sports editor of the *Herald*, ending in the mid-nineties. He was originally from New York, a man who had come out of the progressive tradition in New York City, and had first come to Boston in the early sixties to work for the *Herald-Traveler* newspaper. When busing first started he was on the *Globe*'s "urban team," part of a group of five reporters.

"I used to go around to all the high schools," he said. "Everyone was under incredible stress. They were all city kids, and I identified with them. I thought Hicks was a politician first, and she always played to that. I don't know whether she was really a hater, but she didn't discourage that."

He was in the *Globe* on one of the nights shots were fired into the building, was at ground level of much of the reporting in those early years, the human drama that was taking place all around him. He saw what he calls "quiet heroes and loud villains," like the men who coached basketball teams in the afternoon in empty gyms, because spectators were not allowed.

Most of all, he saw kids get robbed.

Robbed of their education.

Robbed of their childhood.

"It was a heartbreaking time," said Karen Maguire, who grew up in South Boston in the seventies and became a newspaper reporter in Worcester and an editor in Providence.

She was the oldest of five, and graduated from South Boston High School in 1973, the year before the busing started. To her, it had been the ultimate neighborhood school, and back then the neighborhood was her life. Her parents had grown up in the Old Harbor projects. She and her friends went to the movies at the Broadway Theater, which everyone called the Bug House. They took the train downtown to shop at Filene's and Jordan Marsh, the two Boston institutions. They went swimming at Carson Beach, which would become the scene of a mini-riot years later when some blacks tried to go swimming and were chased away by a bunch of angry whites. Her father ran numbers for Whitey Bulger, the South Boston crime boss whose younger brother, Billy, was a state senator, the Bulger brothers arguably the two most powerful men in South Boston then. When she had been just a kid the top floor of her house had been full of telephones and men who answered them, and she never gave it much of a second thought. That was just the way it was.

She was South Boston.

She won a scholarship while at South Boston High School, and the school's headmaster, a local institution named William Reid, who would later be forced out by Judge Garrity, convinced her to use it to go to prestigious Wellesley, and not down the street to UMass Boston in nearby Columbia Point. Wellesley was a woman's college in suburban Boston, not all that far from South Boston in miles, but light-years away in lifestyle.

"William Reid changed my life," Maguire said.

To her, that was the good side of South Boston, the nurturing environment, both the strong sense of place and the sense that you had a definite place in it, the sense that people would help you, that in many ways South Boston then had really been a village. The bad side had been exposed in busing, the clannishness, the fear of outsiders, the sense that the politicians trained you to be able to function in Southie, but they wanted you to need their help.

She had three siblings who went through South Boston High School, and one of her brothers supposedly had been on some unofficial "hit list," after the stabbing of a student there. She saw what it did to them, how different their high school experience was compared to what hers had been. And when she came home on weekends from Wellesley her freshman year and saw the hate and the mothers with their angry faces she knew that it never should have come to this.

"They should have started busing with younger kids," she said.

When she did come back from college on weekends there also was the sense that she had left, and in South Boston in those days you could pay a price for that, too.

"You weren't supposed to forget your roots," Maguire said. "There was an expression if people thought you were doing that. That you were going 'up beyond your raising.'"

She hasn't lived in South Boston in a long time, but she knows there's still a mystique about South Boston. It's been featured in movies like *Good Will Hunting*, in which Matt Damon plays the South Boston kid who must leave the neighborhood to find his dreams, and *The Departed*, with its crime and tribal rules.

"If you come from South Boston you're somehow supposed to be more authentic," she said with a smile. "But I know this. South Boston in the seventies was a grim, grim time."

And when she does go back, whether for a reunion or a funeral, in many ways it's as though she never left. There's still the sense of solidarity, that people will do anything for you, that Southie takes care of its own, that there really is something to the Southie mystique, something palpable, as real as the memories of once going swimming at Carson Beach, or taking the train downtown from Broadway station.

With only one difference.

Many of the people who come back for such gatherings can't afford to live there anymore.

———

The Democratic National Convention came to Boston in 2004, held in what was then called the Fleet Center, the place where both the Celtics and the Bruins play.

It was where a young senator from Illinois named Barack Obama first jumped into the national spotlight, and where Boston's John Kerry got nominated. It also was where the "New Boston," which had had its beginnings back in the sixties, was on full display, a vibrant city, an intellectual, technological, and financial center. In many ways it had become the model for the new economy, one based on information and services.

"Boston is a terrific city," Ted Landsmark said that year, twenty-eight years after being attacked in City Hall Plaza. "It's a much more interesting place than it was twenty-five years ago. Boston has finally grown up. It's a far more cosmopolitan place than it was in the mid-seventies."

Now the president of the Boston Architectural College, he also had said in 2004 that he had gone to college with George Bush, and law school with Bill and Hillary Clinton, had attended the same prep school as John Kerry, and "that there is a lot more to my life than this one event."

He also had been hired by Flynn in 1988 to work in his administration, a symbolic appointment that said the city was in a new era, that the divisiveness and animosities of the past were in the past tense.

The year 2004 was a good year in Boston. It was the season the Red Sox finally won the World Series for the first time since 1918, almost as if there was a public exorcism, all the old ghosts finally put to rest. Bucky Dent. Bill Buckner. The "Curse of the Bambino." All of it. It had long ago taken on a life of its own, had almost become as much a part of the Red Sox as Fenway Park,

the story line that got dragged out every year like some old tired
script, and now it was finally gone. The Red Sox were the best
team in baseball, their tortured past finally put to rest.

Bucky Dent went on to become the MVP of the '78 World Series,
as though emotionally energized by his home run. The following
year he played a running back in a television movie, *The Dallas
Cowboys Cheerleaders.* He went on to play in the major leagues
through the '84 season, and was an All-Star three times, but it was
that one swing on an October afternoon in Fenway Park that gave
him baseball immortality. In one of those curious twists of fate,
his home run became mythic, to the point that to innumerable
Red Sox fans Dent obviously hit his home run to win the game in
the ninth inning, so significant has it become in Red Sox infamy,
and not in the seventh inning of a game where four more runs
were scored after his home run. No matter. The '78 playoff game
long ago became known as the "Bucky Dent Game," or as he's
commonly referred to in New England, Bucky "Fuckin'" Dent.

Some of that got reinforced after the Red Sox's unbelievable
collapse in the '86 World Series, when they were one strike away
from winning for the first time since 1918 and a slow ground
ball rolled through the legs of first baseman Bill Buckner, the
symbolic moment of the Sox's collapse.

So they became the two bookends of Red Sox frustration,
Bucky Dent and the ball rolling through Billy Buck's legs, as if
only the cruelest baseball god could have come up with those
two improbable scenarios. They were the epitome of the "Curse
of the Bambino," the silly belief that somehow the Red Sox were
forever cursed for once selling Babe Ruth to the Yankees, the

catchphrase that continued to grow in popularity as the Sox moved through the nineties and into the new century still not having won a World Series, the Red Sox becoming synonymous with old curses and heartbreak, as though no matter what, the Sox would always find a way to lose the big one.

It would take until finally winning in 2004 to eradicate all that, to sweep it away into the dustbin of baseball history once and for all.

By then, things were different. The Yawkey Trust was gone. There was a new ownership group. And two of the biggest stars were Dominicans, David Ortiz and Manny Ramirez. And it was even possible to walk through Fenway Park and see some black faces in the stands. Not a lot, mind you. But some. More than there used to be. The scars of the past are still there, but time changes, time has the potential to heal, and on those magical nights in 2004 the franchise's past seemed far away.

Dent got into coaching after his playing career was over, even managed the Yankees for eighty-nine games in the mid-eighties before being fired by Steinbrenner. Then again, he had played in the Bronx Zoo; he knew that managing for Steinbrenner had a short shelf life.

He now runs a baseball school in Delray Beach, Florida, and what sets it apart is that there's a replica of Boston's left-field wall. Dent and his partner had it built in 1988, and the scoreboard shows a game between the Red Sox and the Yankees in the top of the seventh inning, with the score 3–2.

"Why does it say the Yankees are winning?" one of the campers asked one day, in a scene captured in a *Sports Illustrated* article.

Dent just grinned.

It's been a long time now since that '78 playoff game.

One night in the summer of 2008 Jerry Remy was honored in a pregame ceremony in Fenway Park for his career as the longtime color man on the station that televises the Red Sox games. Of all the members of that team, he is the one who is now most in the public eye, more well known and popular now than when he was playing. On the field with him that night were Fisk, Evans, and Burleson, and if you didn't know better it could have been a '78 reunion. Rice and Eckersley are frequent commentators on the Red Sox postgame shows on another station.

In August, Yastrzemski was rushed to Massachusetts General Hospital complaining of chest pains, and had triple bypass surgery, another reminder that no one stays young forever, not even these players who can seem all but frozen in time.

Tiant still lives in suburban Boston, is a frequent visitor at Fenway. Lee lives in northern Vermont, but often pops up around New England, still "the Spaceman," still baseball's Merry Prankster, out there in his own fairy-tale world where everyone is still young and strong, and life is always a baseball game. His hair is white now, complete with a beard, a left-handed version of Father Time. One of his stops a few years back was in Warwick, Rhode Island, where he warmed up for a charity softball game throwing knuckleballs, wearing a red baseball cap with a blue "B" on it.

"I was saving the knuckleball for when I got old," he said that day. "I was going to pitch until I was seventy years old. That was my goal. Never age and play ball every day of my life."

That had been said with a smile, but there was a bittersweet tone to it, too. As though he knew he left baseball too soon.

He also had said that day that his dream was to get the '78 Red Sox together again, and as fate would have it, in August

2008 there was another game between the '78 Yankees and the '78 Red Sox.

It was held in Scranton, Pennsylvania, in a place called PNC Field. It featured nine former Yankees and nine former Red Sox in something called a Legends Reunion.

And eight thousand people came out to watch.

At one point Chris Chambliss stood on second base, Roy White was on first, and Bucky Dent was at the plate.

Mike Torrez had seen this before.

And so what if it was staged? Or at one point the Yankees' Oscar Gamble put an Afro wig on, to look more like he looked back there in '78? Or that Lee was miked throughout the game for a running commentary? Or that Torrez's first pitch to Dent went over his head?

"It brought back a lot of memories," Torrez said.

No doubt.

It was the first time these players had played against each other in thirty years, and it resurrected Lee's wish from years before, his dream of bringing the '78 Red Sox together again, that team that was almost great, that season that had taken place in one of the most turbulent eras in Boston history, and played in one of the greatest playoff games ever. A team that, even now, so many years later, is still remembered, as if you can close your eyes and it is still 1978, disco on the radio, the Sox ahead in the seventh inning of a playoff game, just a handful of outs away from immortality.

"We're all going to be spring eternal, no one is ever going to age," Bill Lee had said. "There will be no sore arms, no aches and pains. We'll just play every day in the sun and no one will ever get old."

And no one ever heard of Bucky Dent.

NOTES

The seminal book on busing in Boston is *Common Ground* by J. Anthony Lukas, but I also was aided by *Boston Against Busing* by Ronald Formisano, *Southie Won't Go* by Ione Malloy, *The Soiling of Old Glory* by Louis Masur, and *All Souls* by Michael Patrick MacDonald. All are essential for a true understanding of the era.

For an appreciation of the '70's the best book I found was *The Seventies*, by Bruce Shulman, which puts the decade into context. That, combined with innumerable articles on the decade gleaned from the Internet, provide the cultural backdrop.

There are many books that deal with Red Sox and Yankee history, and right there near the top of the list are the two by Glenn Stout and Richard A. Johnson, one on the Red Sox century and one on the Yankee century. Peter Gammon's *Beyond the Sixth Game* is the definitive book on the Red Sox of the era, and there is no better book on race and the Red Sox than Howard Bryant's *Shut Out*.

You also can never go wrong with anything Dan Shaughnessy

writes about both Red Sox and Fenway Park history, and anything Peter Golenbock and Bill Madden write about Yankee history.

I also was aided by Lou Piniella's book, *Sweet Lou*, written with Maury Allen, Roger Kahn's *October Men*, Jonathan Mahler's *Ladies and Gentlemen, The Bronx Is Burning*, and Sparky Lyle's *The Bronx Zoo*. All are must-reads for understanding the Yankees of the era.

Secondary sources used in various chapters are as follows:

PROLOGUE

Newspaper articles in *Providence Journal*, *Providence Evening Bulletin*, *Boston Globe*, and *Boston Evening Globe*.

Scene with Yankees in Boston hotel on eve of the game comes from a *Sports Illustrated* article by Jonathan Schwartz, as does interplay between Mike Torrez and Ron Guidry before game.

CHAPTER ONE

Newspaper articles from Providence and Boston.

Scene of Ted Kennedy at the Government Center from *Common Ground*.

Fenway history from *Red Sox Century*.

Background on Mickey Rivers from *Balls*.

Background on George Steinbrenner from *October Men* and *Yankees Century*.

Background on Jim Rice from a 1988 *Providence Journal* magazine story.

CHAPTER TWO

Background on Boston from *The Hub* by Thomas O'Connor.

Background on Bill Russell comes from *Go Up for Glory* and *Second Wind*.

Background on Reggie Smith and George Scott comes from *Lost Summer* by Bill Reynolds.

Overview of Boston's racial episodes in the late '60's comes from *Lost Summer* by Bill Reynolds.

Background on Louise Day Hicks comes from *Common Ground* and *New York Times*, *Boston Globe*, and *Boston Phoenix* articles.

CHAPTER THREE

Background on Yankees comes from *Yankees Century*, *October Men*, and *The Bronx Zoo*.

Scene with Billy Martin and Reggie Jackson in Fenway Park in 1977 comes from *October Men* and *Ladies and Gentlemen, The Bronx Is Burning*.

CHAPTER FOUR

Background on Don Zimmer comes from *Zim: A Baseball Life* and from interviews with Jerry Remy, Fred Lynn, and Bill Lee.

Background on Bill Lee comes from "The Wrong Stuff," a 1978 *Sports Illustrated* story, articles in Providence and Boston newspapers, and from interviews with Lee.

Scene with Zimmer at Fenway Park comes from *Red Sox Nation: An Unexpurgated History of the Boston Red Sox*.

CHAPTER FIVE

Background on South Boston comes from *Boston Against Busing*, *South Boston, My Home Town*, and *All Souls*.

Background comes from *Common Ground* and newspaper articles in the *Boston Globe*.

Scenes from in and around South Boston High School come from *Southie Won't Go*.

CHAPTER SIX

Providence and Boston newspaper articles.

The Greatest Game.

Sweet Lou.

CHAPTER SEVEN

Common Ground.

The Assist.

Jimmy Breslin column in the *Boston Globe*, excerpted in *Shut Out.*

Background on Peter Gammons comes from *Dispatches from Fenway* and interviews with Leigh Montville.

Background on Pixie Palladino comes from *Boston Against Busing* and article in *Boston Globe.*

CHAPTER EIGHT

Articles in Providence and Boston newspapers.

Material on Mike Torrez from article from Boston.com and from *Red Sox Nation: An Unexpurgated History of the Boston Red Sox.*

Material on Goose Gossage from *The Goose Is Loose.*

CHAPTER NINE

The scene in City Hall Plaza is from *The Soiling of Old Glory.*

The front pages of the *Boston Globe* and the *Boston Herald.*

Fallout from incident in City Hall Plaza in *Boston Against Busing* and *Southie Won't Go.*

CHAPTER TEN

The Yankee Century.

Sweet Lou.

Red Sox Century.

CHAPTER ELEVEN

Overview of decade comes from *The Seventies*, and innumerable Internet articles on the decade.

Material on Boston in the '70's comes from the *Boston Globe*, and various online articles from Boston publications.

Background on Kevin White comes from *Common Ground* and articles in Boston newspapers.

Articles on day of the game from *Boston Globe* and *Boston Evening Globe*.

CHAPTER TWELVE

Sweet Lou.

The Goose Is Loose.

Articles in Providence and Boston papers.

EPILOGUE

Red Sox Century.

People magazine story on Ray Flynn.

Time magazine story on 1983 mayoral election.

Newspaper obituaries on Louise Day Hicks and W. Arthur Garrity.

BIBLIOGRAPHY

Bradley, Richard. *The Greatest Game: The Yankees, the Red Sox, and the Playoff of '78*. Free Press, a division of Simon and Schuster, Inc. New York. 2008.

Bryant, Howard. *Shut Out: A Story of Race and Baseball in Boston*. Beacon Press. Boston. 2002.

Bulger, William M. *While the Music Lasts: My Life in Politics*. Houghton Mifflin Company. Boston, New York. 1996.

Formisano, Ronald P. *Boston Against Busing*. The University of North Carolina Press. Chapel Hill & London. 1991.

Gammons. Peter. *Beyond the Sixth Game*. Houghton Mifflin Co. Boston. 1987.

Golenbock, Peter. *Red Sox Nation: An Unexpurgated History*. Triumph Books. Chicago. 1992.

———. *Wild, High, and Tight: The Life and Death of Billy Martin*. St. Martin's Press. New York. 1994.

Gossage, Richard, with Russ Pâté. *The Goose Is Loose*. Ballentine Books. New York. 2000.

Johnson, Richard A. *A Century of Boston Sports*. Northeastern University Press. Boston. 2000.

Kahn, Roger. *October Men: Reggie Jackson, George Steinbrenner, Billy Martin, and the Yankees Miraculous Finish in 1978*. A Harvest Book, a division of Harcourt, Inc. Orlando, Austin, New York, San Diego, Toronto, London. 2003.

Lauter, Jack. *Fenway Voices*. Yankee Books. Camden, Maine. 1990.

Lee, Bill, with Dick Lally. *The Wrong Stuff*. The Viking Press. New York. 1984.

Lukas, J. Anthony. *Common Ground: A Turbulent Decade in the Life Of Three American Families*. Vintage Books, a division of Random House. New York. 1986.

Lyle, Sparky, with Peter Golenbock. *The Bronx Zoo: The Astonishing Story of the 1978 World Champion New York Yankees*. Triumph Books. Chicago. 1979.

Madden, Bill. *What It Was to Be Young and A Yankee*. Warner Books. New York. 2007.

Mahler, Jonathan. *Ladies and Gentlemen, The Bronx Is Burning: 1977, Baseball, Politics, and the Battle for the Soul of a City*. Picador. Farrar, Straus, and Giroux. New York. 2005.

Malloy, Ione. *Southie Won't Go: A Teacher's Diary of the Desegregation of South Boston High School*. University of Illinois Press. Urbana and Chicago. 1986.

Masur, Louis P. *The Soiling of Old Glory: The Story of a Photograph That Shocked America*. Bloomsbury Press. New York. 2008.

O'Connor, Thomas H. *South Boston, My Home Town: The History of an Ethnic Neighborhood*. Quinlan Press. Boston. 1988.

——. *The Boston Irish: A Poltical History*. Northeastern University Press. Boston. 1995.

——. *The Hub: Boston Past and Present*. Northeastern University Press. 2001.

Pepe, Phil. *Catfish, Yaz, and Hammerin' Hank: The Unforgettable Era That Transformed Baseball*. Triumph Books. Chicago. 1988.

Piniella, with Maury Allen. *Sweet Lou*. G.P. Putnam & Sons. New York. 1986.

Reynolds, Bill. *Lost Summer: The 1967 Red Sox and the Impossible Dream*. Warner Books. New York. 1992.

Robbins, Mike (ed.). *The Yankees vs. Red Sox Reader*. Carrol & Graf Publishers. New York. 2005.

Scoggins, Chazz. *The Game of My Life: The Boston Red Sox*. Sports Publishing, LLC. 2006.

Shaughnessy, Dan. *Fenway: Dispatches from Red Sox Nation*. Crown Publishers, Inc. New York. 1996.

Shaughnessy, Dan, and Stan Grossfeld. *Fenway: A Biography in Words and Pictures*. Houghton Mifflin Company. Boston, New York. 1999.

Shulman, Bruce J. *The Seventies: The Great Shift in American Culture, Society, and Politcs*. The Free Press. New York, London, Toronto, Sydney, Singapore. 2001.

Stout, Glenn, and Richard A. Johnson. *Red Sox Century: One Hundred Years of Red Sox Baseball*. Houghton Mifflin Company. Boston, New York, 2000.

———. *Yankees Century*. Houghton Mifflin Company. Boston, New York. 2002.

Sullivan, George. *The Picture History of the Boston Red Sox*. The Bobbs-Merrill Co. Indianapolis, New York. 1979.

Swidey, Neil. *The Assist: Hoops, Hopes, and the Game of Their Lives*. Public Affairs. New York. 2007.

Tan, Cecilia. *The 50 Greatest Yankee Games*. John Wiley & Sons. Hoboken, NJ. 2005.

Tager, Jack. *Boston Riots: Three Decades of Social Change*. Northeastern University Press. Boston. 2001.

Zimmer, Don, with Bill Madden. *The Zen of Zim: Baseball, Beanballs, and Bosses*. Thomas Dunne Book. St Martin's Press. New York. 2004.

———. *Zim: A Baseball Life*. Sports Illustrated. New York. 2001.

Yastrzemski, Carl, with Gerald Eskenazi. *Yaz: Baseball, the Wall, and Me*. Doubleday. New York, London, Toronto, Sydney, Auckland. 1990.

Courtesy of the Institute for International Sport

Bill Reynolds is an award-winning sports columnist for the *Providence Journal*. He has written five books, including *Fall River Dreams*, and cowritten three more. *Cousy*, Reynolds's bestselling work about the Boston Celtics' iconic point guard, was called an "insightful, astute biography" by *Sports Illustrated*. His book with Rick Pitino, *Success Is a Choice*, was featured on the *New York Times* bestseller list for several weeks. Reynolds lives in Providence, Rhode Island.

Printed in the United States
by Baker & Taylor Publisher Services